PELICAN BOOKS

DEPRESSION AND THE BODY

Dr. Alexander Lowen is the creator of bioenergetics, a revolutionary method of psychotherapy designed to restore the body to its
natural freedom and spontaneity through a
regimen of exercise. The foremost exponent of
this method of incorporating direct work on
the body with the psychoanalytic process, Dr.
Lowen practices psychiatry in New York and
Connecticut and is the executive director of the
Institute of Bioenergetic Analysis. He is married and lives in New Canaan, Connecticut,
with his wife and son. Dr. Lowen's *Bioenergetics*
and *Pleasure* are also published by Penguin
Books.

By Alexander Lowen, M.D.

BY ALEXANDER LOWEN, M.D.

DEPRESSION
AND THE BODY

The Biological Basis
of Faith and Reality

Penguin Books

Penguin Books Ltd, Harmondsworth,
Middlesex, England
Penguin Books, 625 Madison Avenue,
New York, New York 10022, U.S.A.
Penguin Books Australia Ltd, Ringwood,
Victoria, Australia
Penguin Books Canada Ltd, 41 Steelcase Road West,
Markham, Ontario, Canada
Penguin Books (N.Z.) Ltd, 182–190 Wairau Road,
Auckland 10, New Zealand

First published in the United States of America by Coward, McCann &
    Geoghegan, Inc., 1972
Published in Pelican Books 1973
Reprinted 1974, 1976

Printed in the United States of America by
George Banta Co., Inc., Menasha, Wisconsin
Set in Baskerville

To John C. Pierrakos, M.D.
Dear friend and close associate

Contents

Contents

Preface

The primary goal of psychiatric endeavor, in the present as in the past, is to bring the mentally ill person into touch with reality. If the break with reality is severe—that is, if the patient isn't oriented in the reality of time, place, or identity —his condition is described as psychotic. He is said to suffer from delusions that distort his perception of reality. When the emotional disturbance is less severe, it is called a neurosis. The neurotic individual is not disoriented, his perception of reality is not distorted, but his conception of reality is unsound. He operates with illusions, and consequently his functioning is not grounded in reality. Because he suffers from illusions, the neurotic person is also considered mentally ill.

Reality, however, is not always easy to define. Which beliefs are illusions and which are sound are often a difficult determination. The belief in spirits that was once widely held by most people would today be regarded as illusory. Similarly the vision of a spirit would be regarded as a delusion. But with the increasing acceptance of extrasensory phenomena our conviction that reality excludes such experiences is becoming shaky. Too narrow a view of reality may also prove illusory. Not infrequently the person who prides himself on being a "realist" can be shown to have hidden illusions.

Preface

There is one indisputable reality in the life of every person, and that is his physical or his body existence. His being, his individuality, his personality are determined by his body. When his body dies, his being a person in the world ceases. No individual exists apart from his body. There is no form of mental existence independent of a person's physical existence. To think otherwise is an illusion. But this statement does not deny that a person's physical existence has a spiritual as well as a material aspect.

From this point of view the concept of mental illness is an illusion. There is no mental disturbance that is not also a physical disturbance. The depressed person is physically depressed, as well as mentally depressed; the two are really one, each is a different aspect of the personality. The same thing is true of every other form of so-called mental illness. The belief that it is "all in the head" is the great illusion of our time, ignoring the fundamental reality that life in all its various manifestations is a physical phenomenon.

The proper term to describe disorders of the personality is "emotional illness." The word "emotion" connotes movement and has, therefore, both a physical and a mental implication. The movement takes place on a physical level, but the perception occurs in the mental sphere. An emotional disturbance involves both levels of the personality. And since it is the spirit that moves the person, the spirit is also involved in every emotional conflict. The depressed individual suffers from a depression of his spirit.

If we wish to avoid the illusion that it is "all in the head," we must recognize that true spirituality has a physical or biological basis. Similarly we must distinguish between faith and belief. Belief is the result of a mental activity, but faith is rooted in the deep biological processes of the body. We will not comprehend the true nature of faith unless we study these processes in men and women who have faith and in those without it. The depressed person is, as we shall see, a person who has lost his faith. How and why he lost it will be the main subject of this book. In the course of this analysis we will arrive at an understanding of the biological basis of the sense of reality and the feeling of faith. The importance of this inquiry cannot be exaggerated, for the loss of faith is the key problem of modern man.

DEPRESSION AND THE BODY

1. Why We Become Depressed

Depression and Unreality

Depression has become so common that one psychiatrist even describes it as a "perfectly normal" reaction, provided, of course, it does not "interfere in our daily tasks." * But even if it is "normal" in the statistical sense of referring to how the greatest number of people feel and behave, it cannot be considered a healthy state. According to this definition of normality, a schizoid tendency with its concomitant feeling of alienation and detachment would also be "normal" when it embraced a majority of the people, provided it was not so severe as to cause individuals to be hospitalized. The same could be said of myopia and lower back pain, whose incidence is so high today as to be the statistically normal condition of modern man.

Since not everybody gets depressed, is schizoid, suffers from myopia, or is troubled by lower back pain, are we to regard these individuals as abnormal? Or are they the truly normal individuals while the larger number suffer from varying degrees of pathology, both psychological and physical? No one can realistically expect a human being to be joyful all the

* Leonard Cammer, *Up from Depression* (New York, Simon & Schuster, 1969), p. 9.

time. Not even our children, closer to this emotion by nature, are constantly joyous. But the fact that we rise only occasionally to heights of joy is not an explanation for depression. The base line for normally healthy human functioning is to "feel good." A healthy person feels good most of the time in the things he does, his relationships, his work, his recreation and his movements. Occasionally, his pleasure rises to joy and may even peak at ecstasy. He will also occasionally experience pain, sadness, sorrow and disappointment. However, he will not get depressed.

To understand this difference let me compare a person to a violin. When the strings are properly tuned, they vibrate and emit sound. One can then play a glad or a sad song, a dirge or an ode to joy. If the strings are improperly tuned, the result will be cacophony. If they are flaccid and without tone, you will get no sound at all. The instrument will be "dead," unable to respond. That is the condition of the depressed person: *He is unable to respond.*

Being unable to respond distinguishes the depressed state from all emotional conditions. A person who is disheartened will regain his faith and hope when the situation changes. A person who is dejected will spring up again when the cause of his condition is removed. A person who is blue will light up at the prospect of pleasure. But nothing evokes a response from the depressed person; often the promise of a good time or pleasure serves only to deepen his depression.

In severe cases of depression the lack of responsiveness to the world is clearly evident. The severely depressed person may sit in a chair and stare at nothing in particular for hours on end. He may lie in bed throughout a good part of the day unable to find the energy to move into the stream of life. But most cases are not so severe. The patients I have treated for depression were not so disabled. They were generally able to carry on with the routines of living. They had jobs they seemed to handle adequately. They were housewives and mothers who were performing the necessary activities. To the casual observer they appeared normal. But they all complained of being depressed, and those who lived with them and knew them well were aware of their condition.

Margaret is typical. She was young, about twenty-five, and married, as she said, to a very fine man. She held a job which she found fairly interesting and about which she voiced no complaints. In fact there was nothing about her life that displeased her, yet she said she suffered from chronic depression. I would not at the outset have said that Margaret was depressed, because when she came into my office, she always smiled and talked about herself very excitedly in a high-pitched voice. No one meeting her for the first time would guess the nature of her problem unless he was astute enough to see that her manner was a mask. If you observed her carefully or caught her off guard, you would notice that at times she became very quiet, and as the smile faded, her face grew blank.

Margaret knew she was depressed. It required an effort of will simply to get up in the morning and go to work. Without it she would lie in bed and do nothing. And, in fact, during an earlier period in her life, there were times when she actually felt immobilized. This no longer happened, however, and there had been a general improvement in Margaret's condition over the years. But there was still something missing in her personality. There was an inner emptiness and a lack of real pleasure. Margaret was hiding something from herself. Her smile, her volubility and her manner were a façade pretending to the world that everything was all right with her. When she was alone, the façade crumbled and she experienced her depressed state.

In the course of her therapy she made contact with a deep feeling of sadness. She realized that she felt she had no right to express her sadness. Yet when she gave in to it, she would cry and the crying always made her feel much better. She could also grow angry at the denial of her right to express her feelings. Kicking the bed with her legs and pounding it with her fists brightened her and lifted her spirits. The real work of the therapy was helping her find the cause of her sadness and eliminating the need for her façade of gaiety. As Margaret got in touch with her feelings and learned how to express them directly, her depression lifted.

In succeeding chapters I will discuss the treatment of depression in some detail. Margaret's case was not presented to show that the therapy of depression is simple or that the results are quick and sure. Some patients get well, others do not respond. Each case is different, each person is unique, and each personality has been shaped by innumerable factors. But whether a patient responds favorably to treatment or not, we can delineate certain common features in all depressive reactions. Let me offer several other cases.

David is a homosexual in his late forties who had achieved considerable success in his profession. He was depressed because, as he said, he had lost much of his sexual potency. Through his work, which he pursued zealously, he had many acquaintances, but he had no close or intimate person to share his life. He was lonely, and it would seem he had every reason to be depressed. But there were observable personality traits in David which suggested other causes.

David's face was a mask, but unlike Margaret he made no effort to mobilize any expression. It was, in fact, so frozen that it had a deathlike quality. His jaw was set and grim, his eyes were dull, and his body had a boardlike rigidity. He complained of a bad back and suffered from angina. His breathing was extremely shallow and his voice thin and flat. Looking at David, I wondered whether he wasn't more dead than alive.

He was equally lifeless in so far as the expression of any feeling was concerned. He just didn't *have* much feeling. After working with him for a long time, helping him to breathe more deeply and to loosen his body, I finally succeeded in getting him to break down and cry as he responded to my interest in him. But it only happened once. David was a stoic. Despite his desire to get well, he was not prepared or able to surrender his unconscious stoicism and indifference. Apropos of this attitude, David recalled an incident out of his childhood that provided some insight into his behavior. His mother, to whom he was still attached, had become hysterical. She was crying and wailing. David had shut himself in his room to get away from her, but she came to his door and alternately demanded and begged him to come out. Despite her pleas, David did not respond. He closed himself up, and in a sense he has remained closed up to this day. David reminded me of the phrase "Grin and bear it" except that in David's case it was "Grim and bear it."

Being locked in, David had always been lonely and to some degree perennially depressed. As he grew older, he tightened up even more. His steadily deepening depression was the direct result of the loss of feeling with its corresponding reduction in vital functioning. This reduction slowly eroded his sexual potency. It was not true that he became depressed because of the loss of potency. Rather, his sexual potency faded as his life faded and as his life forces became depressed. He would still bear up and carry on, but he was functioning more like a machine than a human being. He even went to a gym regularly to make sure his body would stay in good running condition.

Some time ago I treated a psychologist who came into therapy ostensibly to learn the bioenergetic approach to emotional problems.* George had many problems, which we openly discussed, since they were revealed in the physical expression of his body. For one thing, he often assumed an idiotic, clownlike expression which belied his keen intelligence. For another, his body was muscle-bound despite the fact that he had never been an athlete or gone in for any form of body-building exercise. His tight and overdeveloped musculature was due to its work in binding and holding in his feelings.

After the therapy had made considerable progress, he remarked one day, "I feel that I have overcome my depression. I have always been somewhat depressed." This remark came to me as a surprise. He had never mentioned being depressed before, and, strangely, I had not considered that possibility. He never complained of any difficulty in going to work and I knew that he found considerable interest and satisfaction in his profession. He seemed in most respects an active participant in life. In the eyes of the world, then, he would be considered normal.

But George was depressed in his emotional aliveness or responsiveness. He was heavyhearted, his spirit didn't soar, he felt chained, weighed down. His depression wasn't severe enough to cripple him, but it *was* depression nonetheless. This is the common form of depression. Observing people in and outside my office, I have come to the realization that it is very common. Most people lack the inner excitement that would add verve to their lives. They carry on but with a determination that is often grim and with a rigidity characteristic of a machine. The grimness, rigidity and dullness of their inner life is clearly manifest in their bodies and directly reflected in their lives.

* A. Lowen, *The Language of the Body* (New York, Collier Books, paperback 1971).

I shall present one more case, a severely depressed woman who felt suicidal. This patient, whom I shall call Anne, had previously undergone psychoanalytic therapy for a number of years. Her suicidal feelings were of recent origin and seemed to stem from the realization that she was a failure as a woman. This was coupled with the fact that she was approaching forty and had never married. Anne was an intelligent woman who had been successful alike in her career and her creative pursuits. With the collapse of her morale, work became difficult and her creative urge diminished. Several other factors contributed to her collapse, but all were related to the loss of the feeling of femininity and womanhood.

When I first saw Anne, she *looked* collapsed. Her body was flabby, her muscles lacked tone, the skin of her face sagged, her color was poor. She lacked the energy to breathe deeply and her constant comment was "It's no use." When a patient utters these words, what he generally means is, "It's no use trying. I can't make it." But I had the impression that Anne was saying, "It's no use *living*. I simply can't make it." So overwhelming was her sense of failure that she was actually prepared to die. Her body revealed her resignation. But how had she reached that point and what was her struggle about?

Anne's history revealed that at the age of four an event occurred which had a decisive influence on her life. For about a year and a half she had been in the habit of watching her father urinate, often touching his penis and holding it. Then one day he turned on the child, saying, "Leave me alone, you slob." One can easily imagine the little girl's humiliation at the sudden rejection. She felt crushed and withdrew from any physical contact with her father and mother. But of equal significance is the fact that she turned against her own body and against her sexuality.

In her adult life Anne became involved in several lesbian

relationships. She also had an extended affair with a married man. None proved satisfying, for Anne could not allow herself to want or need another person deeply. She had been too badly hurt and her heart was closed. Her way, then, was to give of herself, her intelligence, her creativity and her breasts. All of Anne's sensuality had become localized in her breasts. They were her only source of erotic pleasure, but even this she finally denied herself. About a year before I saw her, she underwent plastic surgery on her breasts, ostensibly to firm them up and make them more attractive, but in view of her subsequent severe depression one can question her conscious motivation. The result was a loss of all feeling in her breasts.

I would guess that the unconscious motivation behind the operation was the wish to cut off all erotic feeling in the body. Her body with its desires had been the cause of her trouble in the first place and had continued to be a source of frustration and dissatisfaction. Her mind, on the other hand, was pure, her intelligence alive, her creative potential great. How tempting it was to forsake the body and live in the clean, ethereal atmosphere of the psyche! But Anne was not a schizoid or schizophrenic personality, and this degree of dissociation was impossible for her. She could deaden her body, but she could not escape it.

Anne's interest in her father's penis was completely innocent. This must, I think, be stated in order to understand the devastating effect of this experience. It stemmed from two sources: One was the natural curiosity all children have concerning the male genital organ, the symbol of procreative life; the other was a transference from the nipple and the breast. This transference occurs when the primary object is unavailable. The lack of a satisfying relationship to her mother not only forced Anne to make such a strong transference to her father but was in itself the fundamental predisposing cause for her depressive tendency. (The role of the mother in the depressive phenomenon will be more fully discussed later.) By her father's rejection Anne was denied the right to find erotic gratification through touch or contact with her father's body. This, in turn, led her to deny the possibility of pleasure in her *own* body. Such an attitude is the basis for a depressive tendency.

What is common to these four cases and to all depressive reactions is the unreality that pervades the person's attitude and behavior. The depressed man or woman lives in terms of the past with a corresponding denial of the present. Anne, for example, maintained the sense of rejection she experienced from her father through her own continual rejection of her body. Thus the past was perpetuated and the trauma of the past was inevitably reenacted in the present. Margaret persisted in denying her sadness, although there was no valid reason in her present situation to justify such behavior. And David found the same morbid satisfaction in his continued isolation and loneliness that he experienced as a child when he closed himself off from his demanding mother. Of course the depressed person is unaware that he lives in the past, for he is also living in the future, a future as unrealistic in terms of the present as was the past itself.

When a person has experienced a loss or trauma in childhood that undermines his feelings of security and self-acceptance, he would project into his image of the future the requirement that it reverse the experience of his past. Thus an individual who experienced a sense of rejection as a child would picture the future as promising acceptance and approval. If he struggled against a sense of helplessness and impotence as a child, his mind would naturally compensate this insult to his ego with an image of the future in which he is powerful and controlling. The mind in its fantasies and daydreams attempts to reverse an unfavorable and unacceptable reality by creating images that exalt the individual and inflate his ego. If a significant part of a person's energy focuses on these images and dreams, he will lose sight of their origin in childhood experience and will sacrifice the present to their fulfillment. These images are unreal goals and their realization is an unattainable objective.

Each of the depressed patients discussed earlier had made such a commitment to an unreal future. Margaret saw it as a time in which there would be no sadness, no pain, and no discord. And she would contribute to this future by the denial of her own feelings of sorrow and resentment. In David's image of his future, he saw himself as admired and loved for his stoicism, completely ignoring the fact that such an attitude prevents communication and actually leads to isolation. George harbored a secret, Walter Mitty-like image of power, which was embodied in his overdeveloped muscles but which ignored the fact that these same muscles chained and bound him. And when I pointed out to Anne that she was barely breathing, she answered, "What's the use of breathing?" But if she didn't breathe, there would, indeed, be *no* future for her intelligence or her creativity. Her dream of a future in which the body was denied in favor of the mind was an impossible one.

The unreality of the depressed person's attitude is most clearly manifest in the degree to which he is out of touch with his body. There is a lack of self-perception; he doesn't see himself as he is, since his mind is focused on an unreal image. He isn't aware of the limitations imposed by his muscular rigidities, yet these limitations are responsible for his inability to fulfill himself as a person in the present. He doesn't sense the disturbances in his bodily functioning, his reduced motility and inhibited respiration, for he identifies himself with his ego, his will and his imagination. The life of his body, which is life in the present, is dismissed as irrelevant, since his eyes are on a future goal that alone has meaning.

The Pursuit of Illusion

Depression is common today because so many people pursue unreal goals that have no direct relation to their basic needs as human beings. Every person needs to love, and he needs to feel that his love is accepted and in some degree returned. Loving and caring relate us to the world and give us the sense of belonging to life. Being loved is important only in so far as it facilitates the active expression of our own love. People don't get depressed when they are the loving ones. Through love you express yourself and affirm your being and identity.

Self-expression is another basic need of all human beings and of all creatures. The need for self-expression underlies all creative activity and is the source of our greatest pleasure. This theme was elaborated in a previous book.* Here it is important to recognize that in the depressed individual self-expression is severely limited if not entirely blocked. In many people it is limited to a small area of their lives, generally their work or business, and even in this defined area, self-expression is restricted if the person works compulsively or mechanically. The self is experienced through self-expression, and the self fades when the avenues of self-expression are closed.

The self is fundamentally a bodily phenomenon, and self-expression therefore means the expression of feeling. The

* Alexander Lowen, *Pleasure: A Creative Approach to Life* (New York, Coward-McCann, 1970).

deepest feeling is love, but all feelings are part of the self and can be appropriately expressed by a healthy personality. In fact the range of feeling a person can express determines the breadth of his personality. It is well known that the depressed person is closed off and that activating any feeling such as sadness or anger, which can then be expressed in crying or striking out, has an immediate and positive effect on his depressive state. The avenues through which feelings are expressed are the voice, body movement and the eyes. When the eyes are dulled, the voice flat and motility reduced, these avenues are closed and the person is in a depressed state.

Another basic need of all human beings is freedom. Without freedom, self-expression is impossible. But I do not mean just political freedom, although this is one of its essential aspects. One wants to be free in all life situations—at home, in school, as an employee, in social relationships. It is not absolute freedom that is sought, but the freedom to express oneself, to have a voice in the regulation of one's affairs. Every human society imposes some limitations on individual freedom in the interest of social cohesion. Such limitations can be accepted, however, only if they do not unduly restrict the right of self-expression.

There are, however, internal prisons as well as external ones. These internal bars to self-expression are often more powerful than laws or forcible restraints in limiting a person's ability to express himself. And since they are often unconscious or rationalized, the person is more strictly imprisoned by them than he would be if they were external forces.

The depressed person is imprisoned by unconscious barriers of "shoulds" and "shouldn'ts," which isolate him, limit him, and eventually crush his spirit. Living within this prison, he spins fantasies of freedom, concocts schemes for his liberation, and dreams of a world where life will be different. These dreams like all illusions serve to sustain his spirit, but they also prevent him from realistically confronting the internal forces that bind him. Sooner or later the illusion collapses, the dream fades, the scheme fails, and his reality stares him in the face. When this happens, he becomes depressed and feels hopeless.

In pursuit of our illusions we set up unreal goals—that is, goals which if achieved would, we believe, automatically set us free, restore our right to self-expression, and make us capable of loving. What is unreal is not the goal but the reward that is supposed to follow from its achievement. Among the goals so many of us pursue so relentlessly are wealth, success and fame. In our culture there is a mystique about being rich. We divide people into the "haves" and the "have-nots." We believe the rich are privileged in that they have the means to fulfill their desires and therefore to realize themselves. Unfortunately for many people it doesn't work out that way. The rich, as well as the poor, get depressed. No amount of money can provide the inner satisfactions that alone make life worth living. In most cases the drive to gain wealth diverts energy from activities that are more creative and self-expressive, resulting in an impoverishment of the spirit.

Success and fame are in a slightly different class. The drive for success and fame is based on the illusion that not only will they increase our self-esteem but also they will increase our esteem among others and gain for us the acceptance and approval we seem to need. Yes, they do add to our self-esteem and they increase our prestige in the community. But these apparent gains do little for the inner person. Too many successful people have committed suicide at the height of their achievement. No one has found true love through fame, and few have overcome their inner sense of loneliness because of it. No matter how loud the applause nor how wild the crowd's acclaim, it doesn't touch the heart. Although these goals are glorified in a mass society, *real life is still lived on a very personal level.*

We can define an unreal goal, therefore, as one to which an unrealistic expectation is attached. The real object behind the drive for money, success or fame is self-acceptance, self-esteem, and self-expression. To be poor, a failure or unknown is for many people to be a "nobody" and therefore to be at once unworthy of love and incapable of loving. But if one believes that wealth, success or fame can change a "nobody" into a "somebody," he is suffering an illusion. The successful person may appear to be a "somebody" because he is surrounded by the outer signs of importance: clothes, cars, home, celebrity. He may present the image of a "somebody," but images are superficial phenomena which often have little relation to the inner life. In fact, when a person has to project the image of being a "somebody," it indicates that on the inside he feels himself to be a "nobody." This feeling results from the dissociation of the ego from the body. The person who identifies with his ego and denies the importance of the body, in effect, has no body. The loss of the feeling of the body which is equivalent to feeling oneself a "nobody" forces one to substitute an image based on a social, political, or economic position for the reality of the body.

If we seek to know the real person behind the façade of social behavior, we must look at his body, sense his feelings, and understand his relationships. His eyes will tell us if he can love, his face will show if he is self-expressive, and his movements will reveal the degree of his inner freedom. When we are in contact with an alive and vibrant body, we sense immediately that we are in the presence of a "somebody," regardless of his social position. And regardless of what we are taught, life is really lived on this personal level, where one body relates to another or a body relates to the natural environment. All the rest is stage setting, and if we confuse the setting with the drama of life, we are indeed in the grip of illusion.

An unreal goal necessitates an approved mode of being, for behind this goal is the need for approval. The goal was originally set in childhood, and the desired approval was that of the parents later transferred to others. I shall illustrate this aspect of the problem with another case history.

I treated a young woman who consulted me because of a severe depressive reaction following the breakup of her marriage. She had discovered that her husband was sexually involved with another woman, and it came to her as a shock. She was a modern, sophisticated person, well aware that such things commonly happen. Further, the relationship between husband and wife was not without conflict; the husband did not earn enough money and my patient used her ingenuity to provide a comfortable home for him and their child. In addition, there were sexual problems in the marriage. My patient, Selma, had never reached a climax in the course of the sexual act.

Was Selma depressed because she had lost her husband's love? It is difficult to estimate how much love exists between two people, but as I worked with Selma, I did not have the impression that she suffered grief because of the loss. She was lonely, but loneliness is not the equivalent of depression. And she still had her child and her home to take care of.

Selma was shocked because she hadn't anticipated that she could be deceived and that she was so vulnerable to the deception. She suffered a real loss in self-esteem. She had regarded herself as superior to her husband in many ways. She believed herself more intelligent, more sensitive, and more realistic. She felt he needed her. She could help him further his ambition and achieve success. She saw herself as an inspiring force and as the director and manager of his affairs.

It is easy to see why Selma would be shocked, functioning as she did with this picture of herself in mind. She could not conceive that her husband would turn to another woman, since she saw herself as all any man could want, the perfect little wife. This inflated self-image was abruptly punctured by the deception. Her ego collapsed, and Selma was plunged into depression.

The unreal goal Selma was pursuing was a relationship in which she would feel *completely* secure because the other person could not dream of doing without her. The need for such absolute security denotes the presence of a deep inner personal insecurity, which emerged in the course of her treatment. Her parents were divorced when she was young, and she was deeply hurt by the loss of her relationship with her father. There were other emotional deprivations in her early years which shaped her personality, creating a need for an inordinate amount of security. But Selma was unaware of it and had even transferred it to her husband. *He* needed security, she maintained, and she would give it to him by a wholehearted devotion to his interests.

The unreal goals to which Selma had consecrated her energy were to be a perfect wife and mother and to obtain thereby the constant and unwavering love denied her as a child. One goal was internal, the other external, but both were impossible to attain. The striving for perfection reduces an individual's humanity and becomes self-defeating. It can operate only to make another person appear less than perfect. In Selma's attitude to her husband we can detect a note of contempt and we can suspect an underlying hostility. She expressed many bitter and negative feelings toward him as she worked her way out of her depression.

The search for an unwavering love is also self-defeating. What Selma wanted was more than the commitment of a husband to share his life with a woman. She wanted the man bound to her out of his need and admiration. But no one wants to be bound, it is a limitation on one's individual freedom. Selma's husband could react to this unexpressed demand only with a latent resentment and rebellion, which eventually drove him to another woman.

The investment of energy and effort Selma had made in attempting to fulfill her unreal goals was considerable. It began before her adolescence and only ended with her collapse. When it came, she was exhausted—physically depleted as well as psychically depressed. And her depression can be viewed as nature's way of calling a halt to a senseless waste of energy and giving her time to recuperate. Pathological as a depressive reaction is, it is also a recuperative phenomenon. The collapse is like a return to an infantile state, and, with time, most people recover spontaneously.

Unfortunately, recovery is not permanent. As soon as his energy returns, the formerly depressed person renews his endeavor to fulfill his dream. Sometimes this rebound from the depressed state is so sudden and uncontrollable that the person goes into a high as far above the ground as he was previously below it. These wild mood swings from depression to elation and even mania presage another depressive reaction to follow. The elation is due to an exaggerated conceit that *everything will be different this time,* the way an alcoholic swears he has touched his last drop. It never is. As long as an unreal goal persists in the unconscious and directs behavior, depression is inevitable.

If depression is common today it is because much of our

lives are lived in unreality, much of our energy is devoted to the pursuit of unreal goals. We are like stock market speculators playing for paper profits that very few of us cash in for real enjoyment. This investment in equities that lie outside ourselves as human beings overinflates their real value. A bigger house, a newer car, more appliances, and so on have a measure of positive value, they can contribute something to life's pleasure. But if we look to these things as a measure of our personal worth, if we expect their ownership to fulfill our empty lives, we set the stage for an inevitable deflation, which will depress our spirits just as surely as the stock market speculator becomes depressed when the speculative fever fades and the market crashes.

We are liable to depression when we look to sources outside the self for fulfillment. If we think that having all the material advantages our neighbors possess will make us more of a person, more at peace with ourselves and more self-expressive, we will be sadly disillusioned. When disillusionment sets in, we will become depressed. Since this is the attitude of so many people today, I believe we will see a rising incidence of depression and suicide.

The Inner-Directed Person

From the viewpoint of a tendency to depression, people can be divided into two categories, the outer- and the inner-directed. These are not absolute categories but merely convenient terms for describing attitudes and behavior; actually many people fall in the middle, but most show a preponderance of one or the other of these patterns. For reasons which will become apparent soon, the outer-directed man or woman is vulnerable to depression where the inner-directed is much less so.

Broadly speaking, the inner-directed person has a strong

and deep sense of self. Unlike the outer-directed person his behavior and attitudes are not easily influenced by the changing patterns of his environment. His personality has an inner stability and order and rests on the firm foundation of self-awareness and self-acceptance. He stands on his own feet and he knows where he stands. These qualities are lacking in the person who is outer-directed. He shows strong dependent tendencies, requiring others to lean on emotionally. Then, when their support is withdrawn, he becomes depressed. He has what is called an "oral" character structure, which means that his infantile needs to be held, to be accepted, and to experience body contact and warmth were not fulfilled. Feeling unfulfilled, he has no reason to have faith either in himself or in life.

One difference between the inner- and outer-directed person is where he puts his faith. The inner-directed person places his faith in himself. The outer-directed person puts what faith he has in other people and so risks constant disappointment. He is forever seeking something outside himself to believe in: a person, a system, a belief, a cause, or an activity. On a conscious level he is very much identified with his outside interests. Offhand, this might seem a positive approach; on the surface it appears he is involved and doing things. But the doing is for others, and it is done with the unconscious expectation that the others will recognize his worth and respond with love, acceptance, and support. The inner-directed person acts and does things for himself. His primary identification is with himself as a person, and his activities are an expression of who he is. He finds his fulfillment in his response to the world rather than in the world's response to him. Whatever unsatisfied needs he had as an infant, and we all have some of them, he doesn't expect them to be satisfied by others now.

It would be easy to divide people into independent and

dependent types and to equate the inner-directed person with the former as I have equated the outer-directed person with the latter. I have avoided this classification because appearances are often misleading. The outer-directed person often acts very independently. He often sets himself up as the one who is needed and so appears to be the independent one. Such behavior is a clear indication that the person is outer-directed and therefore really dependent underneath his self-sufficient façade. And, as we saw, this role is intended to fulfill his dependent needs while he hides them from himself and others. The person who can openly express his dependent needs is not as likely to become depressed as the person who hides them behind an appearance of independence.

Another important difference between these two personality types lies in the way they recognize their problems and define their desires. The inner-directed person knows what he wants and expresses it concretely. He may say, for example, "I feel I'm pushing myself too hard and need to let down," or he may observe, "My body is too tight and my breathing too shallow. I need to open up." He speaks personally from a position of self-awareness. The outer-directed person cannot do this; his demands are general and couched in broad terms like "I want love" or "I want to be happy." This style of speaking denotes a lack of self-awareness and strong feeling that would ensure him the self-centeredness possessed by the inner-directed man.

An inner direction is given by a strong feeling that allows only one course of action. This does not mean that the inner-directed person is dominated by a single feeling and moves only in one direction. Such an attitude would imply a rigidity, which would inevitably collapse when the person could no longer maintain the required tension. In a healthy person feelings are constantly changing. One can be angry, then loving, sad, then joyful. Each strong feeling creates a new direction that is the organism's personal response to its environment. All true emotions have this personal quality. They are direct expressions of the life forces within the person.

Faith can be seen as an aspect of feeling. The more one feels, the stronger is his faith. One doesn't feel faith. What one normally feels are the different emotions. But when one acts on an emotion or strong feeling, one acts on faith—faith in the validity of one's feelings, faith in one's self.

The person who lacks faith has suppressed all his strong emotions. In their place he has substituted a set of beliefs or illusions to guide and direct his behavior. He may, for example, be a radical student who believes that violence is the only means of overthrowing an established system which he views as oppressive. In behalf of this belief he may muster considerable energy and evoke what may appear to be genuine feelings. But his feelings are not personal. He is not angry because of a personal insult. He is not sad because of a personal loss. He has set aside his personal feelings in favor of what he believes to be the needs of others. And by this very action he betrays that he is an outer-directed person. Too often these people become depressed when the cause for which they struggle and suffer meets a reverse.

I am not arguing against involvement in causes. But it seems that our first concern must be the advancement of our own well-being. If each individual could do for himself, if he could take care of his own needs, the world would inevitably be a better place. However the inner-directed person is not selfish. He is self-centered, and a true self-concern makes him aware that he depends on the welfare of all others in his community. He is a true humanitarian because he is conscious of his own humanity, his own being as a person.

Transferring our problems to others and demanding their

solution by others is a mark of the outer-directed person. It is, sadly, also the mark of our time. Regretfully we watch the gradual erosion of the sense of personal responsibility. Without intending to, psychoanalysis has unfortunately contributed to this situation. Having shown in every thorough analysis that the individual is not to blame for his handicaps and misfortunes, it has without saying so encouraged the opposite tendency—the tendency for the suffering individual to place the blame on society. If society is at fault, then society should remedy the problem. Since society is all the *other* people, no one individual feels personally responsible.

Society is a vague entity, it lacks real power. What happens is that the burden for all our personal and social ills is shifted to the government. It is difficult to conceive how the government can overcome our depressive reactions, cure our schizoid tendencies, protect us against anxiety, and so on. When individual citizens forgo their personal responsibility to keep the community clean, orderly and safe, it becomes difficult for the government even to provide essential services. It is an illusion to believe that all the government has to do is to come up with more money and all our social problems will be remedied. Such illusions characterize the outer-directed person.

A combination of faith and personal responsibility is at the core of every religious system. If the individual did not assume a responsibility to uphold the moral and ethical principles that add the flesh of life to religious beliefs, religious faith would be meaningless. Faith and belief form an integrated whole when both are part of one's daily life. For people who possess this combination the tendency to depression is greatly reduced.

However it is also true that many people who become depressed have shown an apparent degree of personal responsibility similar to their apparent independence. They have made the effort to stand on their own feet, but we can surmise from their subsequent depression that the effort was not wholehearted. Analysis always reveals in these cases that the effort was not made for its own value but as a means of gaining approval and acceptance. This dissembled responsibility is vastly different from the sincere religious belief that each mature individual is responsible to himself and to his God for the quality of his life. One can only be impressed by the strength and courage of truly religious people in facing great difficulty and hardships. Such resoluteness is not common today.

When a person becomes depressed, it is a clear indication that he has not been standing on his own feet. It is a sign he lacks faith in himself. He has sacrificed his independence for the promise of fulfillment by others. He has invested his energies in the attempt to realize this dream—the impossible dream. His depression signifies his bankruptcy and disillusionment. But when properly understood and handled, the depressive reaction can open the way to a new and better life.

Many people are helped to overcome their depression by therapy—therapy that helps the patient get in touch with his feelings, his inner being. This, in turn, helps him regain a measure of self-possession and independence. In the process it reorients him to the personal self. When successful, it finishes by restoring an individual's faith in himself. If he is to overcome his depressive tendency, he must end by becoming an inner-directed person.

2. Grounding in Reality

Elation and Depression

Since the depressive reaction is what brings a person into therapy and is his main complaint, we tend to overlook the fact that it is generally part of a cycle that consists of a high and a low. In most cases the depressive reaction is preceded by a period of elation, the collapse of which plunges the individual into depression. If we are to comprehend fully the depressive reaction, we must also understand the phenomenon of elation.

The signs of elation are not difficult to discern. The elated person is hyperactive, his speech is more rapid, his ideas seem to flow freely, and his self-esteem is conspicuous. Further development of this phenomenon leads to the condition of mania. Psychoanalysis has long been concerned with the problem of mania and depression. Otto Fenichel sees the depressive reaction as being primary, which it is historically. He says, "The triumphant character of mania arises from the release of energy bound in the depressive struggle and now seeking discharge." * Seen from the point of view of the ego, there is some validity to this interpretation. In the depressed

* Otto Fenichel, *The Psychoanalytic Theory of Neurosis* (New York, W. W. Norton & Co., 1945), p. 408.

state the ego is tied to the collapsed body, having been over-whelmed by feelings of hopelessness and despair. It struggles to get free, and when it does, it rises triumphant like a gas balloon released from the hand of a child, becoming steadily more inflated as it goes upward. There is an increase of ex-citation in the manic condition, but this increased excitation or energetic charge is limited to the head and to the surface of the body, where it activates the voluntary muscular system producing the characteristic hyperactivity and exaggerated volubility. This direction of flow, upward rather than down-ward, does not lead to discharge, which is a function of the lower end of the body. It serves instead to focus attention on the individual and represents an attempt to restore the sense of infantile omnipotence that was prematurely lost. Fenichel recognizes the illusive character of mania, saying, "The mania is not a genuine freedom from depression but a cramped denial of dependencies." *

The elated state is only a lesser degree of this reaction. The ego of the elated individual is also overexcited, as if in an-ticipation of some extraordinary or miraculous event that would realize the person's deepest desire. We can compare this reaction to that of a child who has been separated from his mother and now anticipates her return with intense ex-citement. For a very young child the return of a lost mother (or the restoration of her love) is his deepest desire. Her love represents the fulfillment of all needs.

Every depressive reaction rests on the loss of mother love. I shall discuss this aspect of the problem in a subsequent chapter. Here it is important simply to know that this loss has not been accepted as irrevocable. The hope of restitution, generally unconscious, provides the motivation for the up-ward swing of energy, which results in elation. Unfortunately,

* Fenichel, *op. cit.*, p. 410.

the elated individual is unaware of the dynamics of his reaction and of the fact that he unconsciously regards the people around him as substitute mother figures who will love him, take care of him, and even feed him. Their initial interest in him appears to support this transference. But as his elation grows, people are disturbed by it and withdraw. There is no possibility of their satisfying his unconscious expectations, and sooner or later the elated individual will feel rejected. Then the bubble of self-confidence and self-esteem that accompanied the feeling of elation will collapse and a depressive reaction will ensue. The collapse is a bioenergetic phenomenon. The energetic charge that had overexcited the peripheral structures retreats to the center of the body, the region of the diaphragm, stomach and solar plexus. The omnipotence of the ego changes to impotence. Through no effort of will can the depressed person continue to mobilize himself.

People who suffer depression have unfulfilled oral needs—to be held and supported, to experience body contact, to suck, to receive attention and approval, and to be warmed. These are called oral needs because they correspond to that period of life, infancy, when oral activity dominates life. This is the same as saying that these individuals were deprived of mother love or of the fulfillment that a secure and unconditional love would provide. If this deprivation determines a person's basic character structure, that structure can be described as an oral personality.* In the adult these unfulfilled needs are revealed by an inability to be alone, a fear of separation, excessive talking or other activity, boasting or other maneuvers to gain attention, a sensitivity to cold, and a dependent attitude. If the deprivation is less severe, we say the individual has oral traits or an oral tendency in his personality.

* A. Lowen, *Physical Dynamics of Character Structure* (New York, Grune & Stratton, 1958).

Oral needs unsatisfied in childhood cannot be fulfilled in adult life. No amount of substitute mothering can give a person the security he failed to get in childhood. As an adult he must find this security within himself. No matter how much attention, admiration, approval or love one gives the oral personality, it does not fill his inner emptiness. This fulfillment can be achieved by an adult only on an adult level; that is, through love, through his work and through his sexuality. The dream that one can reverse the past is an illusion. When a patient is encouraged to regress to an infantile state in therapy, the purpose is to have him experience the deprivation and to confront the conflicts and feelings it caused. The objective is to overcome his unconscious infantile fixation and thereby to help him function more fully as an adult in the present. As long as his oral needs continue to influence his behavior, he will be subject to cyclical mood swings of elation and depression.

I have seen this happen so often with oral personalities that when I work with them, I caution against becoming elated. If they do become elated, I warn against the forthcoming depression. Such advance warning is always helpful, since it introduces a note of reality into their thinking, acting like a brake on the mood swings so that when depression ensues, it is not so severe. In a state of elation one thinks that everything will work out splendidly. But it can't if a person's underlying problems have not been worked through. Keeping such a patient "down" keeps him more in touch with these problems and therefore facilitates their resolution.

"Down" also has another meaning. As opposed to the up, which is toward the head, down is toward the lower part of the body, the legs, and the ground. The down state for any person is closer to his reality. Actually, when a person falls from an elated state into depression, he goes so far down that he seems to be buried in a hole in the ground from which he cannot see the light of day. It becomes necessary, then, to help him pull himself out, but this can be done only if the patient recognizes that he never really stood on solid ground. The hole was always there, camouflaged perhaps by some twigs and leaves, but not strong enough to act as a solid base for the personality. The patient never really trusted this covering, for he had never allowed the full weight of his being or his body to rest on it. He had tried to hold himself up from above by his ego or will and had fallen into depression when this illusory support collapsed. But his reaction each time was to rise higher off the ground instead of building a firm base on which to stand. When he is elated, he is up, "up in the air," "up in the clouds," and his feet do not "really" rest on the ground.

In a healthy person there are no mood swings of elation and depression. He always has his feet on the ground—the base line from which he operates. He may become excited by some event or prospect which brings the energy strongly into his head, but his feet never really leave terra firma. His feeling may be one of pleasure or even joy, but rarely is it one of elation. If the event or the prospect proves ultimately disappointing, he may be saddened, somewhat dejected, but not depressed. He does not lose his ability to respond to new situations, as the victim of a depressive reaction does.

When people swing between highs and lows, it indicates that bioenergetically they have lost the sense of their feet resting or standing on solid ground. I think the same could be said of a culture that swings between highs and lows, between an overoptimistic enthusiasm that all its problems will be easily solved and the despair that they are insoluble. If people keep their feet on the ground, they can view their problems realistically, seeing that they are mountainous but knowing that human beings with faith have moved mountains.

While the highs portend the lows, they should also be seen as an attempt to escape the low feelings one has inside oneself. This is the only explanation for the desperation with which so many young people seek through drugs to get high. The drug trip or flight lifts their minds up and out of their bodies—away from the low down-in-the-hole feelings they would otherwise have. It is hard to blame young people for seeking this escape when doctors prescribe other drugs to accomplish the same purpose for their parents. I am not blaming the doctors either, since desperation, depression, and despair are forms of living death which are often intolerable to bear. Unfortunately no drug is of lasting help. The high it induces is always followed by a low, and so a psychological dependence on the drug is created, which can be as devastating as any physiological dependence. Our salvation can lie only in understanding the lows and accepting them, for they, at least, provide some solid ground on which to build.

Alcoholic highs are, of course, no different from drug highs or other manic or elated episodes. The person who takes a drink to get high obviously needs something to lift him out of a low feeling. I am not saying that everyone who takes a drink is running away from depression. If one *needs* a drink, it is a bad sign. The person who can take or leave alcohol, can enjoy its mild relaxing and stimulating effects. It is the person who seeks the high that we are talking about. When he is high he is almost literally off the ground, his balance is disturbed, his feet are unsteady, and he may actually feel that there is a space between his feet and the earth.

Everyone knows an alcoholic high is followed by a low. When there are physical symptoms, we call it a hangover. But even without any physical aftereffects the next day's mood is down. This increases the need for another drinking episode, if one can't face his low feeling. Coming down from a drug high may be somewhat different. The effects of drugs are generally longer lasting than those of alcohol. The person coming down from a drug high may not feel low the next day because drugs are more potent agents in cutting off feelings than alcohol. Marijuana highs tend to leave the person in a state of apathy, which may not be experienced as low because it is not experienced at all. Some people may claim that they have taken trips from which they emerged feeling elated. I will not dispute this claim, since there are exceptions to every generalization. But it is not the common experience.

Some people must be desperate indeed if we can judge by the fact that they try to stay high all the time. Hard-line drug addicts fall into this category. So painful is the low that the high must be maintained at all costs. But I occasionally meet a person who asks, "Well, why can't we stay high all the time?" Such a question reveals his degree of unreality. I suppose one can stay high on drugs until one cracks up or dies, but those are final descents which permit, in the latter case, no further upward movement. Nothing stays up all the time, not even a tree or a mountain. But how long it does depends on how well it is rooted in the ground in the case of a tree or how solid its base in the case of a mountain. For a tree, up doesn't mean high, it means erect.

I have spoken of a depressed person's falling into a hole in the ground. Actually the hole is in his feelings or, more precisely, in his body. The hole in one's feeling is the sense of inner emptiness of which many individuals complain, notably people with an oral character structure. The hole in the body is a lack of sensation in the belly. I described earlier in the case of the oral character how the charge retreats from his head end to the center of the body. It doesn't flow through that region into the lower part of the body. It is held in the midsection out of fear—an unconscious fear—that there is no ground to rest on, nothing or nobody to hold or support him if he lets go. As a result of this holding, the lower part of the body is energetically undercharged, which contributes greatly to the sense of insecurity. And the belly containing the guts also lacks feeling or charge. When feeling is absent there, it is as if one didn't have any guts when it came to standing on one's own feet and taking a position in life. The empty belly, the deep fear that one lacks "guts," or that one will not be able to stand up in a crisis is a gaping hole in the personality.

In Japanese thinking, the belly is regarded as man's vital center. It is called *hara*. As Karlfried Durckheim points out, the Japanese "realize that life on earth both in its need and in its fulfillment can be rightly achieved only if a man does not fall out of the cosmic order and if he maintains his contact with the great original unity. Enduring contact with it is shown by the man who keeps his unshakeable centre of gravity in that centre which is *hara*." * Thus in the figure of Buddha, as in that of the other great teachers, the belly is shown as the center, "from which all motion flows and from which it receives its force, direction, and measure." † Whether or not we accept this Japanese view, we must recognize that the belly is that part of the body in which the individual life has its inception and from which it emerges into the light of day.

According to the Japanese, if a man has *hara*, it means he is centered. It also means he is balanced both physically and psychologically. A balanced person is calm, at ease, and as long as he remains that way, his movements are effortless and yet masterful. *Hara* is the secret of Zen archery, for the man

* Karlfried Durckheim, *Hara, The Vital Centre of Man* (London, George Allen & Unwin Ltd., 1962), p. 27.
† *Ibid.*, p. 26.

who possesses it is attuned through his vital center to all the forces in the external world. Thus his movements are not willed but flow naturally as the response of his total being to a situation.

One may well ask: Why is the belly so important? The answer is that it is the *seat* of life. Literally one *sits* in one's belly and so one has contact through it with the pelvic floor, the sexual organs and the legs. If one pulls oneself upward into the chest or the head, this essential contact is lost. The upward direction is toward consciousness and the ego. In a culture which overemphasizes these values, the correct bodily posture is belly in, chest out. In ancient mythology the diaphragm was equated with the surface of the earth. Everything above the surface was light and therefore conscious. Below the surface was darkness, which represented the unconscious. By holding oneself above the diaphragm, one splits consciousness from its deep roots in the unconscious. The importance of the belly and the significance of *hara* is that only if one is in one's belly, feeling-wise, is the split between consciousness and the unconscious, between the ego and the body, between the self and the world avoided. *Hara* represents a state of integration or unity in the personality on all levels of life.

A person who has *hara* is, of course, an inner-directed person with all the appropriate qualities. Actually, *hara* represents an even higher state, one of transcendence in which an individual, through the full realization of his being, feels himself part of the great Unity or Universal. Such a person has faith not as a matter of belief, which is a function of mind consciousness, but as a deep inner conviction which he feels in his guts. Only such a faith has true sustaining power. This view makes us realize that real faith cannot be preached. It can be gained only by experiences which reach into and evoke gut sensations.

To be fulfilled is to be filled full, and that means a full

belly whether of good food or good feelings. This is not the same as a paunch, which is an accumulation of fat on the outside of a tight, constricted abdominal wall. That the fullness of the belly is a sign of an organism's vitality was dramatically demonstrated to me many years ago. My bitch had given birth to her first litter—ten live pups. As this was also our first experience with whelping, my wife and I were at a loss on how to handle the situation. If left alone, the stronger pups would get all the milk, leaving the weakest to die. At the end of the first day we called a veterinarian. His solution was simple. He divided the pups into two groups, the stronger and the weaker. The weaker ones got first crack at the teats. When they were through, the stronger were allowed to nurse. To separate the pups, he picked each one up and felt its belly. Those with full bellies were considered the stronger. Under this arrangement all ten pups thrived.

Grounding the Individual

Getting feelings into the belly so that a person can sense his guts and into his legs so that he can sense them as mobile roots is called grounding the individual. The person thus grounded feels he has the solid support of the earth under him and the courage to stand up or move about on it as he wishes. To be grounded is to be in touch with reality; the two are synonymous in our language. We often say that a person fully in touch with reality "has his feet on the ground" or that he is "well grounded." It follows that when an individual is grounded, he no longer operates on the basis of illusions. He doesn't need them. On the other hand, the person who holds onto his illusions, whether he really needs them or not, keeps himself up in the clouds and so prevents himself from becoming grounded. Every good psychiatrist works to dispel his patient's illusions, which is why some people call him a shrink. This is a much easier task to do once the person has become depressed or down because, temporarily at least, his illusions have lost their power to keep him hung up.

However, under no conditions is grounding a simple task. There are deep anxieties standing in the way. I have mentioned the fear that there is no one to lend support should the person let go. Verbal reassurances to the contrary are well-meaning but empty gestures. The person who opens his heart to others quickly discovers that he is not alone. Almost every-one responds warmly to a person whose heart is open. But to reach this openness of being, he must go through his anxiety about feeling alone to learn that it is no longer relevant.

The average individual is also afraid that if he lets himself down, he may never rise again. Within his belly are feelings of deep sadness and despair to which he is afraid to yield. He has committed his energies to the struggle to overcome them. Giving in to them would be experienced, therefore, as a personal failure, a defeat of the ego and a seeming loss of integrity. Yet he longs to surrender, for the struggle no longer makes sense, since it has become a struggle against the self. He is frightened, but if he is working with a therapist who has brought others through their personal hell, he can take courage from the faith of his doctor. A psychiatrist has to be a man of "faith"—that is, he has to be grounded himself— if he is to impart some faith to his patients.

When a patient begins to allow sensation to develop in his belly, he will invariably cry. He will cry both from the sad-ness of a life without faith and the gladness that a life with faith may be possible for him. It is not just tears that will flow. His whole body will be convulsed with sobs, sometimes pain-fully, sometimes pleasurably. By cutting off belly sensation he had suppressed his crying as a child when he found it failed to bring him the love, security and comfort he needed. As sensation returns, so do these feelings, not once but over and over again until the pain of the past is fully washed away.

Then as the feelings develop deeper in the belly, touching the pelvic floor, they will change into sexual sensations, which for most human beings are a major source of anxiety. To understand this anxiety we must distinguish between sexual and genital sensations. Genital sensations are part of the sexual, but the reverse is not true. Sexuality is a function of the whole body, including the genital apparatus when that is operative in adult life. Genitality, on the other hand, is a limited aspect of the total sexual response. In many individuals, the genital function is split off and dissociated from the body's feelings just as, at the other end of the organism, the ego is also dissociated from these same feelings. Sexual anxiety attaches to body sensations, not to genital sensations. These bodily sensations can be very frightening, whereas purely genital sensations, as are involved in a male erection, for example, pose no threat to the personality.

What, you may wonder, are these sexual sensations? They are the melting and streaming sensations deep within the body that in both men and women precede genital excitation. When they occur, they indicate that sexual desire is flowing through the body and is not limited just to the head and genital organs. But, then, why are they so frightening? Because they are the beginning of a dissolution that will culminate in the ecstasy of a full orgasm but which to the neurotic or schizoid personality are first experienced as a dissolution of the self, a surrender over which he has no control, a letting go from which there is no return. Everyone seeks this dissolution, this surrender and letting go, but few have the faith that would allow it to happen. In our insecurity we hang onto our precious selves, to our egos and to our genital potency, and we are not prepared to surrender everything in the name of love.

In most people there are anxieties connected with the urinary and anal functions that must also be resolved. Most of us have learned the lesson that these functions can cause us much pain, shame and humiliation if not rigorously controlled. We have been praised for such control and punished when it failed. We have been taught that it is wrong to let nature take its course, that one must be in control at all times. Now, we cannot let go of our tight asses and uptight pelvic floors. We are afraid that the bottom will fall out of things if we do. We don't really know how to relax the contracted muscles that surround our body's lower apertures.

Finally, there is the anxiety that accompanies standing on one's own feet. It is not that we are afraid of it, but true independence signifies being alone. The fear of being alone, I would say, is probably the overriding anxiety of our time. No one really wants to be alone. We are gregarious by our very nature, but in many people the fear of being alone rises to irrational heights. Out of this fear they will go to any length to conform. They will forsake their individuality because of it, assuming, erroneously, that the person who is a true individual, who dares to be himself in opposition to others, will be ostracized or rejected. This fear fosters the mass society with its mass media, mass entertainment, and so on.

And yet, strange as it may seem, it is the mass individual who is truly alone, who lacks the deep and intimate personal relationships that unite people. And it is the individual who stands alone, on his own feet, who feels and knows the unity that relates man to man and man to woman. Being true to himself, he attracts people, and his responses to them are genuine and heartfelt. In his feeling he is never alone, whereas the mass individual feels alone even in the crowd. The true individual doesn't play games, he doesn't barter a pat on the back for one in return. He gives of himself generously and he takes of others freely.

The fear of rejection associated with standing on one's own feet stems from early experiences in the home. In many homes a child is often made to feel rejected if he doesn't accept the dictates of his parents. Some mothers do not hesitate to withdraw their affection if their children oppose them or become negative. Either the child goes along with parental demands or he is made to feel an outsider. We shall see the effect of this kind of child rearing in a case study to be presented later.

But behind this superficial submission there is a sense of rebellion that grows more perverse with time. In the most depressed patient one can uncover the attitude (generally buried deep) "I was made to feel unwanted, now I don't really want anything." This perversity may seem to unite rebels in a common cause but rarely in a common feeling. People with a lack of faith are not kindred spirits, although they may find themselves on the same side of a protest or demonstration.

Treating the depressed patient, one must understand his perversity and accept his rebellion. Only by his rebellion can he mobilize the feelings that will free him to be a true person. His protest is against a system that denied him the right to be himself and deprived him of the security associated with this right, with loving and being loved. But it is not in rebellion that he will find the faith he needs or the ground on which to stand. The rebel is still an outsider who longs to belong but can't or won't admit it.

We don't ask a patient to give up his rebellion but to go beyond it to a faith in life that transcends any system or its ideology. By grounding him in the feelings of his body, in his animal sexuality, and in the earth from which he came, we restore him to the family of man and to the kingdom of nature. We return him to that basic faith that sustained his earliest ancestors, the faith that he was made for this world and that the world was made for him. How and why grounding an individual can accomplish these goals requires further exploration.

Grounding is a bioenergetic concept and not just a psychological metaphor. When we ground an electrical circuit, we provide an outlet for the discharge of its energy. In a human being grounding also serves to release or discharge the excitation of a body. The excess energy of the living organism is constantly being discharged through movement or through the sexual apparatus. Both are functions of the lower part of the body. The upper part is mainly concerned with the intake of energy either in the form of food, oxygen or sensory stimulation and excitation. These two basic processes of charging up and discharging down are normally in balance. Within the body there is an energetic pulsation; feeling moves upward toward the head when we are in need of energy or excitation and downward toward the lower end when discharge is necessary. If a person cannot adequately charge up, he will be weak, undercharged, and show a lack of vitality. If he cannot adequately discharge, he will be hung up. One gets hung up on some illusion and is unable to come down to earth until the illusion collapses. But one will not stay down unless one is grounded in the function of discharge.

The function of discharge is experienced as pleasure. We know this from common experience, which tells us that the discharge of any state of tension or excitation is pleasurable. We also know it from the pleasure of sex when the discharge of feeling has been intense. Sigmund Freud pointed it out and Wilhelm Reich documented it. We have felt the pain of an inability to discharge a state of tension. We can surmise that the hung-up individual is in a state of pain. However he does not consciously experience his pain. He has deadened himself to it by rigidifying his structure. And he is afraid to release the rigidity because that would evoke the pain. When a hung-up condition becomes second nature to a person, he also loses the awareness of his rigidity. What he does sense is a lack of pleasure in his life, which forces him to intensify his drive for money, success or fame, or to attain whatever goal his illusion has set for him. He becomes caught in a vicious cycle spiraling higher and higher until the illusion collapses and he plummets into depression.

Grounding facilitates the experience of pleasure, which then motivates a person to reach out for more charge in every area that promises pleasure. The process of life may be viewed bioenergetically as charging up with excitation → discharging down with pleasure → more charging up (more excitation) → more discharging down (more pleasure). If you cut off or reduce an organism's capacity to experience pleasure, you immediately limit all its outgoing impulses. When a person loses the pleasure of being alive, his breathing is restricted, his appetite wanes, and his interest in life declines. The oscillating flow of feeling or energy in the body is like a great pendulum which keeps life moving easily and effortlessly. In the hung-up person the flow is reduced; in the depressed person it seems to come to a stop. In effect, any disturbance in grounding is like a destruction of some of the roots that maintain the life of a tree. Destroy these roots and see how long it will stay upright and alive.

Grounding roots a man in his basic animal or bodily functions, and by doing so it nourishes and supports his spiritual striving, which is associated with the movement of feeling and energy to his head. As his feet go down into the earth, his arms reach out and up to heaven, his eyes open to the glory of the universe, and his spirit soars in exultation at the miracle of his life, his consciousness, his being part of it all. This upward surge of feeling from one's roots in the ground is the bodily counterpart of all spiritual feeling. It is the basis of all religious experience. It is the miracle of life moving against gravity and feeling its own surging force.

When a fruit falls to the ground, the seeds it contains normally germinate and seek to implant themselves in the earth. This process is facilitated if the fruit and the seeds are ripe or mature. Both germination and implantation are handicapped if the fruit is prematurely separated from the tree. A child prematurely separated from his mother is in the same situation. His natural inclination is to get back to the mother in order to complete the aborted maturation process. Without realizing it, all his available energy is invested in this attempt. But if the separation is definitive, the original connection cannot be restored any more than a fruit can be reattached to the tree. No matter how strenuous the attempt, it is destined to failure. This is the dilemma of the oral personality and it explains his predisposition to depression.

The process of grounding an individual is therefore a process of helping him complete his maturation. In the course of the years while the person had grown physically, he had remained immature emotionally. He had not learned to stand on his own feet, for he still expected too much from others. His belly wasn't full because he kept waiting and hoping for others to fill it for him. This was his unreality. But no one can be his surrogate. He must do it for himself, albeit with the help of a therapist.

How is this done? In bioenergetic therapy we start with

breathing just as the Oriental or the yoga does in his practice. Breathing holds the secret of life, for it provides the energy through the metabolism of food to keep the flame of life burning. But it does more than that. As Durckheim says, "In breathing we partake unconsciously in the Greater Life." * The reason for this statement is that breathing is a total body process of expansion and contraction which is at once conscious and unconscious. Healthy breathing is very largely unconscious, but through the body sensations that arise from full and deep breathing we become conscious of the pulsating aliveness of our bodies and sense that we are one with all pulsating creatures in a pulsating universe.

To achieve this state of unity and self-realization, one's breathing must have a deep abdominal quality. The inspiratory wave starts from within the belly at a place the Japanese call the vital center of man. As it moves upward to the throat and mouth, it produces an inhalation. The expiratory wave proceeds in the opposite direction and results in an exhalation. These waves can be observed passing through the body either as full and free or as restricted and spastic movements. Each area of tension blocks the wave and distorts the perception of the pulsation. One can find such blocks extending from the head to the feet.

To show how they disturb the natural breathing pattern, I shall describe a few of these blocks. If the belly is held flat and the buttocks tight, there is little abdominal involvement in the breathing movements. Breathing is either thoracic or diaphragmatic with little sensation developing in the lower part of the body. These muscular tensions developed in the abdomen as a means to curb sexual feelings, to control the excretory functions and to diminish the pain caused by a persistent crying that failed to evoke a positive parental response.

* Durckheim, *op cit.*, p. 152.

Diaphragmatic tensions which developed as a result of fear also cause the lower ribs to be elevated. This has the effect of splitting the unity of feeling in the body by creating a ring of tension around the waist.

The upper half of the body often has its own specific tensions which interfere with natural deep respiration. A rigid chest wall will reduce sensation in this part of the body, specifically those sensations and feelings associated with the heart. When the heart is enclosed in a rigid thoracic cage, one's love is not free, it is restrained and confined. Muscular spasticities in the shoulder girdle, which inhibit the natural movements of reaching out or striking out, also affect one's breathing. They prevent a deep expiration, which would evoke sensations in the pelvis, by hanging the individual up (as if on a coat hanger) and holding against the normal letting-down phase of the breathing cycle. Shoulder tensions also raise the body's center of gravity.

Most important here are the tensions in the muscles of the throat and neck. These tensions develop to block and inhibit crying and screaming. By constricting the passageway for air, they reduce the oxygen intake and lower the organism's energy level. Throat tensions frequently extend upward into the head and mouth because they are also part of a general inhibition of sucking. The mammalian animal is by nature a nursing and sucking creature. In breathing we suck in air. I have found in my work with patients that any disturbance in the normal sucking pattern is reflected in a corresponding disturbance of the breathing pattern.

Finally, there is a ring of tension encircling the base of the skull. In the back of the neck these tensions can be palpated in the spasticity of the small occipital muscles. In the front of the head they can be palpated in the tightness of the musculature that moves the jaw. These tensions affect the motility of the jaw, which is held in either a retracted or protracted position. Each of these positions has a specific meaning: The retracted jaw denotes an inhibition of self-assertion, the protruded jaw is defiant and unyielding. Since the jaw tensions include the internal pterygoid muscles, which insert into the base of the skull, this ring of tension is actually a layer that blocks the flow of feeling from the body into the head.

There are other patterns of chronic musclar tension which disturb the respiratory waves and block the full and free flow of excitation in the body. Spasticities in the long muscles of the back and legs create an overall body rigidity which impedes the flow of excitatory waves. In other cases there are areas of collapse in the body where a pattern of rigid holding has broken down under stress. These areas of collapse are powerful barriers to the flow of excitation and feeling.

Every therapeutic approach that aims to ground a person must effect a significant release of these muscular tensions. In bioenergetic analysis this is done by bringing a person into contact with his tensions, that is, helping him perceive them. One can ask a patient to make certain expressive movements which would activate the immobilized area, or one can put selective pressure on the tense muscles to produce an immediate release. Next, the patient must become aware of the meaning of these tensions: (1) what impulses or actions are unconsciously restrained by the tension, (2) what role does the tension play in the energy economy of the body—that is, how does it act to limit feeling and excitation—and (3) what effect does it have on behavior and attitudes? If these tensions are to be released other than temporarily, insight into their origin is necessary. A patient should understand the relation of his bodily attitudes—his tension patterns—to the experiences of his life, especially those of his childhood. Finally, some degree of abreaction must occur. The impulses blocked by the muscular tension should be allowed expression within the controlled setting of the therapeutic situation. Thus patients may be encouraged to voice their negativity or scream their hostility against their parents when such actions are pertinent to their feelings, with the condition that such behavior is not to be acted out in real life.

I do not want to give the impression that the therapeutic work of grounding a patient is limited to the physical aspect of his problem. The psychic aspects require as much attention as their physical counterpart. Roughly speaking, I would say that the therapeutic time is equally divided between these two sides. Every valid modality of psychotherapy has its place in the armory of a good therapist. Bioenergetic analysis is distinguished by the fact that it is body oriented, which provides a visible and objective basis for both its diagnostic observations and therapeutic improvements.

As the various muscular tension patterns are reduced, one can quickly see the difference in the patient's body. A marked brightening of the face and eyes indicates a greater flow of excitation there. Increased color and warmth in the feet not only are signs of improved circulation but denote a greater energy charge. A diminution of a high, contracted arch or better muscle tone in flat feet is a positive sign. Most important, however, is the fact that the legs change from passive organs used only to support the trunk to active organs of relationship. This change is readily apparent to a trained observer. It becomes clearly evident when the natural motility of the pelvis is restored by opening its connection to the legs. The wave of respiration can be seen to pass through his whole body and into his legs.

On the subjective side the patient reports feeling his legs and feet in a new and more vital way. He senses that he is "in them" not just "on them." He is aware of his contact with the ground and feels more rooted. He says he feels connected with his body, his sexuality and the ground. To be so connected is not an ideal of health; in my opinion *it is the minimum of health*. Not to be connected or grounded is an indication of pathology on the organismic level.

Some Bioenergetic Grounding Exercises

While it is true that most people may need the help of a therapist to work through the anxieties that prevent them from being fully grounded, there is much one can do for oneself to promote the process by practicing some simple bioenergetic positions and exercises. In fact my patients are encouraged to do these exercises regularly, since I believe that what one does for himself is more valuable in the long run than what others do for him. If some anxiety develops in the course of the exercises, one should try to understand it in terms of one's childhood experience and to go "with it."

The first step toward grounding is to learn to stand with knees slightly bent. Standing with knees locked back as so many people do immobilizes the whole lower half of the body. Take a position with the feet parallel and about six inches apart and bend the knees so that the weight of the body is balanced between the heels and the balls of the feet. The rest of the body should be straight, with the arms hanging loosely at the sides. The best results will be obtained if one stands barefoot or without shoes. If possible, hold this position for about two minutes.

The mouth should be slightly open so that the breathing can develop easily and fully. Let the belly out but don't force it. Holding the belly in restricts breathing and is unnecessary work. You don't have to hold yourself up by your guts if you will allow your legs and back to serve this function, as they were intended to do. The breathing movements should ex-

tend into the belly. The back should be straight but not rigid, the buttocks and pelvis should be allowed to hang loose and free.

The purpose of this exercise is to bring you into touch with your legs and feet, and this will happen as sensation develops in them. Put your attention into your feet and try to maintain your balance between the heels and balls of the feet. As you do this, you may find some involuntary tremors occurring in the legs or body, your legs may begin to vibrate or to shake. These involuntary movements are an expression of the flow of feeling in your body. Allow them to develop to the extent that you are comfortable with them. Sense your body and see if you can feel its aliveness. When the position becomes painful or if you think that your legs will collapse, change the position to exercise 2.

In the second position the feet are placed eight inches apart

EXERCISE 2

with the toes turned slightly inward. With the knees flexed, bend down until the fingertips touch the ground and let the head drop. Then, keeping the fingertips on the ground, straighten the knees gradually until some vibration develops in the legs. If the hamstring muscles at the back of the thighs are too contracted, this may produce some pain. Do not attempt to extend the knees fully and stiffen the legs, as this will destroy the value of the exercise.

Again, in this exercise, as in the one above, the mouth should be open and the breathing allowed to develop easily and fully. All the weight of the body should be on the feet, the fingertips merely serving as points of contact. The body should be balanced between the heels and balls of the feet.

This position even more than the first one tends to produce some vibration in the legs. It does not, however, happen to everyone in the first trial, and in persons who unconsciously hold themselves in tight control, it may take many repetitions of the exercise to occur. The nature of these vibratory movements is explained more fully later. Their occurrence increases the amount of feeling in the legs and feet, which is the aim. The position should be held for one to two minutes but never if it becomes too painful or too tiring. One will also notice that both exercises deepen one's breathing and increase the circulation to hands and feet. Occasionally tingling sensations, or paresthesias, may develop in the extremities. They are a sign that one has been breathing more deeply than normally. They fade out when breathing returns to normal.

If done regularly, these two exercises will do much to increase one's being grounded. Patients who have used them report many positive benefits. For example, an analyst who attended a bioenergetic workshop, during which he was made aware of the fact that he always stood with locked knees, wrote to me afterward, "Standing with bent knees feels unnatural. It gives me the impression that I am groveling. But I notice, too, that I feel more secure and better balanced. My friends says that I look trimmer and more alive. I am certainly more conscious of my legs all the time." With continued practice the bent-knee position becomes the more natural postural attitude. One becomes aware, then, that locking the knees puts one into a passive position because it shifts the weight of the body to the heels and eliminates the flexibility of the knees' action. This knowledge is apparently common to trainers of athletes; I was surprised to hear an announcer say that one football player learned to overcome his tendency to fumble by bending his knees while catching the ball.

Another story told by a patient shows the value of the

second exercise. He was a singer and an actor. At auditions while others were practicing their scales in the wings, my patient grounded himself by bending over and getting his legs to vibrate. Consequently, instead of being keyed up and then breaking under the stress of the audition, my patient felt relaxed and sang easily and effortlessly. He attributed part of his success in getting jobs to this maneuver.

The body naturally stiffens to meet an expected shock. This reaction prevents the collapse shock can produce, but it also immobilizes the body and limits its ability to cope with the stressful situation. Normally the initial stiffening reaction is followed by a mobilization of one's forces for fight or flight as adrenalin is discharged into the bloodstream. As soon as the body goes into action, the musculature relaxes. But if one remains in the stiffened position (rigidity), the relaxation does not occur and the impact of the shock is not abreacted. The organism is not released and continues to be in a state of emergency.

Locking the knees is part of this stiffening reaction, which also includes holding one's breath and alerting the exteroceptive receptors, especially the distance sensors, sight and sound. By the very fact that a person habitually stands with locked knees, it can be inferred that he holds himself in a state of emergency. He is unaware of the significance of his bodily posture, since it has become second nature to him. He has lost touch with his first or original nature. Were it not for the fact that a sense of emergency is so prevalent and that we are constantly keyed up to meet one crisis or another, people would be more conscious of being out of touch with their original or animal nature. We can accept an emergency state of being only as long as we are unaware of its deleterious effect on our bodies. We may even pride ourselves on the ability to tolerate pressures and stress, not realizing that we create unnecessary emergencies to gain this spurious ego satisfaction.

The individual who "can't take it" is looked upon as a weakling. If he should give way to tears, that would be a further humiliation. He has become conditioned by an insidious upbringing to regard collapse or failure as a moral stigma. Yet the person who cannot collapse, who cannot give way, give in and let down is doomed to a continual attrition of his vital energies that will inevitably destroy him. He will be subject to the illnesses caused by persistent stress: lower back pain, arthritis, cardiovascular disease, gastrointestinal disturbances such as ulcers, colitis, and others. It seems to me wise to learn to collapse in appropriate situations and to give up unnecessary struggles. Letting down returns a person to the solid security of the earth and allows him to renew his energy and strength at the sources of his being. One is reminded of the story of Hercules' fight with Antaeus, the son of Gaea, Mother Earth. Antaeus had the power of regaining his strength by touching the earth with his feet. Every time Hercules knocked him down, he sprang up with renewed vigor. Hercules felt himself tiring and was in danger of losing the battle when he realized Antaeus' nature. In the end Hercules strangled him by holding him high in the air. One cannot but think, too, of Germany and Japan, which after having been beaten and devastated in World War II are today among the most successful nations of the world.

We cannot be grounded if we are too frightened by the prospect of failing or falling, for then all our energies will be directed upward. But why *are* we so frightened? Our lives do not depend on success, yet we must have gained the impression that they do. To uncover the source of this fear, I use a simple exercise, asking the patient to stand on one leg and bend the knee as far as it will go without raising any part of the foot off the ground. The other leg is extended backward

off the ground. The arms are extended and the hands rest *lightly* on two chairs placed alongside the person. The chairs are used for balance, not for support. On the floor six inches from the patient's foot is a folded blanket.

The patient is asked to hold this position as long as he can, breathing easily and deeply, and to feel the weight of his body on his foot. When he can no longer maintain it, he is directed to let himself fall on his knee onto the blanket. There is no danger of injury through this exercise, yet most people are afraid to let themselves fall. Some will struggle to maintain the position indefinitely, while others will fall prematurely as an act of will rather than surrender. Many lower themselves to the floor gradually. This exercise is repeated twice on each leg. On the fourth time I ask the patient to say, "I give up," as he falls. When this exercise is done in my office, I can gauge from the tone of the patient's voice and his manner of saying it whether his surrender is genuine or false, that is, whether he really felt like giving up or simply said it in response to instructions. In both cases, however, the implications of this action are discussed with the patient.

Exercise 3 is generally preceded by the other two exercises so that a certain amount of sensation and feeling have already developed in the person's body. It is not surprising, therefore, that many patients when they first fall or when they say "I give up" will break into sobs. To feel oneself fall and not be hurt seems to relieve some deep anxiety. Having fallen, the patient feels secure in the closeness to the ground. Lying on the ground, one has temporarily abandoned the struggle against gravity and the compulsion to do something. But so few people seem capable of letting go in this simple way. They feel they have to be up and doing.

Why is falling and surrender so difficult even in this symbolic way? In my discussion with patients the following reasons became apparent. There is the association that to fall is to be helpless. To be helpless is to be vulnerable. One can often analyze this feeling in terms of the patient's experience with his parents. He may have felt himself locked in a power struggle with them; that if he didn't resist their demands, he would be overwhelmed and negated. If he couldn't fight back, at least he wouldn't give in. Holding on and not letting go became, then, a final expression of individuality and integrity. Patients also say that to fall is to be alone. If a man falls, he will be left behind and no one will be there to pick him up. If this was one's experience as a child, it is not difficult to understand the fear of falling. The act of falling evokes the feeling of aloneness, which the individual is loath to reexperience. One must keep up with the crowd, whose rush is so great that few dare turn back to assist the fallen. And there is also in many people a stubborn pride that says, "You weren't there for me when I needed you as a child, now

I will not let myself get into the position of needing anyone again." Such complex and hidden motivations destroy our capacity to surrender to love or to fall into the easy and deep slumber a baby knows.

This exercise has another value. With the whole weight of the body on one leg and foot a patient feels that leg more intensely. He can also learn that his legs can hold him up as well as let him down. He develops more feeling in the feet and can sense what it means to have his feet literally on the ground.

Bearing in mind what this exercise aims to accomplish, the reader can do it at home regularly. It should always be followed by relaxation. After the person falls for the fourth time, I suggest that he remain down, on both knees, with the hands extended, together and flat on the floor. With the forehead on the hands the person is in the position of Moslem

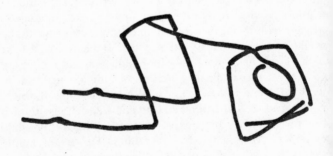

EXERCISE 4

prayer. The value of this position is that the head is close to the ground, which symbolically drops the ego below body level. It also allows the soft front or ventral side of the body to hang loosely, especially the belly. The rear end should be pushed back as far as possible. This will allow the breathing to develop into the deep abdominal cavity. It can also serve to relax some of the anal and gluteal tensions. One should hold this position for two minutes in order to feel the relaxing effect of letting the belly hang freely.

Another position that I use to help patients feel the vital center of their being is a variation of exercise 2. After a patient has adopted the position of exercise 2 and held it for about a minute, I ask him to bend his knees all the way and to hold his hands straight out, just off the floor. The weight of the body should be pitched forward, but the heels should not come off the ground. The position is illustrated below.

EXERCISE 5

The patient is asked to hold this position as long as he can but not excessively. The position puts a strain on the quadriceps muscle of the thigh and is difficult to maintain for any time if these muscles are tight and contracted. This position forces the breathing deep into the pelvis. I do not mean that one breathes air into the pelvis. The crouched position forces one to use and to expand the deep abdomen in order to make a full inspiration. The result is that one feels the pelvic cavity come alive, and for many people it is one of the best ways to accomplish this.

In this position as in all others it is important for the person to breathe easily but deeply through his mouth. Mouth breathing is used in these exercises because the positions are stressful and one needs as much oxygen as one can get. It also allows the jaw to hang loose, which diminishes the tension normally present in the jaw muscles when the mouth is closed. Fuller and deeper breathing charges the organism and promotes the development of vibratory movements in the legs. One will frequently find very strong tremors developing in the legs in this exercise. This is partly due to the strain the leg muscles are subject to. As they tire, their ability to hold against the tendency to collapse weakens. In some people the knees will begin to shake, which is different from the natural vibratory movement. In the shakes the knees move from side to side, a well-known sign of fear. The natural vibratory movements are small up and down oscillations or minute quivers. When these exercises are done regularly, the tight muscles gradually relax. Feeling flows more easily into the lower part of the body and into the legs and feet. A number of my patients have found that the physical condition of their feet and legs improved significantly as a result of these exercises. Although such an outcome can be anticipated, it is not the primary goal. The primary aim is to ground an individual in the reality of his body and of the earth, not as an intellectual concept but as a feeling experience.

When one senses that the leg muscles are beginning to tire while doing this last exercise, one should let oneself fall onto the knees and assume the position described in exercise 4, which is one of relaxation and surrender. We should not be afraid to surrender, for we are surrendering to our bodies, to the earth, and to life. We are surrendering to the only force that in the final analysis can sustain us. It is the living force in the soil which passes into the bodies of all plants and animals. If this force fails us, then neither intellect nor will can ensure our survival.

In this section I have described some of the simple bio-energetic exercises which are regularly used in bioenergetic therapy to help a patient become more firmly grounded. There are others which further the same objective. For example, sitting on one's haunches native-style is recommended. Some exercises work directly with the feet, such as placing the sole on the handle of a tennis racket and pressing down to excite the muscles of the longitudinal arch. One can also improvise special positions or exercises to help a person work through specific areas of tension or holding. They will work, though, only if the individual understands that their aim is to release him from patterns of muscular tension or holding, which limit his motility and block his ability to relate.

In our culture people have a great need to "let down." I have mentioned that as a society we are keyed up to meet continual crises. If a person can't find a natural way to let down through the body, he will be tempted to use drugs or alcohol. If he does not let down naturally, he will find himself cast down, sooner or later, into depression.

3. The Energy Dynamics of Depression

The Depressive Condition

In the preceding chapters I showed that the depressive reaction occurs only in individuals who pursue unreal goals and who are not grounded in reality. I pointed out that the depressive reaction results from the collapse of an illusion, not a conscious illusion but one that was operative in a person's behavior. Most psychiatrists view the depressive reaction as due to a loss of self-esteem. If this loss is responsible for the depressive reaction, we must probe into the foundations of self-esteem to learn why it is vulnerable to destruction. I believe this calls for another look at the depressive phenomenon and especially at the energetic processes that underlie self-assurance, self-confidence and self-esteem.

The word "depression" is loosely used today to describe any low mood. But not all low moods are depressed states, and a clear distinction must be drawn between them. If we fail to make this distinction, we will fall into the error of regarding the depressive reaction as normal under some conditions. For example, we will assume that it is perfectly natural for a person to become depressed when he suffers a loss, financial, personal or otherwise. Long John Nebel took this position during a radio interview with me on NBC. He asked, "Don't you consider it normal for a person to become depressed when a job promotion which he has anticipated for some time falls through?"

He was surprised when I answered, "No. The normal reaction to this situation is disappointment."

"What is the difference between them?" he asked.

The depressive reaction immobilizes a person. He is unable to muster the desire or the energy to carry on his usual activities. He feels defeated, is pervaded by a sense of hopelessness, and as long as the depressive reaction continues, he doesn't see any use of further effort. Disappointment may leave a person feeling sad, but it doesn't immobilize him. He can talk about his disappointment and otherwise express his feelings, something the depressed person cannot do. As a result of his disappointment he may reevaluate his aspirations or find other means to realize them. He does not have the sense of hopelessness that characterizes the depressed person. Neither his interest in life nor his energy is seriously affected.

In contrast to disappointment there is often no apparent reason for the depressive reaction. In many cases it occurs when everything appears to be going well, sometimes just at the point when the person is on the verge of or has just realized his ambition. For instance, one man became depressed when he sold his business for more than $1,000,000. This had been his goal for a number of years, and he had worked energetically to achieve it. Yet when the sale was consummated, depression set in. I heard a similar story from another of my patients who became depressed when he was offered a large sum of money for a business he had built up and considered selling. It is common to hear of men who become depressed when the retirement which they have looked forward to for so many years becomes an actuality. Or for theatrical people to become depressed when the success and fame for which they struggled is at hand.

The apparent contradiction between success and depression can be explained if we assume that success was not the person's real goal. If it was love, for example, and the achievement was unconsciously conceived as a means of obtaining love, it is clear that the failure to do so could result in a severe disappointment. But since these people are not grounded in their bodies and are out of touch with their feelings, they fail to sense their disappointment. Being unable to express any feeling, they go into a depression.

It may not always be possible to relate its onset to an immediate cause. The depressive reaction may develop so insidiously that by the time it is full blown the person may have forgotten the specific event that triggered it. But knowledge of the catalyst is of little help even in those cases where it is known. The woman who came for treatment in a state of depression because her marriage collapsed was as helpless to combat it as the person whose depression is without obvious cause.

We experience many low states in life which are not depressive reactions. In addition to disappointment, one can be dejected by a refusal or disheartened by an unfortunate event. Each has an emotional tone of sadness distinguishing it from the depressed state. If one is out of touch with this feeling, one gets depressed. A simple illustration is the following: A patient will often answer my initial inquiry, "How do you feel?" with the response, "I feel depressed." Looking at him, however, I observe that his face is sad, sometimes close to tears. When I point this out, he may say, "Why, yes. I *do* feel sad." Surprisingly, the recognition and acceptance of a feeling changes the quality of the mood. The patient no longer feels as depressed as he did when he blocked his awareness of the feeling of sadness.

Psychotherapists have long known that getting a patient to cry or to become angry breaks the grip of the depressive reaction. Crying is the more appropriate emotion, since the depressive reaction is linked with a sense of loss. Freud, who studied the depressive reaction in the form of its more severe manifestation as melancholia, believed that it was caused by an inhibition in the expression of grief. In some cases the grief could be traced to the loss of an important love object in an individual's early life. Later psychoanalysts related it to the suppression of anger and rage at the deprivation caused by the loss of the loved object. I have found that it matters little which emotion is expressed. The expression of *any* emotion is sufficient in most cases to lift the person out of his depressive mood.

Since depression is caused by the suppression of emotion, it cannot itself be regarded as one. It represents the absence of emotion. It is not a true feeling; one doesn't "feel" depressed, and it should not be confused with a real feeling, such as feeling "blue," a state embracing elements of sadness and loneliness. Feelings and emotions are organismic responses to events in the environment; the depressed state is a *lack* of responsiveness. Feelings change as the outside situation changes, causing a different response from the organism. The proper company, for example, can lift a person out of his blue mood; the individual in a depressed state, however, remains unresponsive.

Depression is a loss of an organism's internal force comparable in one sense to the loss of air in a balloon or tire. This internal force is the constant flow of impulses and feeling from the vital centers of the body to the periphery. Actually, what moves in the body is an energetic charge. This charge activates tissues and muscles in its path, giving rise to a sensation or feeling. When it results in action, we call it an impulse—a pulse from within. In the depressed state impulse formation is sharply reduced both as to number of impulses and their strength. This diminution produces a loss of feeling on the inside and a loss of action on the outside. We can speak therefore of depression being an internal collapse, meaning that the ability of the organism to respond with appropriate impulses to environmental events has greatly diminished.

Thinking in terms of impulses and the force they exert clarifies our understanding of the nature of depression. Impulses exert an outward pressure and normally result in some form of expression. Expression literally means outward-moving force. Behind every desire, feeling, or thought is an impulse, which may be defined as an energetic movement from within the organism to the outer world. Each impulse that carries through to the outside represents a desire, evokes a feeling, is associated with a thought, and ends in an action. Thus, for instance, when we have the impulse to strike someone, it represents the desire to stop that person from causing us pain, it carries with it the feeling of anger, it is associated with thoughts relating to the situation that provoked the impulse, and it ends in a blow.

An impression is the opposite of an expression. When an impulse affects another person, he receives an impression. The impulse need not be a blow; it may be a look, a gesture or a word. The impression is the result of an external force acting on the body. In a living organism, impressions evoke some response from the organism which constitutes a recognition of the impression. Inanimate objects do not generally react to external forces. I can, for example, press my thumb into a ball of putty and leave an impression, but the putty does not sense the impression and does not react to it. For an object to react, it must contain some internal force. An inflated balloon will react to the pressure of my thumb because it contains such a force. It will first become distorted, then resume its original shape after the pressure is removed. A deflated balloon will not do this. This oversimplified analogy helps explain why the depressed person does not react like a normal person to the stimuli proceeding from his environment. He may sense them like any normal person, but his undercharged body and deflated spirit render him incapable of responding.

The Suppression of Feeling

We do not express all our impulses all the time. In the course of growing up we learn which to reveal and which to hold back. We also learn when certain impulses can be expressed and also the proper manner of their expression. The conscious holding back of an impulse is done by the voluntary muscular system of the body, which is under the control of the conscious mind or ego. It occurs at the surface of the body just before the impulse is released in action. Actually the muscles that would be involved in expression are set to act but are blocked by a command from the mind. The inhibitory command does not affect the other components of the impulse. We remain conscious of the desire, in touch with the feeling, and aware of the thought. It is only the action that is blocked.

The suppression of impulses is another matter. All components of an impulse are blocked when suppression occurs. The word "suppression" means that the impulse is pushed down under the surface of the body, below the level at which perception occurs. One is no longer conscious of the desire or in touch with the feeling. When the memory or thought of the impulse is pushed back into the unconscious, we speak of repression. Memories and thoughts are repressed, impulses and feelings are suppressed. The suppression of impulses is not a conscious or selective process like the act of holding back their expression. It is the result of the continual holding back of expression until that holding back becomes a habitual mode and an unconscious body attitude. In effect, the area of the body that would be involved in the expression of the impulse is deadened, relatively speaking, by the chronic muscular tension that develops as consequence of the continual holding pattern. The area is effectively cut off from consciousness by the loss of normal feeling and sensation in it.

The deadening of part of the body has an effect on its overall functioning. Each area that becomes deadened reduces the vitality of the whole organism. It limits to some degree the body's natural motility, and it acts as a restriction on the function of respiration. Thus it decreases the organism's energy level and indirectly weakens all impulse formation.

In situations where the expression of an impulse would evoke a threat to a child from his environment, the child will consciously try to suppress that impulse. He can do this by decreasing his motility and limiting his breathing. By not moving and by holding one's breath one can cut off desire and feeling. In effect, in a desperate maneuver to survive, one deadens the whole body. If this deadening goes far enough, it produces the schizoid personality I have described in a previous book.* This personality is extremely prone to depression for this very reason. In the schizoid personality all impulse formation is diminished.

A child will also actively suppress an impulse when it becomes too painful because of continued frustration. A child who has lost his mother in a crowd, for example, will cry from the pain of the loss, but he will not or cannot cry indefinitely. After a time he will stop because the pain is

* A. Lowen, *The Betrayal of the Body* (New York, Macmillan, 1969).

too intense and the effort too exhausting. We are assuming for our discussion that no one comforts the child. In his exhausted state the child becomes numb. But the numbness will pass, and when it does, the child will cry again if he has not found his mother. Each time, however, the crying will become progressively weaker. It is a desperate situation, for a child who is left alone to cry could die. René Spitz has recorded such cases. Normally, in this situation, the child soon finds his mother and the trauma is short-lived.

However, if the mother is not just lost but dies and the child is left unloved, the situation takes on a chronic and serious character. No amount of crying will restore the mother, and each outburst serves only to increase the pain of the loss. Sooner or later the child will give up. He will stop crying and wailing, but he will also stop every effort to reach out to the environment. The child will lie in his bed, unresponsive, in a state of depression which, if prolonged, can result in death.

The situation is only slightly less tragic when a mother is physically present but emotionally absent—that is, emotionally unresponsive to the needs of the child. In one sense she is lost. The child will cry for a closeness she cannot give him, and he will continue to cry until it becomes too painful to long for the unavailable. Unlike a child without a mother, he will survive, but in the process he will have learned to suppress both desire and feeling.

An infant cannot accept the loss of mother love. He is too dependent on a mother or a mother substitute for his survival. He cannot, therefore, release his grief as adults can who have lost a loved one. But even some adults have great difficulty in venting their grief. I believe this is owing to the partial suppression of the impulse to cry in early childhood. As a result this impulse is not fully available in later life.

The impulse to cry will be suppressed in children for reasons other than the actual disappearance of the mother. Many mothers cannot tolerate a child's crying. Unable to respond because of her own hangups, she reacts to the child's persistent weeping with hostility or by withdrawing her love. She may make it a practice not to pick up the crying child when he wants to be held to teach him that she cannot be commanded by such tactics. She engages in a power struggle with the child and, being stronger, she wins out. If his crying alienates the mother, the child is forced to suppress it. When the mother reacts with anger and hostility, the effect on the child is greater. He may at first intensify his crying, but he soon learns that this is not a wise procedure and will suppress his crying in the interest of survival.

Effective as it is, it is very difficult to get a depressed patient to cry. If you ask him to reach up his arms and say "Mama," the answer often is: "What's the use?" or "She never came" or "She wasn't there." These remarks are reasons to cry. One cries because mother was unresponsive, but such reasons do not touch the depressed patient. He has suppressed most of the feeling associated with a mother, and he has lost the ability to express a sense of longing. But this is not true of other patients, and the technique is often effective with those who do not suffer from depression. It will generally release a flood of tears and sobs. Actually, the depressed person lacks the energy to express feeling. When his energy is restored, crying or the expression of other feelings becomes possible.

Another set of feelings that are often suppressed in children are anger, negativity and hostility. It is not difficult to conceive that in some homes their expression would elicit severe punishment. This may be less true today in our permissive homes, but it was certainly true previously. A young child does not have the ego development necessary for the conscious control of impulse expression. He still lives in an all-or-nothing world. Faced with continued conflict with a parent, a young child will often suppress his negative and hostile impulses. At first they are not completely controlled and break through in hysterical outbursts, but their direct and immediate expression becomes blocked, and in time the feelings themselves are suppressed. When this happens, one sees the picture of the good, obedient child who obeys all mother's orders and wishes. It is, of course, the portrait of an automaton.

In my experience few patients have the ability to express their negative or hostile feelings directly and convincingly. I test for this by having them say "No" as loud as they can while hitting or kicking a bed. In almost all cases the effort lacks conviction. I don't believe my patients are exceptions to the general population. An inability to say "No" seems to be structured into most people. My associates and I have tried this exercise in professional workshops throughout the country, and we have encountered the same difficulty everywhere. We can only conclude that these impulses were suppressed when these people were young.

It seems old-fashioned in this day of apparent sexual liberation to talk of sexual feelings being suppressed in childhood. The fact is, however, that it is still happening and probably more than before. Sexual feelings are suppressed not only because they are taboo, but also because they are dangerous to the child. They pose a danger when a parent is openly or surreptitiously seductive. I believe that seductive behavior by parents is more common today than in past generations because of our sexual sophistication. One proof is the growing incidence of homosexuality, which, in my opinion, can always be traced to a seductive parent. In this connection we should remember that I am talking about sexual feelings in the body and not genital sensations. These bodily feelings are suppressed by sucking in the belly and contracting the pelvic musculature. The effect of this defensive maneuver is to "cut off" feeling in the lower part of the body, which prevents the individual from feeling grounded. It also strongly disturbs the respiratory function by limiting breathing to the chest and diaphragm.

It may be asked, assuming that incest does not occur, what the actual danger to a child of a seductive parent may be. The child, however, cannot afford to make this assumption, since incest does occur and, surprisingly, frequently at that. But there are other dangers involved. If the parent is unaware of his seductive behavior and the child responds, he is seen as the sexual aggressor and is rebuked and often humiliated. We saw this happen to Anne, one of the four cases presented in the first chapter. It would be very easy for a parent to transfer his own sexual guilt to the child in this way. On the other hand, if the parent accepts the child's response, without engaging in any overt sexual actions, the child is sucked into the parent's orbit and loses his independence. The child who is sexually involved with a parent, on a feeling level, cannot say no to that parent. By becoming a satellite, the child loses not only his independence but his sense of self or identity. Consequently, the child has no choice but to make every effort to suppress his body's sexuality.

The suppression of feeling creates a predisposition to depression, since it prevents the individual from relying on his feelings as a guide to behavior. His emotions do not flow in sufficient strength to give him a clear direction; that is, he lacks what it takes to be an inner-directed person. He loses faith in himself and is forced to look to the outside world for guidance. He was conditioned to do this by his parents, whose love and approval he needed. As an adult he makes every effort to gain love and approval from the outside world and he does this by proving that he is worthy of the response he seeks. The effort will be a tremendous one, for the stakes are high, and the individual's total energies will be mobilized and committed to this undertaking.

How one proves he is worthy of love depends on parental values. For some worthiness is attained through achievement, for others through service and self-denial. Some parents demand the child distinguish himself; others require conformity, submission, and hard work. The child who tries to meet these demands (rarely openly stated) is headed for depression; the child who rejects them will become a rebel and an outsider. In both cases, however, the energy that should be available for pleasure and creativity becomes bound into a way of life that is unfulfilling. The submissive person will get depressed when his effort fails to produce the sought-for reward, but the rebel will also get depressed when he finds that his defiance is in behalf of a lost cause.

To a man or woman who didn't get needed love and approval as a child, my advice is "Forget it." Once one attains adulthood, the issue is closed. Return to infancy is impossible. If a person tries to do so, he sacrifices his present—that is, his adulthood—in this vain attempt. The needs that seemed so imperious when one was small and dependent are meaningless now. The breast can no longer fulfill an adult. The holding and support so vital in early years do not add to one's independence and maturity. One has to accept his loss and go on living and growing.

The seeming exception to this principle is the therapeutic situation. A therapist will often function as a substitute mother or father. He will offer love and approval and he may encourage a patient to regress to an infantile state. This is not done, however, with the idea that it will make up for the patient's earlier loss but to help him reexperience that loss and express the grief associated with it. The therapeutic task is to help a patient find his way to self-love and self-acceptance and to develop a faith in himself to replace the one he failed to get from his parents.

Suicide and Negativity

Depression is a form of dying, emotionally and psychologically. The depressed person not only has lost his zest for life but has temporarily lost the will to live. He has, to the degree of his depression, given up on life, which is why depression is so often accompanied by suicidal thoughts, feelings or actions. Yet few adults ever actually die from depression other than by the willful act of taking their own life. An analysis of the motives behind suicide will offer some insight into the depressive state.

The act of suicide has multiple motivations in the unconscious. The attempt at self-destruction is, as most psychologists agree, a call for help, a desperate maneuver aimed to draw attention to the desperation of one's situation. Attempts outnumber actual suicides by about ten to one. Most are not *designed* to succeed. A young woman may cut her wrists, but at such a time and place that her act will be discovered before it is too late. Another may take an overdose of sleeping pills anticipating that she will be found before she dies. Afterward these people often admit that they didn't want to die. They wanted help and they wanted their plight taken seriously. The attempt often accomplishes the needed attention, and many people are alive today who, after having tried suicide, found their way to a more meaningful life through the help it brought.

But attempts also succeed, and the desire to die is part of the motivation of this act. The reasons given for this desire can be summed up in the statements *"Life is not worth living,"* *"There is no point to living,"* and *"I can't go on this way."* I cannot argue with these statements when made by a patient, since I am not in their situation and can offer no promises. I do point out, though, that it is not the body that wants to die. If that were the case, they would die peacefully as a wild animal does when it dies naturally. Suicide is a conscious and deliberate act in which the ego turns against the body because the body has failed to measure up to the ego's image. That image is always power and masculinity in men and sex appeal and femininity in women. So overwhelming can the sense of failure on this level be that it can lead to self-destruction.

The *"You have failed me"* which underlies self-destruction is aimed both at the self and at others. Suicide is as much a rebuke to those who profess an interest in the individual as it is a rejection of the bodily self. And since it always serves to make the family of the deceased feel guilty, it must also be viewed as a hostile and negative act toward them. Associates of one psychiatrist who had an unusual number of suicides among his patients told me that he went out of his way to assure his potential suicides of his support. *"Call me any time you need me,"* he is reputed to have told all patients. Then, why so many suicides? The only conclusion I could arrive at was that his patients had a need to say, *"You failed me,"* and he *failed* to recognize this need. If one overlooks or tries to deny this feeling in a patient, one may push him to a point where he *has* to prove it by the extreme measure of taking his own life.

In a paper entitled "Mourning and Melancholia," to which further reference will be made later, Freud expressed the view that suicide was motivated in part by sadistic and hostile feelings. "It is this sadism, and only this, that solves the riddle of the tendency to suicide." His reasoning was stated earlier: "The sufferers [from melancholia] usually succeed in the end in taking revenge, by the circuitous path of self-punishment, on the original objects, and in tormenting them by means of the illness, having developed the latter so as to avoid the necessity of openly expressing the hostility against the loved ones." * Freud did not mean that the depressive reaction is a deliberate maneuver to hurt the loved person. He did say that there is a relation between depression, suicide and the suppression of hostility which should not be overlooked if we are to understand the depressed individual and his suicidal tendency.

When a person commits suicide, it means he cannot live with himself. He can no longer endure the negative and hostile feelings within him, and he cannot express these feelings except through some destructive act. This is why murder and suicide often occur together, the murder, of course, before the suicide. One of the effective ways I have found to help a potential suicide is to point out that his act is partly directed at me, that it is a way of getting back at me for my presumed failure. This approach often angers the patient and then the hostility comes out against me in a less self-destructive way.

But is not the emotional dying of the depressed person a similar rebuke? Depression like suicide can produce a great deal of guilt in the family of the depressed person. It can also be viewed as a cry for help. *"Look! I can't seem to do it for myself anymore!"* However, if we are to help the depressed person, it cannot be done by being supportive while his underlying negativity is left untouched. One cannot give him

* Sigmund Freud, "Mourning and Melancholia" in *Collected Papers* (London, Hogarth Press, 1953), Vol. IV, p. 162.

the love and approval he lacked as a child. To pretend to do so is unreal and he will remain in his depressed state if only to prove to you that *"You, too, have failed me."*

On the conscious level the depressed person is saying, *"I can't respond"* while proclaiming at the same time his desire to get well. In his unconscious there are deeply buried resentments which add up to an *"I won't respond."* Being unaware of these resentments, he cannot express them. On the surface he presents himself as a person who would do anything to get out of his depression. But he is like a swimmer with an anchor attached to his leg. No matter how hard he struggles to rise to the surface, the anchor drags him down. The suppressed negative feelings with their accompanying weight of guilt are like the anchor in the analogy. Release the swimmer from his anchor and he will rise naturally to the surface. Release the suppressed negative feelings in a depressed person and his depressive reaction will be over.

Are there suppressed negative feelings in every case of depression? My unequivocal answer is yes. These feelings could be demonstrated in every case I have seen. Demonstrating their existence, however, is very different from releasing them, and only their release has a positive effect on the depressive condition.

The presence of these negative feelings in a person's unconscious is responsible for the collapse of his self-esteem because they undermine the foundations of a solid self-awareness. Every depressed person has previously operated on the basis of a denial of his negativity. He has invested his energy in the attempt to prove himself worthy of love. Whatever self-esteem he built up rested on perilous foundations. The collapse was inevitable. At the same time, the energy that went into the effort to realize the illusion was diverted from the real goal of living—pleasure and satisfaction in being. The process of energy renewal which depends on pleasure was greatly weakened. In the end the person finds himself without a base to stand on and without the energy to move.

The Lack of Energy

Depression is marked by the loss of energy. This must be recognized if we are to understand and treat it. The depressed person complains of a lack of energy, and most observers agree the complaint is valid.

Everything about the patient indicates his impoverishment. All major organismic functions, those involving the whole body as opposed to single organ systems, are depressed. The quantity and extent of movement are reduced. Cinematic studies support this observation, revealing a marked decrease in body movement in the depressed as compared with the normal individual. This decrease is clearly evident in the severely depressed person who just sits most of the time, barely moving. But even in the less depressed person there is a noticeable diminution in spontaneous gestures and a visible lack of facial change. The depressed face droops and the skin seems to sag as if it lacked the energy to maintain its tone. The normal play of facial movement—eyes, mouth, brow, and so on—is absent.

This low energy level can be directly related to a decrease in his metabolism. I mentioned earlier the loss of appetite common in the depressed state. More important, however, is the decrease in oxygen intake due to marked diminution in respiratory activity. Not only is the patient's breathing restricted by his underlying neurotic or schizoid personality, but it is further diminished by the depressive reaction. The relation between depressed mood and depressed breathing is so direct and immediate that any technique which activates breathing loosens the grip of the depressive mood. It does so by actually increasing the body's energy level and by restoring some flow of bodily excitation. Generally the increased breathing will lead sooner or later to some form of emotional release, either to crying or anger.

The question that cannot be answered is: Has the depressed person suffered a sharp decrease in his energy level *because* of his disillusionment and loss of interest or is his loss of interest the *result* of the reduction in his available energy? This cannot be answered because we are dealing with two related aspects of a single organismic function, namely, the ability to keep life or feeling flowing. When this flow dwindles measurably, we speak of depression. When it stops, that is death. On the other hand, when the flow is strong, it maintains a high energy level by increasing metabolic activity and at the same time stimulating an interest in life.

Therapeutically, it is easier and more effective to work with a patient from the physical or energetic side of the personality than from the psychic or interest side. Anyone who has lived with or treated a depressed person knows how difficult it is to activate him by arousing his interest. His resistance to taking an active interest in the world is enormous. In part this is due to a deep negative attitude of which he is unconscious and which must be uncovered and worked through for a lasting result. But in large part his resistance stems from a sense of depletion and exhaustion arising from his lack of energy. If the depressive tendency is not too strongly structured in the personality, there is often a spontaneous recovery of energy and, with it, of interest. Generally this recovery is only temporary unless the person can find ways to sustain his energy and maintain his interest.

A phenomenon that needs explanation is the difference between the amount of energy a person displayed before his depressive reaction and the low energy level he shows in

The Energy Dynamics of Depression

the depressed state. The contrast is often striking and also puzzling to people who knew the patient before he became ill. Patients, themselves, frequently remark on it. One told me, for example, "Before I got depressed, I was the best worker in the company. I could work faster than anyone else." The same is true of the alcoholic who seems intensely energetic until drinking gets to him and his capacity to work falls apart. Both the depressed person before his illness and the alcoholic before his drinking problem became serious were compulsive workers. The collapse of the compulsive drive at once reveals its pathological nature and its weakness. (The seeming energy of the compulsive worker is misleading.) Such similarities also show that alcoholism is a cover-up for depression. The alcoholic drinks to avoid becoming depressed, although the two symptoms often appear together in some individuals.

I have pointed out that the collapse ushering in the depressive reaction can be due to a disillusionment, sometimes produced by an event which shatters the person's dream. But such cases are less frequent than those in which the depressive reaction cannot be traced to a specific event, and here the energy factor is most apparent.

Martin, for instance, was referred to me because of a severe depressive reaction. He sat in his house all day unable to do any work or to respond to his surroundings. Before Martin became depressed, he was a hardworking man, a house painter by occupation. He told me that he was one of the best, that he could work ten hours a day "like a machine." Driving himself, he saved money, which he invested in real estate. As if this wasn't enough for one man, he spent nearly every evening at fraternal and church meetings, where he was intensely active. It was, consequently, quite a shock to his friends when he suddenly lost interest in all activity.

Martin could offer no reason for his collapse, and in the

course of treatment I could not find the specific event that triggered it. Very likely it was something small. It only takes the slightest prick of a pin or the touch of a lighted cigarette to burst a balloon. But in view of Martin's history the specific event would not be all-important. He had maintained his intense pace for almost eighteen years. How long *could* he have gone on? A man is not a machine, which needs only a constant fuel supply to keep it operating. A man needs pleasure and a feeling of satisfaction in his life. Pleasure was alien to Martin. He knew only work. Even sex had lost its appeal long before his depression struck. Over the years he had shown progressively less interest in his wife and family. The other pleasures men seek—boating, fishing, bowling, and so on—Martin disdained.

He was a compulsive worker, not a creative one. In a culture that values productivity, Martin would pass for normal, despite the fact that during his working years his emotional life was quite depressed. When we assume that such a person is energetic, we ignore the fact that it takes more energy to be emotionally alive than to function as a machine. Whatever self-esteem Martin had prior to his depression was not a self-esteem based on being a person. If he had prided himself on his working capacity, he now faced the realization that this is not the true measure of a man.

Something was radically amiss, and I believe Martin's depression was inevitable. A pattern of self-denial began early in his life associated with a need to prove his worth through work. Despite his religious affiliation, he lacked faith, and despite his solid citizenship, he was not a grounded individual. To me the surprising thing was that he had not collapsed sooner.

I believe it a fair assumption that depression occurred when Martin, the machine, ran out of steam. He had exhausted his vital reserves in the effort to maintain an impossible image. I believe that if he had had more energy available, his depressive reaction would merely have been postponed. He was like a man who runs until he collapses from exhaustion and then lacks both the energy and the desire to get up again. And Martin looked that way.

Regardless of the catalyst to the depressive reaction, it does not occur until the person has reached a breaking point. If an individual has not arrived at that point, I don't believe he will give up his struggle to realize his illusion. Proof of this is that when the individual recovers his energy and asserts his interest in life again, it is still oriented toward the pursuit of the elusive goal. Thus just as interest is tied to a high energy level, disillusionment and loss of interest are related to a low one.

Helping a person regain his energy is a first step in the treatment of depression. Yet even when a person's normal level of energy is restored, he is not free from his tendency to depression—only from the depressive reaction itself. Whatever that "normal energy level" is, it cannot be regarded as the equivalent of health. It falls short of the requirement for healthy living and functioning. It provides enough force to power the ego drives, but it does not sustain the pleasure motivation. It can keep the upper half of the body activated, but it fails to extend into the legs and ground. It takes energy to stay up, it takes real energy or vitality or inner strength to keep one's spirits constantly up, and the person who tends to depression doesn't *have* that kind of energy.

The tendency to depression is an indication of an undercharged organism. Healthy, vital people do not get depressed as individuals. If their culture does so, it may affect them, but it is not the kind of depression psychiatrists see in their office. This is a selective, personal reaction with its roots in cultural phenomena but not directly caused by them. We will examine these roots in a later chapter; at this point we must look at the energy factor more closely.

Physicists define energy as the capacity to do work and measure it by the work done. The work involved in the living process, however, is not mechanical. The energy of life is used for growth, reproduction, excitability and emotional responsiveness. It is at work throughout the animal kingdom, moving organisms toward the fulfillment of their needs and toward self-expression, which leads to creativity and is experienced as pleasure.

Since the organism is a self-contained system, its ability to function effectively depends on its state of excitability or, if you wish, aliveness, although excitability is the preferred term. Within the limits of its biological structure, an organism with more energy has a higher level of inner excitement. It moves more quickly than others of its kind, is more alert and more responsive. It is also better coordinated in its movements and therefore more effective. The higher charge is manifested in the brightness of its eyes and the motility of its body.

Excitement and depression are opposite qualities. When a person is excited, he is not depressed. When he is depressed, his level of inner excitement is reduced. In elation and mania the level of excitement flares briefly but fades quickly too. A healthy person can sustain his level of excitement at a fairly high pitch. The metabolic fires burn with a hot flame and the brightness of the flame remains relatively constant. We cannot ignore the fact that it takes energy to keep these processes going.

Energy moves into an organism in the form of food, air and exciting stimuli. It is discharged in the form of movement or other body activity. Input and output are always in balance if we consider growth as one aspect of body activity. If the input is diminished, the output falls off. But it is equally true that if the output declines, the input is spontaneously lessened. The output is motivated by the striving for pleasure. Every activity of every animal organism aims at pleasure immediately or in the future. This statement includes the corollary, that the organism also moves and acts to avoid pain.

When pleasure is missing, the motivation to move diminishes correspondingly. The energy output declines and the organism's energy level decreases. When the lack of pleasure is due to a structured incapacity for it, we have a person whose emotional responsiveness is limited and, by the same token, one whose inner level of excitability is low. Such a person is a candidate for a depressive reaction, since he already possesses a depressive tendency.

When the problem of depression is tackled therapeutically, each of its several aspects—lack of faith in the self, pursuit of unreal goals, failure to be properly grounded, diminished energy level—should receive attention. It is not enough, for example, to suggest a new interest to a depressed person unless he can derive some pleasure from it, and this may not be possible if he has unconscious guilts and anxieties about pleasure. These may have to be worked out first. In doing so we will confront his lack of identification with his body and we will observe his lack of grounding. This, then, brings us inevitably to the energy base of the depressive phenomenon.

Some years ago I treated an analyst who related his depression to an inability to read the literature in his field. He asked if I could help him overcome this block. When I examined him physically, I found his body was as depressed as his spirits. He was a heavy man about fifty years old, whose breathing was very shallow. His body motility was extremely limited due to severe muscular tensions binding him like chains. I might add that he had had about twenty years of previous analytic treatment.

My initial reaction was not positive. I did not believe I could do much for him and pointed out to him the severity of his body problem, especially his poor breathing. He said, "I am not interested in breathing, just in getting over my inability to read." I was reluctant to turn him down without giving bioenergetic therapy a try, but I was doubtful of any positive result. We both agreed, however, to see what could be done.

We worked on his problems for about forty sessions, once a week, combining a physical approach with verbal analysis. Despite the fact that some interesting and important material emerged, we made very little progress. He told me about sexual experiences he had had with his sister when he was a young man which he had not revealed to any previous analyst, so I understood why he had suppressed feeling to such a severe degree. But he was not prepared or desirous to regain a feeling life. He had cut off an active interest in the life of his body, and I believe that this was related to his depression. It was definitely involved in our inability to break the grip of his depressive reaction. This case confirmed my feeling that one can build neither a sustaining faith nor a true self-esteem on a limited interest in life.

4. A Case of Depression

The Problem

Would you believe that a person could be almost continuously depressed for more than twenty years? That was the story Joan told me when she first consulted me. She was in her early forties, twice married and twice divorced. She had a child from her first marriage who was now away at college. Joan lived alone, but this didn't trouble her. She *was* disturbed, however, by a lack of desire to do anything and by the loss of interest in her friends. She found it painful to be with people, even those she had known for many years. She felt that her life was empty and meaningless—a common complaint of people who are depressed.

As we talked together, I learned that Joan was an extremely sensitive person. She was personally acquainted with many literary and artistic figures and had published some of her own poetry. The state of the world upset her, and she expressed deep concern about America's involvement in the Vietnam War. There was an elegance in Joan's manner which indicated she was a woman of refinement and taste. She had traveled extensively throughout her life. A sizable inheritance received many years ago at the death of her father made her financially independent, and she was able to live in better-than-average circumstances.

Apart from her depressive condition, Joan also complained bitterly about the lack of a meaningful love relationship in her life. She had been in love several times and each time she had hoped it was the answer to her need. The promise was never fulfilled, however. The men Joan fell in love with seemed incapable of maintaining a mature relationship with a woman. After a shorter or longer period these relationships fell apart and Joan was left with a sense of disappointment, which always deepened her depression. Despite these repeated disappointments, the idea of fulfillment through romantic love still remained with Joan as the dream to which her life was committed.

The physical signs were clear: Her voice was low in timbre and intensity. She sat quietly as she spoke, with a languid expression in her body. Her smile was superficial; not once did her eyes brighten during our conversation. Despite her story of long-standing depression, she did not wear its marks on her face. Her mouth was not drawn down, her skin did not sag, and she did not have the hangdog look one sees in the chronically depressed. The outstanding quality of her facial expression was its immobility; the normal play of feeling was completely absent.

Joan had undergone analysis many years earlier. But while the analysis had helped at the time, it had failed to alter her basic attitude. About a year before she consulted me, she was in treatment with a Reichian therapist whose approach emphasized the importance of the body and the central role of breathing in restoring feeling. Bioenergetic therapy is an extension and development of Reich's basic concepts, and Joan's belief in the validity of the body approach motivated her to seek my help. Her initial response to her Reichian therapist was positive; she made some initial improvement, but it was not sustained and she relapsed again into depression. I found later that the same thing was repeated in the course of our own work.

We shall study Joan's personality and the treatment to illustrate the bioenergetic approach to depression. After a short case history the first thing I do is to look at a patient's body. It tells me who he is and what is going on with him. The body is often more revealing than a patient's verbal statements since these reflect what is in the individual's conscious mind while the expression of the body directly demonstrates the person's unconscious attitude to the world and himself; how he moves, the degree of motility in the body, the amount of feeling in the eyes, the depth of his breathing, the warmth and color of the skin, all these, plus other indexes, reveal an individual's life-style. They are one aspect of his reality and can be correlated with the other aspect of his reality, which is the psychic or inner life. It is necessary to achieve this correlation if a patient is to find out who he is.

When Joan first stood before me in her leotard, I was struck by the pose and expression of her body. She looked as if she were a statue and her face had the expression of a person expecting to be admired. I could, indeed, admire her well-shaped body and regular features. Unfortunately for Joan, however, what she wanted was love not admiration. And no one can love a statue with the warmth and passion one reserves for another human being. Joan was bound to be continually disappointed. She was not, of course, aware that in her unconscious bodily attitude she was identified with her pose and the role it implied. Consciously, she thought of herself as a woman seeking and able to give love. But to the degree that this statuesque quality affected her personality, she was incapable of either. There is no warmth in a statue.

In fact there is no life in a statue. Yet Joan was no statue but a live person. To the degree that she had identified unconsciously with the image of the statue, however, she was immobilized by her pose, which diminished her life. She did not see herself as posing, and consequently she was out of touch with the reality of her bodily attitudes. In view of the unreality in Joan's personality it was not difficult to see why she would be depressed.

This analysis of Joan's problem suggests two approaches to its solution. Joan must be made aware of her bodily attitude and its meaning. She must be brought into contact with the reality of her bodily functioning, since this is the basic reality of individual existence. And concomitantly, the experiences that early in life forced Joan to surrender her true personality and assume the image of a statue must be made conscious. It would be important to ascertain who imposed this image, whose admiration it was designed to secure, what terror froze Joan into immobility.

Her story reminded me of the myth of Pygmalion, the Cyprian sculptor who made an ivory statue of a beautiful maiden and fell in love with it. When the statue failed to respond to his embraces, Pygmalion was heartbroken. Taking pity on him, Aphrodite endowed the statue with life. Joan probably identified with Galatea, the statue brought to life by the goddess of love. There is a connection between this Pygmalion myth and the stories of Cinderella and Sleeping Beauty. In all three an innocent young woman is restored to life or happiness through the love and devotion of a hero or prince. I will assume that Galatea had been turned to stone by some malevolent influence which could be overcome only by its opposite, the power of love.

The two directions of therapeutic effort—to help Joan get in touch with her body and to keep her in touch with her past—are merely different approaches to the same goal, the reality of the person. A body is the repository of all experience and it is also the summation and expression of the living experience of the individual and his species. Working with the body, therefore, facilitates the recall of repressed memories and suppressed feelings. But it is also important to proceed from the psychological side. The interpretation of dreams, the analysis of the transference situation, and the use of conscious fantasy uncover feelings and evoke sensations that liberate the body. When and how one uses each of these approaches depends on the personal orientation of the therapist and on his sensitivity and skill. I prefer to begin with the body and to introduce the psychological work as the therapy develops.

In Joan's case, this meant beginning by getting her to breathe more deeply. So shallow was her breathing, one was barely aware of it. When she made a special effort to breathe deeply at my suggestion, it was done by an effort of will, forcibly and not freely. Her breathing did not spontaneously deepen when she was over the stool,* as often happens. Yet

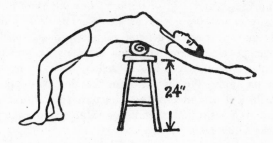

THE BASIC BIOENERGETIC BREATHING EXERCISE

* Some of the specific exercises used in bioenergetic therapy, as well as a description of the stool, are reported in my previous book, *Pleasure: A Creative Approach to Life.*

her condition was not surprising. A statue doesn't *need* to breathe. If her breathing was full and free, it would be impossible to see her as the prized image. By inhibiting her breathing, Joan was able to keep her feelings suppressed. It was essential, therefore, to make her conscious of this inhibition and to loosen her body so that some abdominal breathing could develop. Her statuesque quality was not merely a psychological metaphor; her body was extremely rigid as befitting a statue, although it lacked the wooden or stony hardness occasionally seen.

Following the breathing exercise over the stool, the patient is asked to bend forward, with knees slightly flexed and with fingertips lightly touching the ground. This position reverses the backward arch of the body and brings the person down closer to the ground. If it is maintained for 30 to 60 seconds, a tremor will develop in the legs, and they will start to vibrate. Some degree of vibration is normal when the body or a part of it is held in a fixed position. It can be explained by the natural elasticity of the muscular tissues. It is facilitated in this exercise by the stretch placed on the hamstring and calf muscles at the back of the legs. The vibratory response to this exercise does not occur, however, if the legs are too rigid. For that reason it generally shows up more quickly in younger people. A gross vibration indicates the presence of muscular tension, which is activated by the exercise. A fine vibration implies the absence of such tension. As the body relaxes through the therapeutic maneuvers, the vibration increases in intensity and extends upward to embrace the pelvis and the whole body.

Patients experience the vibration as a current or aliveness in the body which is pleasurable. It also gives them the vivid sense impression that their feet are touching the ground. Some have remarked that after this exercise their feet felt rooted to the floor.

Just as Joan's breathing was very shallow at the outset, her ability to vibrate was so reduced as to be altogether absent. This was to be expected. If her body could be made to vibrate, its rigidity would lessen and the image of the statue would be in danger of falling apart. After considerable work with breathing and kicking, Joan developed some vibration in her legs, but it rarely became intense and did not extend into the pelvis. This condition, however, improved as the therapy progressed.

The simplest way to get a person to express feeling is to have him kick his legs into the bed and say "No" in a sustained and loud voice. Every patient has something to kick about, some protest to voice, and this is especially true of depressed patients. But they more than others have suppressed their negative feelings. When Joan kicked the bed, her movements were mechanical, her voice lacked conviction. Since she could not pretend she had nothing to kick about, I was able to confront her with the fact that she had suppressed her feelings. It is at this point that I generally introduce the analytic work by asking the patient if he had been able to stand up to his parents and voice his opposition to their demands. Joan had never done so. All her forms of self-assertion took indirect channels.

Mobilizing the full range of the voice is one of the most effective ways of evoking feeling. Most patients have suppressed their crying and screaming on discovering that such behavior often elicited a hostile reaction from their parents. Even under the stress of severe pain they will freeze rather than cry out and thus structure the pain into the body as muscular tension. A scream creates an intense vibratory reaction, which temporarily frees the body from some of its rigidity. It was important to get Joan to scream. This is generally accomplished by applying pressure to the anterior scalene muscles in the upper third of the neck while the patient is attempting to scream. The spasticity of these muscles inhibits crying and screaming. It took a lot of work before Joan became free enough to let go. Releasing the scream also enabled her to cry, and both these releases had a positive effect on her mood.

One effect of the focus on the body and its functions is to make the patient aware that his problem is not all in his head. Up to this time he has regarded his depressive reaction as a purely mental phenomenon. In his mind he has struggled with his depressive tendency, seeking to understand its cause and to mobilize his will to overcome its downward drag and self-negating propensity. Each failure to pull himself out of the hole makes him feel more inadequate, more worthless, and more depressed than before. This mental struggle is doomed to failure, since the depressive process is beyond the reach of the conscious mind. Yet this is all the patient knows to do. It comes as a big relief, therefore, to learn that the problem can be attacked from another side and that his failure to resolve it by mental effort is not an adverse reflection on his intelligence or his will.

More important, however, is the resurgence of feeling brought about by the activation of bodily functioning. Starting with an awareness of his body, he progresses to feeling more alive and more hopeful. The change is often dramatic. The depression lifts to varying degrees in all patients, slowly in the more chronic cases, faster in the acute ones.

At the end of each session I could see the life returning to Joan's body. Her eyes brightened, her skin color improved, her voice had more resonance and her body moved more freely. This positive response was more evident when Joan released some of her sadness through crying. She did not, however, cry very deeply. She was unable at this time to confront the tragedy of her life and to muster the anger that lay buried deep within her. These deeply suppressed emotions had to be reached before I could be sure Joan was on solid ground.

As the body work progressed, I began the analysis of Joan's behavior and background and pursued this concurrently with the physical effort. Previously Joan had described the personalities of her parents and the circumstances and patterns of her upbringing. She grew up in a Southwestern community. Her family lived in the country. Her father was a construction engineer who became very successful through hard work. She remembered her mother as a beautiful woman who suffered from tuberculosis. Her home was not a happy one, she said, with her father away most of the time. When he was at home, he seldom spoke to his family and rarely expressed any feeling. She remarked one day that her mother was very lonely. When Joan was twelve, her mother died and Joan said that she wept seeing her father cry. He, however, remarried a few months later.

Joan described herself during childhood as an ineffectual dreamer who read constantly. Her fantasies centered on romantic love and she reports that she worshiped every little boy from afar. To gain some contact with them she engaged in their sports, often excelling at their own games. But this interest disappeared when she became an adolescent. She mentioned that in this period of her life her sexual conflicts were so intense that she was close to agony. She didn't masturbate, which would have provided some relief, partly because masturbation was taboo and partly because she was looking for someone to rescue her. She sought a hero, a prince on a white horse, who would break through the impenetrable thorn hedge surrounding her and bring to life the dreaming princess. Joan was called The Princess by those in her family who at once admired and resented her assumption of a special, seemingly regal, manner.

When Joan was sixteen, a hero did appear. He was a young

man who, struck by her beauty and elegant carriage, took down the license number of her car and obtained her name and address. To her great surprise and exultation he turned out to be a college football hero. For two years it seemed her romantic fantasies might come true. The lovers engaged in every variety of sexual play, but because of their backgrounds, they stopped short of consummating their passion in intercourse. Eventually, they decided it was best to separate.

During the years that followed, Joan was involved with a number of men. Each relationship began with the same high hopes, and each ended when those hopes were dashed as Joan discovered some major flaw in her lover's personality. It did not occur to Joan that she was searching for unreality or that she contributed, through her own personality, to the failure of her relationships. She was not looking for a real man but for the prince of her imaginings who simply did not exist. She could not give herself to a real man, for her heart was imprisoned in the statue which had to be smashed before the true person could be liberated. But the men who were attracted to her admired the statue, not realizing that it was this quality in Joan that defeated their aspirations. She couldn't give herself and they couldn't possess her.

How does a person become a statue and why? Since such a characterological pose, in the sense that it is structured in the body and part of the personality, is not adopted consciously, we must examine the emotional situation in Joan's childhood to find the forces that imprisoned her. In the course of her therapy Joan recalled a significant dream. She dreamed that she was walking down a beautiful marble hall at the end of which she saw her mother standing on a platform as a statue. As she approached her mother, she was horrified to see the statue's arms fall off and crash to the floor. There are many facets involved. For one thing, the dream revealed that Joan has identified with her mother, since she ascribes to her mother the same pose she developed.

I do not know if Joan's mother had the same statuesque bearing. It is rare that a child's identification with a parent leads him to become a mirror image. Generally, the identification has both positive and negative elements, so the child will show attitudes that simultaneously resemble those of his parent but are opposite to them, too. Joan had described her mother as a lonely, suffering woman whose pain was visible. Joan, however, went to great lengths to make sure that no one would see her own suffering. As a princess she was above it, and as a statue she was mute to it.

The mood of the dream tells us something about Joan's relationship to her mother. The marble hall may be beautiful but it is cold and bare. Her mother is not seen as a warm, loving, or vibrant being but frozen in immobility. As Joan approaches, perhaps with the desire to be picked up (most small children would have this desire), she is horrified by her mother's inability to reach out to her or to hold her. Her mother's helplessness, expressed in the image of the statue's arms falling off, appalls her. For Joan, too, has felt helpless all her life, although she had not consciously accepted it. We shall see later why she did not. At this point it is important to recognize the absence of a warm and secure mother-daughter relationship. It explains why Joan didn't cry about her mother's death. Her tears on this occasion were for her father. The loss of her mother had occurred long before her actual demise. This loss is confirmed by the fact that her earliest memory involves her maternal grandmother.

The loss of a mother, physically or emotionally, is, as I have said, the predisposing cause of every depression. To have this effect the loss must occur when the child still has need of a mother figure, when he is dependent on a mother for body contact, warmth, and support. In the case of the loss or absence of the actual mother, a substitute mother can fulfill these needs. But they must be fulfilled if the emotional health of the child is to be ensured. And children will spontaneously turn to any other adult figure in their home environment for their satisfaction if their mothers are incapable of responding.

Joan turned to her father for the closeness and warmth her mother denied her. There are fathers who can provide this kind of support, but Joan's was not one of them. He was seldom at home and he was emotionally unexpressive. But, then, he was not a lonely, suffering, and helpless person. He was a strong, self-made man. He seemed to Joan to be a king, and therefore she could readily imagine herself a princess. In all her fantasies, the prince who would save her was an idealized image of her father. He would have her father's strength and courage, but he would also be more tender and loving. Most important, he would be responsive to her. What she really wanted was her father's love and acceptance, and she adopted her statuesque pose to gain his approval.

Joan also identified with her father. Prior to her adolescence she had competed with boys, wanting to be like them in hope that this resemblance would bring her closer to her father. He was, however, too preoccupied with his work to pay much attention to her. What little he did give her was addressed to her as a girl. He saw her as a growing woman in form but not in feeling. He demanded the suppression of all sexual overtones that normally play between daughter and father, and Joan had no choice but to comply. He wanted a daughter whose appearance and manner would do him credit but whose feelings would not interfere with his life. Joan believed that if she could become what he wanted, he would in turn become the father *she* wanted. In a certain sense she was seduced by her father into becoming the statue of an elegant woman.

Once Joan committed herself to this course, she was doomed to continued disappointment. But she could not of her own free will turn back. All her hopes rested on the realization of a dream based on illusion, not reality. As a statue she had cut herself off from real human contact, yet she believed this maneuver would bring the contact that could fulfill her need. She was betrayed, but she also betrayed herself, though she was not prepared to face this fact. Betrayal evokes a murderous rage in a person. Yet Joan spoke only of love and abhorred violence and hatred. Through the muscular tensions and bodily rigidity she had suppressed the rage and hostility which, since it was directed at the very person from whom she expected her salvation, could not safely be expressed.

In terms of the Vietnam War Joan was a dove. This followed from her conscious devotion to love in all its forms. What surprised me, however, was the vehement attack she made on Lyndon Johnson, when he was President, when the subject of the war casually arose in our conversation. She berated him as an ambitious, heartless, and insensitive man. This description fit her father so closely that the hostility expressed against Johnson was obviously transferred to him from her father. Although I pointed this out to her, she ignored the connection.

It later developed, in the course of the therapy, that she experienced the same sense of betrayal by me. She had turned to me in the beginning with the feeling that at last she had found her salvation. Of course I promised no such thing, and I warned her repeatedly of the difficult times ahead. Yet her seeming need for salvation was so strong that it overrode all rational considerations. And it set her up for a disappointment that she would regard as a betrayal. This enabled us, however, to work through the hostility she had toward men and anchored the improvement she had made.

The Treatment

I have described the basic approach to the problem of depression as both physical and psychological. The physical work involves the mobilization of feeling through breathing, movement and sound. The psychological work aims at the development of insight into one's condition, its meaning and its cause.

Working directly with the body opens up a number of deep conflicts revolving around the relation of a person to his body and to his feelings. The first to surface is between the ego and the body. The depressed individual doesn't trust his body. He has learned to control it and to subject it to his will. He has no faith that it will function normally without the prodding of his will. And in his depressed state it doesn't seem able to do so. He doesn't realize that his body has become exhausted through its long subservience to the demands of an inflated ego. He sees his depression as due to the collapse of his will rather than to physical exhaustion. Thus his primary concern is to reestablish the power of his will, and he attempts to pursue this objective even at the expense of the body's need to recuperate and restore its energy. This attitude will delay his recovery, but that is the nature of the problem.

The second conflict involves the sense of helplessness which the depressed person cannot accept. He had been helpless once before, as an infant or child in a situation he felt threatened his existence, and he had survived and overcome his sense of helplessness by a tremendous effort of will. The collapse of his will now throws him into a feeling of utter powerlessness against which he believes he must struggle. The struggle is intensified by the guilt stemming from the suppressed hostility in his personality. His failure to pull himself out of his low state becomes the occasion for self-deprecation, which serves only to deepen the hole he is in. There is much in the depressed state to indicate the operation of self-destructive forces in the personality.

The will is an emergency mechanism that has great survival value but no pleasure value.* The body doesn't normally function through willpower but by virtue of its innate life force. In the depressed individual this force has been sapped by the subjection of the body to the authority of the will and by the suppression of feeling in the interest of an ego image. Liberating these feelings cannot be accomplished without pain, which adds another element to the conflict between the ego and the body. In the beginning of therapy, however, before these conflicts become conscious, the body approach has an immediate and positive effect. The patient experiences a sense of relief as he comes to realize that a new way out of his difficulties is available.

So it was with Joan. In our first sessions she responded enthusiastically. Nothing could have been, in fact, more effective in overcoming the immobility of her body than the involuntary movements associated with breathing, vibrating, kicking, and screaming. But the conflict between will and feeling has its roots in an earlier conflict between the desire to reach out for a parent who is not there and the pain of doing so. Joan was not aware of the pain and despair connected with these early traumas. All she felt at the beginning was an excitement that now, possibly, her situation would change radically for the better. But the pain was not long in coming and with it also came feelings she had long suppressed.

I had advised Joan to do our exercises regularly at home. Then, six weeks after the therapy began, I left for my summer

* A. Lowen, *The Betrayal of the Body*.

vacation. I got two letters from her pointing up her problem. She had gone to a Caribbean island for a short stay. Writing that she had spent some beautiful days there, she then said, "I wakened in the night [the night before she left] with pain pushing its way through muscles in the waist and pelvis. It seemed as though muscles were unknotting themselves. I cried out with the pain yet that pain was bitter-sweet. My cries changed into 'Yes, Yes!' I went to sleep again wondering mightily. I awakened with a terrible headache—right in the eyes and in the back of my head and neck. I came home. For about five days I was immobilized, too weak to care to answer the telephone. I feel well again now and have resumed the exercises."

I interpret such suffering as "growing pains"—that is, it results from feelings (or energy) pushing their way through tight spastic muscles. It is like the pain one feels when frostbitten fingers are exposed to warmth. The flow of blood into the frozen extremities is extremely painful. The thawing-out process must therefore be done slowly to allow the tissues time to relax. Joan's headache and the pain in her neck had the same explanation. Vital currents pushing through her body were meeting strong resistance. It was too much for her body, which collapsed in order to gain the needed rest.

In another letter written that summer Joan said, "There are times when I feel what must be the whole armature giving way. My shoulders seem looser, as do the muscles about the pelvis, in my back, and even in my calves. My body seems to be in the throes of a conflict like the one between Lucifer and Gabriel. I groan with the terror and sweetness of it. I have felt, obscurely, the currents—and even more obscurely, fear." Prior to this note of fear Joan had never sensed that she was frightened. Her fear, like her anger, was strongly suppressed, and both had to be evoked and expressed before she could get well. We are not accustomed to thinking of a depressed person as being frightened. Very rarely does he manifest any such sign. Fear is effectively held down by the role the patient adopts. What does a statue have to be afraid of? It threatens no one. Then, when the role collapses, the person becomes too depressed to be aware of fear. Yet every person who adopts a pose has been frightened into abandoning his true self, his emotional self. It is the function of therapy to make that fear conscious so it can be understood and released.

Some intimation of Joan's underlying terror had come through a dream. She recalled, "I awakened apprehensive and depressed. It was a very vivid dream and I wanted to forget it." As she described it: "They are going to torment a baby. (I feel the baby is me, but it is dressed like my little brother.) To save it, I steal it and flee from the place in a car with a male companion. It is a wet, dark night. We turn into a wooded place which is new yet somehow familiar, as a childhood environment. The baby is safe, but we are pursued. Our pursuers see us. I follow my companion into a house without doors. I lie on a floor under a table, so as not to be seen, and like a sphinx I face the doorway.

"Our pursuers pass but come back to the house and find us. They do nothing sinister immediately. We are forced to sit at the table while they take their leisure, drinking. I think I am terrified but hope they will not hurt me. Finally they are finished. One of the men approaches me and says, 'We are going to make you lose your function.' [This figure, she said, resembled me.] He is half commiserating but unchangeable and merciless. One of his companions hands him a nauseous mess which he offers me to drink. It is a means of torture. I awaken at 3 A.M."

Her association to the dream was: "My grandmother is

angry at me for being mean to my little brother. The scene reminds me of a table setting when I was a little girl and hiding under the table afraid I was going to be punished." The dream combines a childhood fear with her unvoiced fear of the therapy.

The childhood fear is that she will be punished for being mean to her little brother, the punishment taking the form, according to the dream, of being forced to "drink a nauseous mess," which can be equated with swallowing a humiliation. It can also refer to being made to eat something one doesn't want, which is an insult to a child's personality. The statuesque pose with its implication of superiority can be regarded as a compensation for the sense of humiliation. It may also be considered a form of self-punishment for being mean. Years ago, children were often made to stand motionless in a classroom corner for having done something against the teacher's rules. The attitude exemplified by the statue is also a defense against any meanness in Joan's temperament. A statue can do no wrong. If the statuesque pose is abandoned, this meanness may surface. Joan is, therefore, afraid the therapeutic process will have a destructive effect. This is the meaning of the remark in the dream, "We are going to make you lose your function." The loss of the defensive function, expressed in her body attitude, would expose her meanness and subject her to torture.

Fritz Perls, the founder of Gestalt therapy, tells us that we are at once all the persons in our dreams. Seen in this light, Joan inflicts the torture on herself in the dream as a punishment for the sense of being wrong. The dream is a measure of her guilt.

Joan had other dreams of being tortured, which indicated the severe state of fright she was in. "A tall man keeps me and another woman in an underground place. She is almost insensible with illness and fear. Finally we are brought up into another underground chamber—mud and rocks. Our keeper is seated and served a drink. I know he will get drunk and violent. He orders the other woman, who is young and pretty, to a slide of mud—it is a form of torture. Very ill and incapable of resistance, she goes and disappears down the mud slide. Meanwhile, I climb to a more removed place, seat myself, and glance at our torturer. He has not noticed. When I passed him, he indicated the slide and smiled sadistically. 'Just to punish her a little,' he said. Unnoticed, to my surprise, I have moved further off and, always frightened, escape easily, climbing down a dark, muddy, and rocky landscape."

The torturer, Joan remarked to me, was a composite figure but, she said, "all three are myself." What aspects of her does each figure represent? Because the torturer is male, I would identify him with her father and view him as a representative of her ego. The other woman reminded me of her mother who was ill and who disappeared, and I would therefore equate that figure with her body. Joan escapes, but it is really only her spirit that escapes. She abandoned her body and thus was forced to wander the earth without a home. All of Joan's search for love is really a roundabout way of trying to reclaim her body and recover her identity—that is, to find herself.

The dissociation in Joan between spirit and body, or between ego and feelings, is revealed in another dream. "There is a strike. The cars, including mine, are pooled by the union to transport the workers. Mine, a shaky, old model designed to carry five passengers, is jammed with black and white workers. It is a terribly cold, sunlit afternoon. The canvas top and curtains keep the workers protected. Outside, hanging somehow to the side, her feet drawn up precariously, rides a segregationist. The segregationist (me) is played by comedienne Barbra Streisand."

Commenting on this dream, Joan said, "I am fascinated by the question: Does the unconscious sometimes rib us or is the unconscious so square that it doesn't realize how hilarious this dream is?" What Joan found so amusing was her identification with a segregationist and a comedienne. Knowing Joan, it would be hard for anyone to imagine her in either of these roles. Throughout her adult life she has been a serious advocate of every liberal cause. Prejudice against the blacks was the furthest thing from her mind. But how far removed was it from her body or, more specifically, from her feelings, both of which she attempted to exclude from the car?

To get Joan to face herself honestly one had to help her feel the truth of her body—that it was stiff, scared stiff, frightened into frozen immobility. The work with her body accomplished this gradually. She noted, "I am increasingly aware of the dissolution of a system of muscular rigidity. I feel that the awareness and breakdown is well. At the same time, severe depression threatens. I have less stamina than before. I conclude that my only choice is never to leave my home (body)." On the psychological level, her problem was to accept her fear, her sadness, and her loneliness. On the physical level it was to accept her rigidity and her exhaustion. If she couldn't accept these realities of her being, she was headed for more depression. Her exhaustion tied her to her body and provided the means for her convalescence. Only by giving in to exhaustion can one get over it.

Another dream brought her into contact with her loneliness. "I am sitting in a room looking at a flat, featureless land, except for a sort of tower, very near. My father and his second wife enter unexpectedly. I am obliged to explain my silence and my isolation. I confess, in sudden strength, that I am incurably lonely.

"To lighten my spirits, my father has his wife, Florence, buy theater tickets. I am aware that he is unable to approach me or to take any meaningful responsibility for my plight or for me. At the theater we descend the aisle and I am not surprised to see other members of Florence's family seated there. This imposes a burden of *civility*, which I have neither the interest nor the strength to accept.

"I am walking away through the same landscape and Florence is walking beside me holding the tickets. I say to her, 'I guess my loneliness is pathological.' "

By pathological, Joan meant that she had imposed it on herself. Why? Obviously because she could not reach her father. He was the tower, tantalizingly near but unattainable. This was an important insight, for it helped Joan recognize one of the psychological mechanisms of her depressive tendency. If she could give up trying to win her father's love and accept the fact that it was a dream that could never be realized, she would be free to choose not to be lonely. After the analysis of this dream there was a significant change in Joan's attitude. She became more outgoing and she had some wonderful days, despite the fact that the depressive mood returned at times with severity.

Slowly, other mechanisms underlying her depressive tendency came to light. The following incident revealed an important physical mechanism of her illness: "You remember, perhaps, that several weeks back I began blacking out at the dinner table during a small dinner party. My explanation of this and similar events has been that I cannot drink—not even one drink. I could find no explanation for my behavior but that of alcoholic intoxication.

"The same thing began to happen to me last night at a cocktail party—a party which I found exceptionally nice. For an hour I was relaxed. The following two hours I was,

I realize now, stiffening up. That well-known feeling of suffocating fatigue struck me. I could hardly speak. I managed to leave and stumbled out into the air, which revived me somewhat, and I found a taxi. At home, feeling completely drunk, though I had had during three and a half hours one unfinished vermouth and later a whiskey and soda, I got out of my clothes and, leaving them on the floor, fell into bed, where I did black out. At two thirty in the morning I wakened in a black depression and groaned that I had to live through this again. I drank a glass of milk and took a hot bath, trying to think how it came about. I relived the evening. Suddenly I realized that I was holding my breath. Every part of the breath-holding mechanism was in operation. Suddenly I knew that my drunkenness was oxygen starvation and my fatigue the result of absolutely minimum energy intake.

"This morning, in the light of all you taught me, I understand better the mechanism by which I have been trying to kill myself. The question is, naturally: Why do I do this? Why this extreme of unconscious terror? I recalled that I had a similar experience of terror and breath-holding when I was five or six. I'm still ill with 'hangover' and have consciously to draw every difficult breath. I do not wish to breathe. I see that now."

Actually Joan's difficulty in breathing was as much an "I can't" as an "I won't." The rigidity of her body made natural and easy respiration almost impossible. Only after this had become somewhat loosened was Joan able to identify with her breath-holding as a conscious decision. The first hour of ease and relaxation at the party made it possible for her to recognize the respiratory disturbance that led to terror, fatigue, and depression. To bring her this far had involved several months of therapy in which she was encouraged to breathe, scream, and kick.

The question Joan asked "Why do I do this?" still had to be answered. There can be no simple answer, for if there was, I would not have to write a book about depression. A pattern of behavior that proves to be self-destructive as one grows older did not start that way. Originally it was a means of survival, a way to cope with a trying situation, probably the *best* way to cope with that situation. The pattern becomes structured in bodily attitudes because the situation it was designed to meet—namely, the relationship between a child and his parents—is also structured by fixed attitudes on the part of the parents. In Joan's case, for example, the fact that her mother was unavailable and her father unapproachable forced Joan into a painful state of isolation and loneliness. Her initial attempts to gain attention and affection took the form of screaming, temper tantrums, and acts of rebellion and defiance, which became interlaced with a streak of meanness as they were continually defeated. Joan had no conscious recollection of such behavior, the memories had long since been repressed together with the behavior.

At some point in her life she suppressed every impulse to express her hostility and her anger out of some deep fear that the continuation of such behavior would lead to her complete rejection or annihilation. She became terrified. In desperation she went to the opposite extreme. She withdrew into herself, cut off all her aggressive feelings, and adopted a pose that would ensure approval. I believe she had no choice, that she saw no other possible alternatives. The surrender of her spontaneity and motility was a last desperate effort to get the love and acceptance that she needed. If that should fail, nothing seemed left but deep despair and death.

However Joan is no longer a child and therefore no longer dependent on her parents' love and acceptance for her life and her fulfillment. Why, then, does she continue to hold her breath, immobilize her body, and block her spontaneity? In effect she has remained fixated at that early stage when this first happened, unable to grow up and move out into the world as a mature woman. Her subsequent development was on a conscious and superficial level. The core of her being, her emotional life, was locked up in the child. Associated with the child is the sense of hopelessness, a despair unto death. Her conscious attitude is strongly tied to the belief that restrained behavior, an elegant manner, and a denial of self-assertion are the only conditions for being loved.

We should not underestimate the strength of this belief. The patient, herself, may consciously recognize it as invalid, that in fact it is an illusion. But her recognition is superficial; its aim is to please the therapist and gain *his* approval. The commitment to the illusion is as deep as the despair and desperation that motivated its creation. Joan clung stubbornly to her illusion, for she saw no other way of being. My attack on this attitude was seen as an expression of hostility. Her depression, as Lucy Freeman says, is a cry for love. What I offer, however, is only a sympathetic understanding of her difficulty.

Joan's crisis generally developed in company or at a party. She noticed that when she took a stimulant, she made every effort to suppress the stimulation. She stopped her breathing. What would have happened if she had let the stimulation and excitement grow in her? I believe that as she became more excited, she would have become exhibitionistic, dominated the gathering, and made every effort to draw attention to herself. This may not strike us as being so terrible, but for Joan it posed the danger of possible humiliation and rejection. Still she could not avoid her condition; if she blacked out or crawled away, she felt humiliated, and if she stayed at home, refusing all invitations, the result was the same.

As long as Joan was not free to express herself and her feelings easily and spontaneously, she would feel inadequate. And since she wasn't free, she suffered. The feelings that needed expression were a violent rage deriving from a sense of betrayal, a strong defiance against the demand for her submission, and a deep sorrow that stemmed from the loss of love and the abandonment of her body. She could not afford to let any spontaneity develop, for it could open the lid on a Pandora's box of hostility, negativity, and sadness. Yet the lid had to be opened, the feelings vented—but only in the controlled and protected setting of the therapist's office.

In the succeeding months of her therapy Joan was brought to understand she was not the person she presented to the world. She was not without prejudice, not without some measure of dishonesty, not free from meanness, and certainly not devoid of feeling. This was done partly by a careful analysis of her dreams and behavior and partly by the mobilization of her body through movement and the use of her voice. She was encouraged to scream, and one of her recurrent dreams was of being in a life-or-death conflict with another woman. Screaming, she felt, would save her, but she couldn't make a sound. The other woman was herself and also her mother or grandmother.

She used a tennis racket to beat the couch, at first without much feeling but later with considerable anger at the painfulness of the treatment she had received. She kicked the bed and yelled her defiance and negativity. This was done repeatedly, using different procedures to bring out the suppressed "No." After a while Joan was able to see that her depression, with its consequent inability to move, was her body's way of saying, *"No. I will not try anymore."* By translating this unconscious response into an overt expression, she gradually conquered the depressive tendency. And she was also encouraged to reach up with her arms and to reach out with her lips as an infant would for his mother. This gesture or expression, which was very difficult for her to make, opened Joan's throat for the release of the pent-up longing and crying. If depression is a cry for love, then crying for love is the antidote to depression. To be effective, however, it has to be a crying with all one's being.

The critical work in the treatment of depression is the grounding in reality, in the body, and in one's sexuality. In the foregoing discussion I described in some detail the first two aspects of this procedure. The sexual aspect is the most difficult because it is the most deeply suppressed and because the anxiety connected with the Oedipal situation is very severe. If this aspect of the problem is not resolved, the sense of security provided by the lower part of the body remains shaky and a firm footing or standing cannot be established. When feelings flow into the legs, they also flow into the pelvis and genitals. If either is blocked, the flow is disrupted.

Joan's relation to her father combined both oral and sexual needs. She wanted him to take care of her, to hold and to support her as her mother had not done. She also wanted him to respond to her as a potential woman—that is, with interest in and admiration for her femininity. But above all she wanted to be close to him, to touch him, and to feel his masculinity. These sexual feelings are pelvic not genital, they aim for excitement not discharge. Fulfillment of a child's oral needs helps him reach out to the world with assurance. Fulfillment of her sexual needs allows a girl to accept her sexuality as natural and, as she grows older, to reach out to the world as a woman.

It is extremely difficult for a father to respond to both oral and sexual needs in a child. If he responds to the former, he assumes the role of a mother and loses his masculine image. If he ignores the oral needs and responds to his daughter's sexual needs, his behavior will be experienced by his daughter as seductive, since it will stress the sexual side over the total personality. The problem can be avoided only where both mother and father fulfill a child. This gives the child the sense that he or she has two legs to stand on, a mother and a father.

There are cases, however, where children have been reared by one parent alone with faith, security and self-esteem. In these cases, as far as I know, the single parent has been the mother. The absence of a father is not a serious handicap because his role can be taken by male relatives or by male figures in the community. These men can accept and approve of a young girl's flowering womanhood or a young boy's growing manhood. Neither the mother nor a woman is an adequate substitute for a man in this regard. By the same token I don't believe that a man can substitute for a woman in mothering a child, especially during its earliest years. A substitute mother figure must be a woman.

As we have seen, Joan's mother was unavailable and her father was unapproachable on both levels. This left Joan no choice but to withdraw into herself, to become a dreamer, and to long for fulfillment from a man. Yet she could not give herself, for she had cut off her sexual feelings to diminish the pain of rejection. She was left with genital feelings, which served her oral needs, but she was incapable of having a satisfying orgasm. She was reduced to being a rejected child and so humiliated that in self-defense she became a statue.

A statue is cold and passionless. A child is warm but lacks the capacity for sexual fulfillment. Neither as a child nor as a statue could Joan realize herself as a woman. As the statue broke down, the child emerged. But therapy cannot stop there. It is important to help a patient gain the maturity for satisfying adult living. This can be done only by opening up the patient's sexuality, which resides in the belly as pelvic sensation.

The work with the lower part of the body involves special exercises to restore natural motility to the pelvis. When the vibratory movements in the legs reach the pelvis, it starts to tremble. This is a beginning. As the pelvic tensions are reduced, the pelvis will go into a swinging movement in harmony with the breathing, backward on inspiration and forward on expiration. Reich called this movement the orgasm reflex because it also occurs involuntarily at the climax of the sexual act. When this movement is free, the respiratory wave passes through the pelvis into the legs. Grounding is complete. To open the belly and free the pelvis, it is necessary to analyze the Oedipal situation thoroughly, as well as to reduce the muscular tensions in the lower back and hips which block the flow of feeling into and through this area.

The work with Joan's body, stimulating her breathing and mobilizing her motility, had other positive effects. Her rigidity decreased markedly, and pleasurable sensations began to stream through her body. She began to experience the pleasure of being alive in her body. As these increased, she gained a degree of self-love. She felt loving at times and even lovely and was able to give love rather than to need it. Finally, she decided to move out of New York City, which she hated, and to build a home in the country in surroundings similar to those she knew as a child.

Joan's therapy lasted for about two and a half years. I saw her again when I visited her area two years after our last appointment and found her in very good spirits. She told me that she no longer felt depressed. I noticed that her eyes were bright and her manner lively. Although she was in the company of many people, she was relaxed and at ease. We had some drinks together, which didn't affect her in the least.

She remembered the importance of the exercises we had done and she had made it a regular practice to continue them. I knew that as long as she stayed in touch with her body and aware of her feelings, she would be free from any major depressive reaction.

In subsequent chapters I shall present the cases of other depressed patients I have treated. Joan's case was described in detail because it shows *all* the dynamic mechanisms of the depressive tendency. Each should be studied more closely now, for each is present to a greater or lesser degree in all persons who suffer from this disturbance.

5. The Psychoanalytic View of Depression

The Loss of a Love Object

The phenomenon of depression has elicited the interest of many psychoanalytic thinkers starting with Freud. This is easily understandable, since it has been and is one of the main reasons people seek psychoanalytic help. Freud's interest dates from as early as 1894. His major contribution to our knowledge of this reaction is contained in a paper entitled "Mourning and Melancholia," published in 1917.

In this paper Freud showed that there was a parallel between mourning and melancholia (as the state of depression was then called). Both have many traits in common; "a profoundly painful dejection, abrogation of interest in the outside world, loss of the capacity to love, inhibition of all activity." * There is, however, a loss of self-esteem in melancholia which is absent in grief. When the loss of self-esteem is viewed bioenergetically, the difference between the two conditions is marked. Mourning is an alive and energetically charged activity in which the pain of the loss is expressed and discharged with the full support of the person's ego. In depression or melancholia the ego is undermined by the energetic collapse of the body, resulting in an unalive and

* Freud, *op. cit.*, p. 153.

unresponsive condition. Despite Freud's exclusive focus on psychological factors, one is continually impressed with the clarity and depth of his understanding. He pointed out that mourning performs a necessary work; it enables the individual to withdraw the feelings or libido invested in the lost love object and make them available for other relationships. But this is not easily accomplished. The human mind has a tendency to hold onto the lost object and to deny the reality of its loss. It does this to avoid the pain of the separation. Consequently, if the pain is not released by grieving, the separation is incomplete and the ego remains bound to the lost object and inhibited in its ability to establish new relationships.

In grief the loss is known and accepted; in melancholia it is either unknown or unacknowledged. Why this is so in melancholia puzzled Freud. We shall, however, offer an explanation later. The fact is that the loss is not admitted. The ego identifies with the object and incorporates it. The person continues to function as if the loss had not occurred and modifies his behavior to prevent its acknowledgment. This was made dramatically evident to me in a case I treated some years ago. The patient, a woman in her early thirties, suffered from depression and migraine headaches. Early in our work she told me that her father had died when she was seven years old. In the course of the therapy it became clear that this loss was a grievous one, for she had transferred to her father the longing for love, acceptance and security her mother had failed to provide. Progress in the therapy was steady but slow. Despite many significant improvements, her problems recurred. When it became apparent she was unable to form a satisfactory relationship with a man, I offered the interpretation that she was still clinging to her father's image. She surprised me by saying she had never accepted his loss. In this she was abetted by her mother, who kept telling her, "Your father watches every move you make. He knows everything you do." She was still trying to gain his approval. After this admission there was a profound change for the better and not long afterward her therapy came to an end. She had known that she made a strong transference to me as a substitute father figure and that she was also trying to gain my approval. She experienced this effort then as a struggle she wanted to give up, and she realized that she had to lose me too in order to find herself. When she finally accepted the reality that she was alone and had to stand alone, she was free to be herself.

The person who mourns expresses his grief; he cries, wails, becomes angry at the loss, and may even subject himself to physical insults as a means of venting or discharging his pain. If this fails to occur, the pain must be suppressed in order to be contained. Its suppression results in a reduction of all vital aspects of an individual's personality. His whole emotional life becomes impoverished because the suppression of any feeling operates to suppress all feeling. Thus Freud noted that "in grief the world becomes poor and empty, in melancholia it is the ego itself" that becomes poor and empty.

But while it is true that in depression the ego is severely deflated, we should not regard depression as a purely psychic reaction. If we do, we focus on the ego to the exclusion of the body and fail to see how depression affects the total personality. Depression is a loss of feeling, and Freud concluded in his article "that melancholia consists in mourning over loss of libido." Since libido is the psychic energy of the sexual drive, it can be equated with sexual feeling and, therefore, with excitement in general. To put it in physical terms, the melancholic person mourns the loss of his aliveness. Anyone in contact with a depressed person is aware he is constantly bemoaning his lack of feeling, interest, and desire. In effect, the depressed person has suffered a loss of self, not just self-esteem. Before we attempt to find out *how* he lost his self, let us follow the further development of analytic thought on this subject.

One of the early analysts, Karl Abraham, through his study of manic-depressive patients, related adult depression back to a "primal depression of infancy." He believed that the depressive reaction in an adult was a reactivation of a similar experience the person had gone through as an infant. This infantile depression stemmed from "disagreeable experiences in the childhood of the patient." As a result the infant or child feels hateful toward the parent, hatred mainly directed against the mother. Since this has to be suppressed, the patient is "weakened and deprived of his energy." Thus in depression there is not only a loss of love, but also the suppression of the instinctive response to this loss.

This phenomenon of infantile depression was studied in depth by Melanie Klein, who treated a number of very young children. She postulated that every child, in his normal development, goes through two reaction patterns; the first, called the paranoid-schizoid position, describes the attitude of an infant toward frustration by his mother. The infant regards such frustration as a form of persecution. The second, called the depressive position, occurs when the child develops a conscience and feels guilty about his anger toward the mother. Klein writes, "The object which is being mourned is the mother's breast and all that the breast and milk have come to stand for in the child's mind: namely, love, goodness and security. All these are felt by the baby to be lost, and lost as a result of its own uncontrollably greedy and destructive phantasies and impulses against his mother's breasts." *

* Melanie Klein, "Mourning and Its Relation to Manic-Depressive States," *The International Journal of Psychoanalysis*, Vol. 21, Part 2 (April, 1946).

There is a strange logic in Klein's thinking which sees the hostility as primary and the loss as secondary. In the natural sequence of events a child's destructive impulses, such as screaming and biting, would be seen as a reaction either to frustration or to the loss of pleasure at the breast. When this leads to the irretrievable loss of the breast, it would be natural for a child to become depressed. But such a sequence —frustration, anger, loss—cannot be considered normal development except in a culture which discourages breast feeding or limits it to three, six or nine months. Infants whose access to the mother's breast is regulated by their own need and desire do not develop "uncontrollably greedy and destructive phantasies and impulses" toward this source of pleasure. And if the breast is available to a child for about three years, which I believe to be the time required to fulfill a child's oral needs, weaning causes very little trauma, since the loss of this pleasure is offset by the many other pleasures the child can then have.

We will never fully understand the depressive reaction if we accept infantile frustration and deprivation as normal. It is certainly true that in our culture, with its exaggerated demands on the mother's time and energy, some infantile frustration and deprivation are inevitable. If this cultural situation takes precedence over a child's needs, then the child who fails to adjust becomes a "monster." Actually, he may be the child with more energy and therefore more fight, whereas a weaker and more placid child who makes less fuss would be regarded as more normal. Following this line of thought, the treatment for depression would be a better adjustment to the negative aspects of one's life, whereas I believe that the only real treatment for depression is to enlarge the meaning of life by *increasing* the pleasure of life.

The direct effect on the child of the loss of physical contact with the mother was studied by René Spitz. He observed the behavior of babies separated from their mothers after six months of life because the mothers were in a penal institution. In the first month of separation the babies made some effort to regain contact with a mother figure. They cried, screamed, and clung to anyone who was warm. As these attempts to restore their lifeline to feeling proved unsuccessful, they gradually withdrew. After three months of separation their faces became rigid, their crying was replaced by whimpering, and they grew lethargic. If the separation continued, they became more withdrawn, refused contact with anyone, and lay quietly in their beds.

Both in their bodily attitude and in their behavior these infants showed the same characteristics that are seen in adult depression. In other words, they suffered from what Spitz called "anaclitic depression" to distinguish it from the more involved depressive reaction of adults. Spitz's observations on the effect of premature separation from the mother were confirmed by other studies of this phenomenon. Dr. John Bowlby observed the effect of separation on infants and children who were between six months and thirty months of age when the separation from the mother occurred. In all cases where the separation was prolonged, the child went into a depressive reaction characterized by detachment, unresponsiveness, and apathy.

The same pattern has been observed in rhesus monkeys separated from their mothers. This was done experimentally at the Regional Primate Research Center of the University of Wisconsin. The following is a report of the experiment: "In our experimental analog we reared monkeys with their mothers, then separated them from each other. The young monkeys followed almost identically the patterns of Bowlby's depressed children. First they protested—scampering around their cages in agitation. Within 48 hours the agitation was over, they became quiet and withdrew to the corners of their cages. Their despair continued unabated for three weeks until they were reunited with their mothers." *

In adult depression we are faced with three questions: One, what happened in the person's present to trigger the depressive reaction? Two, what happened in the past to predispose the individual to depression? And three, what is the relation between the present and the past?

I have attempted to provide an answer to the first of these questions in the preceding chapters. I will repeat it here for the sake of continuity. A depressive reaction occurs when an illusion collapses in the face of reality. The predisposing event in the past is the loss of a love object. The loss is always the mother's love and sometimes that of the father as well. But how the two are related finds no real answer in analytic thinking. Freud's statement that the ego has identified with the lost object is a psychological interpretation that bypasses the question of mechanism—namely, the how. The answer must be sought on the biological or body level.

Studies have shown that both human infants and monkey babies need physical contact with the mother's body in order to function normally. This contact excites the baby's body, stimulates his breathing, and charges the skin and peripheral organs with feeling. Eye-to-eye contact of a loving kind between mother and baby is important for the development of a child's visual relationship with the world. By being in touch with the mother's body, the child becomes in touch with his own body and with his bodily self. In the absence of this contact, the child's energy is withdrawn from the periphery of his body and from the world around it. The infantile depression that results from separation is not a

* William F. McKinney, Jr., S. J. Sisuomi, and H. F. Harlow, "Studies in Depression," *Psychology Today* (May, 1971), p. 62.

psychological reaction but is the direct physical consequence of the loss of this essential contact. The effect on the child of a loss of mother love is the loss of the full functioning of his body or a loss of his aliveness.

The same thing happens to an adult who loses an important love object except that the withdrawal from the world and the periphery of the body is only temporary. The normal functioning of the body is too well established to give up what Freud called "the narcissistic satisfactions of living." The body fights back by venting its pain in grief and thereby recovers its aliveness. Reality informs the person that other love objects are available if he can manage to free himself from his attachment to his lost love. But how little of this is available to an infant! Can we expect an infant to release his pain in grief in the hope of finding another mother? A calypso song tells it truly: *"There is only one mother in my life, but I can always find another wife."*

For an infant the loss of a mother is the loss of his world, of his self, and, if definitive, of his life. Should the infant survive, it is because the loss was not definitive; sufficient affection and care were provided to maintain a minimal or certainly less than optimal functioning. The factors here are quantitative. How much is lost depends on the degree of deprivation of loving contact. In this situation, where some part of the self is lost, the child's developing ego will strive for wholeness and completion on the mental level. To do this he must deny the loss of the mother and the self and regard the crippled state of his bodily functioning as normal. The crippling is then compensated by the use of willpower, which enables the individual to carry on, but this way of functioning is no substitute for feeling and aliveness. The denial of the loss forces the person to act so that the loss will not be acknowledged. He will therefore create the illusion that all was not lost and that the lost love could be regained if he only tried hard enough to be different.

No alternatives are available to a child. In the absence of full mother love he cannot attain the full aliveness and functioning of his body. In his helpless and desperate state grief is meaningless. It will become meaningful later when his helplessness and desperation are diminished—that is, when he grows up and gains a measure of independence. But to grieve over the loss of mother love will not restore an adult's bodily functioning. Since the loss is irrevocable—that is, one cannot find another mother—one can grieve for it endlessly. What *is* important is to rebuild the self, to develop the full functioning of the body, and to root oneself into present reality. What an adult can grieve for is the loss of his full potential as a human being.

Any therapy that is to be more than temporarily effective in the treatment of depression must aim to overcome the crippling effect of the loss of love. It cannot really do this by replacing the lost mother with a surrogate in the form of the therapist. Actions such as holding the patient, comforting him, and reassuring him of support have tangible but momentary benefits. The patient has passed the stage of childhood, and to treat him as a child ignores the reality of his being. The unfulfilled child in him must be recognized but its demands cannot be satisfied. The emphasis must be on the crippling of his bodily functioning, for that is the reality of his being. To overcome the crippling, many modalities of therapeutic intervention may be employed—dream analysis, fantasy, body movement, and so forth—but the objective of the treatment must not be confused. Above all it is important to understand the form of the crippling in each specific case, for only so can its effects be ameliorated.

In the previous chapter I described the bodily disturbances

that impaired Joan's functioning as a person and were the underlying cause of her depressive illness. At this point I shall discuss the specific aspects of the crippling that results from the loss of a satisfactory emotional relationship to the mother. They became very clear to me in the treatment of another patient, James.

A Gloomy Picture

James was a young man in his thirties who consulted me because of depression. It was not so severe that he was unable to work, but apart from doing his job, there was little else he could bring himself to do. He found it extremely painful to be with people socially. His sexual feelings were reduced and he felt miserable. This state of affairs had been going on for a long time. In fact, James mentioned on one occasion that he felt bad two-thirds to three-fourths of every month of his life. James was an engineer, but even his work suffered. Getting up every morning was difficult, and he frequently overslept. His constant complaint in the course of the therapy was that he didn't know what he wanted to do. He felt he couldn't make a move.

James believed, at first, that he was paralyzed in life because he suffered from depression. It was only after he had some experience with bioenergetic therapy that he realized it was the other way around; he was depressed because he couldn't move. His body had a heavy, wooden quality, which might have been taken for strength in view of his muscular overdevelopment, but his seeming strength was bought at the cost of his motility and was therefore no asset. All his movements were executed mechanically, and he made few spontaneous gestures. He desperately wanted to feel, but nothing moved him—to either tears or anger. It was hard to budge his solid body, which was almost like a tree trunk. Somewhere inside James was a current of life (the sap still flowed), but it could not break through the heavy musculature that imprisoned his spirit like thick bark.

And a sense of gloom hung over him, manifest in the darkness of his skin, in his overcast face, in his sad eyes that didn't cry, and in the heaviness of his body. James looked gloomy and felt gloomy. He spoke of having a "big ball of cancer" inside his tissues, of which he wished to be rid. But the prospect looked gloomy.

In terms of his personal history James had every reason for gloom. He had no recollection of being close to his mother, and his relation to his father was marked by a sense of inadequacy and of being constantly rejected. At times his father made a gesture of sharing his skills and interests with his son—for example, showing him how to use some tools. But when James gave the first sign that he wasn't master of the activity, he was dismissed as incompetent. He grew up with a sense of aloneness, inadequacy, and a lack of joyful experiences.

James believed the physical approach to his problems would help him. He had previously tried other forms of therapy with little success. At an encounter session at Esalen he had discovered bioenergetics and had come East to undergo the treatment. As a young man he felt awkward while walking and he was self-conscious about his body. He sensed that his heavy body imprisoned his spirit in a dark and gloomy cell and that he would have to break down the barriers of muscular rigidity that barred his way to freedom of self-expression. Mobilizing his body through breathing and movement temporarily lifted his mood and gave him the hope he so badly needed that he could emerge from his gloom.

In the sessions James worked hard at the exercises. When

he bent over the breathing stool, he made every effort to breathe deeply, to yell loudly, and to stay with it as long as he could. An immediate effect was to induce a vibration in his legs when he bent forward. This involuntary movement made him realize that there *was* a vital force within him that could move him if he could only manage to reach it. This proved, however, no easy undertaking. He kicked the bed and said his "No," but for a long time it was done without feeling. He pounded the bed with his fists, but the only anger he felt was directed against himself for being depressed. The massive tensions in his body were a formidable obstacle to feeling and required intensive physical work. Fortunately, despite the lack of feeling, James persisted at the exercises because they *did* make him feel better. His persistence even took the form of having a portable stool made, which he took on business trips and used in hotel rooms.

On occasion some feeling could be evoked. Several times after an intensive workout he was able to cry, which dispelled the clouds for a short time. One technique that almost always produced some feeling was a maneuver designed to evoke fear by simulating a frightened expression. With James lying on his back, I had him open his eyes very wide, drop his jaw, and hold his hands in front of his face while I looked into his eyes. Then I pressed firmly with my thumbs on his face, alongside his nose, and he felt a sensation run through the front of his body and into his belly. It was a feeling of fear, but James did not perceive it as such. He could not let himself feel afraid, but he welcomed the physical sensation in itself, for it made him feel more alive.

During the course of a year James felt better at times, then depressed again at others. It was discouraging because whatever progress we seemed to make would be lost in another depressive reaction. Then the old complaints would appear:

"I don't seem to be getting anywhere" and *"I don't know what I want to do."* However, his body was getting looser and his breathing was freer and deeper. A significant change occurred when James sensed my discouragement. I made no attempt to deny it. No matter how often I pointed out to him that his inability to move could be interpreted as a structured refusal to do so, he could not see it. All he was aware of was that he wanted to move but that some strange force held him immobile. Although this force was part of his personality, he had dissociated his conscious mind from it, and thus it had become an unknown and alien entity within him.

My discouragement seemed to have a positive effect. He stopped complaining and listened. As long as I was encouraging, he could act out his unconscious negativity by refusing to accept my interpretations. He had every right to be negative, but he owed it to himself to express it openly. By denying his negativity he blocked himself off from being impressed by what I said or expressing what he felt.

Instead of self-expression, James' energy went into self-negation, which took the form of chronic muscular tensions. His spastic overdeveloped musculature was a form of internal armor designed ostensibly to protect him from a hostile environment but serving also to bind his energy and reduce his hostile aggression. In every individual one can gauge the amount of suppressed negative feeling by the degree of armoring. In James' case it was substantial. Every chronically contracted muscle inhibits movement and, therefore, in effect, says no. As long as the tension remains unconscious, the patient experiences it as "I can't." He feels justified in his complaint. Making the tension conscious, however, and having the patient identify with it transforms the "I can't" into an "I won't." This opens the door to self-expression, but nothing important happens until the therapist refuses to go along with the patient's overt expression of good intentions. Only by the therapist's insistence on the reality of the underlying negative attitude can a depressed patient be made to accept that reality.

My discouragement had this effect. James opened up sufficiently to take in this interpretation, and from that session on, his whole life took a turn for the better. A relationship he had developed with a girl began to deepen. His sexual responses, which had been slowly improving, became significantly more pleasurable. He became attached to this girl and, as far as he was able, felt some real affection for her. What had been a casual relationship changed into a more serious one. James experienced some feelings of jealousy. The young woman's feelings paralleled his own and so the relationship grew. Some months later they got married.

Shortly after the marriage James became depressed again after having been relatively depression-free for a while. He had been ill with the flu and had stayed home for a few days. It left him feeling weak and edgy. He remarked, "I am turned off everything—job, marriage, sex, etc. I am depressed, but it doesn't seem to have such a grip on me as before." Significantly, he had dropped twelve pounds and his body had lost some of its heaviness.

I knew words would not reach James, so we began to work physically with the breathing and the yelling. My focus this time was on the tension in James' jaw. I could describe it only as resembling the burl of a tree, hard, set, and immovable. One could guess that he was using it to hold on for dear life. I applied pressure with my fists to the sides of his jaw, and as James yelled, I could detect a note of sadness in his voice. He was sad, he said, because he was depressed. I next applied some pressure to the anterior scalene muscles at the side of his neck, and as James continued to yell, he broke into some light sobs. He continued to sob every time he opened his throat to make a sound. Somehow this crying was different. He said he felt it like the crying of a year-old child who is sad about something. He repeated an exercise he had done several times before with no effect. He reached up his arms and said "Mama." Now, however, he began to cry in earnest and realized that his crying was related to her loss.

In this experience James had made a slight contact with the child in him, a part of his personality he had buried and kept hidden all these years both from others and from himself. It was protected by the thick, wooden walls of his heavy musculature, unreachable but also unable to come out. Buried with the child were all the feelings that make life rich and meaningful but also painful. James had been badly hurt and he was grimly determined, unconsciously, of course, not to be hurt again. He would be invulnerable as, indeed, he nearly was.

At the end of the session James appeared a different person. There was a lightness and gaiety about him characteristic of a man released from prison. I had not seen this quality in him before.

Two weeks later I saw him again. He had not lost the effect of the previous session. He observed he did not feel sad and did not think he could cry again. But he had touched only the surface of his longing and his sadness. It was necessary to bring these feelings out more fully.

He began with the breathing (over the stool) to mobilize his body. Then he got the vibrations going in his legs. He was charged up when he lay down on the bed. I asked him to reach out with his arms and his mouth as if he were a baby and wanted to suck. How hard it seemed for him to do this! His lips barely moved forward. I put some pressure on his jaw, and as he said "Mama," he burst into tears. To his surprise it came rather quickly and was repeated each time he made an effort to reach out with his mouth. A baby also reaches with his tongue to suck. So I placed my hand over James' mouth and asked him to touch it with his tongue. This produced even deeper crying. He was aware now how desperately he wanted to reach out and how difficult it was. He sensed a feeling of anger, which cut off his crying, and for the first time he was able to bang his fists into the bed and say "Why" with a tone of conviction. His mourning had begun and he had touched the anger about his loss.

What had he lost? He had lost the pleasure and satisfaction a mother's love could provide, but, more important, he had lost the ability to reach out and open up to pleasure. He had lost the capacity for pleasure, and this is what he could grieve for and be angry about in the present. This is what every person who is deprived of fulfillment as an infant loses. It is not a loss one can adjust to or accept, for it robs life of all meaning. It cannot be compensated for, and all attempts at compensation must end in failure and depression. Only if therapy restores the patient's ability to reach out for pleasure will it be effective in overcoming the depressive tendency.

I believe we can understand now why depression strikes many people just when they seem to reach their goals. Having worked hard for the conditions they believed would make pleasure possible, they suddenly discover that it is not possible. The pleasure is not there for them, since they do not have the capacity to reach out and take it. Actually the pleasure is in the reaching out and opening up, as I pointed out in my previous book.* And this, we must realize, is not just a mental attitude. The reaching is done with the body, and it is blocked by muscular tensions that limit these movements.

* A. Lowen, *Pleasure: A Creative Approach to Life.*

There are two specific movements of reaching out: One is with the mouth and represents the infantile impulse to reach for the breast; the other is with the arms which expresses the child's desire to be picked up by his mother and held close to her body. In adult life these actions become transformed into the kiss and the embrace of affection. Both these movements are severely restricted in depressed patients. The arms may move upward, but the shoulders are retracted and the hands dangle limply from the wrist like wilted flowers. The reaching often has a listless quality, which the patient experiences as *"What's the use?"* or *"She wasn't there,"* referring to the mother. There is a lack of feeling in the arms due to the contraction of the muscles in the shoulder girdle. The forward movement of the lips is similarly inhibited by spasticities in the facial muscles. Most patients have a tight upper lip, which we recognize as an indication of holding back feeling. A tight and rigid jaw, which also expresses a negative attitude, blocks the lower lip from coming forward freely.

If a person can't reach out, he must manipulate his environment so that the pleasure is offered him. But, then, he still can't take it. There is no way out of this dilemma except to eliminate or reduce the muscular tensions. However this cannot be done mechanically. The holding back is an unconscious "I won't," which on one hand is a defense against the possibility of being disappointed and hurt, but on the other is also a spite reaction: *"Since you didn't come when I wanted you, I don't want you now."* Until this negative attitude is made conscious and expressed, the reaching out will remain tentative and incomplete. But since the patient is desperate, lonely and in need of acceptance and approval, he lacks the security to assert his negativity openly. This was James' situation. He needed more grounding.

As I worked with his reaching out and his negative feelings, James improved measurably, remaining free from a depressive reaction for many months. The pleasure in his relationship with his wife increased considerably. But problems began to emerge in his work situation which made him very anxious. He came to the session one day feeling deeply depressed, as badly as before, with the feeling, *"I don't know if I want to live."* Realistically, his work situation did not justify this feeling. Studying him, I realized that he had been unable to consolidate his gains because he lacked sufficient feeling in his feet to maintain his ground in the face of some adversity.

I had been aware of this problem in James' personality for a long time. We had worked with his legs and feet throughout the therapy, but we had never resolved this area of difficulty. To restore to a patient the feeling of being rooted into the earth through his feet is the therapy's final step. It enables him to regain his standing as a person. It gives him the full mobility and motility of his body. He can move freely in life. I might add that James had flat feet, the left foot markedly so. We were forced to focus on this problem.

There are a number of bioenergetic exercises which mobilize feeling in the feet. One, for example, is placing the arch of the foot on the handle of a tennis racket and pressing down till it hurts. I also made James conscious that he didn't fully use his feet in walking. He got very little lift from them. In a sense, therefore, he couldn't lift himself out of his gloom.

James didn't readily accept my interpretation of his difficulties. Only after he developed some feeling in his feet, as a result of the exercises, did he realize how little he had had in the past. When there is a lack of feeling in a part of the body, the person doesn't sense that part and consequently is unaware of the lack. This is the key problem in therapy. James worked with these exercises religiously at home and in the therapeutic sessions. He came out of his last depressive reaction quickly and has remained entirely free from it since then. He learned he must keep his feet on the ground in a feeling way if he wanted to be sure of where he stood as a person.

The significance of a mother for a child lies in the fact that all the infant's pleasure functions depend on her response. If her response is negative, these functions wither and fade. A nursery can provide the physical care a child requires, but only a mother or one who fulfills that role can respond to a child's reaching for pleasure with his mouth with an equal pleasure at the satisfaction of the child's desire. The child who is fulfilled on this level has the inner conviction that he can reach for and enjoy any pleasure that is available. The sweet taste of mother's milk in a baby's mouth nourishes his spirit as the milk itself nourishes the body. And the security that loving contact with the mother provides will be translated into a feeling of security that the earth is there for one and one can stand on it with confidence.

The Reactions to the Loss

Studies have shown that when the loss of a mother occurs, the child reacts to the deprivation violently at first. He will fight with all his strength to restore the lost mother by screaming, crying, temper tantrums, or whatever means he can command. Only after the fight proves hopeless and his energy is exhausted does he slowly sink into a depressed state. The loss is never accepted, it is simply endured.

John Bowlby, who studied the child's reaction to separation, observed that the child went through three phases: In the first he protests the loss; "with tears and anger he demands his mother back and seems hopeful he will succeed in getting her." * Later he becomes quieter, his hope altering to despair. But in the second phase of despair, his hope springs forth from time to time. Eventually, he seems to lose interest in his mother. He may even forget her and not recognize her when she *does* come for him. This third phase is one of detachment. The child is withdrawn and depressed. But even in the third stage there are occasional episodes of angry behavior, often of a "disquietingly violent kind."

It is Bowlby's contention that when a child or an adult reacts with anger to a loss, it is a perfectly normal response. He writes, "So far from being pathological, the evidence suggests that the overt expression of this powerful urge, unrealistic and hopeless though it may be, is a necessary condition for mourning to run its normal course. Only after every effort has been made to recover the lost object, it seems, is the individual in a mood to admit defeat and to orient himself afresh to a world from which the loved object is accepted as irretrievably missing." In the young child the anger is primarily directed against the loved object, the mother, who the child feels has deserted him. Bowlby believes this is a reproach to the mother for leaving and also a maneuver to prevent her from doing it again.

Bioenergetically, the reaction of anger to a loss is the natural response of an organism to pain. The child is angry at his mother for having caused him pain and tries through his anger to prevent the pain or overcome its effect on the body. Pain, in this case produced by a loss of pleasure, causes the body to contract. Feeling and energy are withdrawn from the body surface (the erotic areas) and concentrated in the muscular apparatus. They can be released from this system only by some violent action. Following the angry discharge,

* John Bowlby, "Childhood Mourning and Its Implications for Psychiatry," *The American Journal of Psychology*, Vol. 128, No. 6 (December, 1961).

a further release occurs through crying and sobbing. Only after these reactions have taken place is the energy available for the body's pleasure functions. If a full release has not occurred, the organism is biologically blocked from reaching out again to the world for pleasure.

There are important differences, however, between a child's loss of a mother or her love and the adult's loss of a loved object. An adult has the objectivity to realize that the loss was not deliberately caused by the object and so his anger is not directed against the object. An exception to this statement occurs in divorce situations where, because the separation is deliberately produced, it often provokes in the one who suffers the loss a violent anger at the other for leaving. Another difference is due to the fact that an adult can replace a lost loved object (one can find another mate), but a child cannot replace a lost mother. If a satisfactory replacement could be found for the loss of mother love, the trauma would not be severe. But how can we ask a child who has lost this love to accept his defeat and reorient himself to the world? Without a mother, all the child's pleasure functions (reaching out) become frozen and his pain is a continuing one. To deaden the pain, he must deaden his body, and this is why so many of our chronically depressed patients have relatively lifeless bodies.

The intensity of the anger must be directly proportional to the pain experienced, which is also directly related to the amount of pleasure lost. Thus a child who had a satisfying relationship with his mother will react more violently than another on losing it. This is the reason why breast-fed babies tolerate less frustration than bottle-fed babies. While this may pose a problem for some parents, I can only say "more power to them" (the babies). For it is by not accepting the frustrations and separations that a child gains the emotional health needed for living in these troubled times. All my depressed patients have attempted to adjust to a deprivation they should not have experienced, and in each case the adjustment subsequently failed.

Psychoanalysts have also been aware that underlying the depressive tendency is a conflict of love and hate for the loved object, always the mother but frequently also the father. Karl Abraham believed that the paralysis of feeling in the depressed person was due to equal feelings of love and hate blocking any movement. The hatred is repressed and turned inward against the self, and in this process it forms a negative layer over the feeling of love, which cannot then be expressed. In suicide the self-hate is acted out, but this action also contains the unconscious wish to destroy the person responsible for these feelings.

The hatred of a child for his mother must be viewed as a natural response to separation, rejection, or the withdrawal of love. When a mother withdraws her love, whether deliberately or unintentionally, she is, in effect, being destructive to the child, since the latter's emotional welfare is almost entirely dependent on her love. The child's first response to this withdrawal is one of anger or rage. But most mothers believe their actions stem from necessity—that is, from factors beyond their control—and they react to the child's anger with threats and punishments. Sandor Lorand showed that one of the factors responsible for depression was "the threatening, frustrating, punishing attitude of the mother." *

The hostility which some parents, and especially some mothers, vent on young children is unbelievable. Joseph Rheingold studied the abuse to which some children were

* Sandor Lorand, *The Technique of Psychoanalytic Therapy* (New York, International University Press, 1946).

subject and was appalled at the degree to which mothers act out on their children their repressed hatred of their own mothers. He says, "We deal simply with the transmission of destructiveness from one generation to the next; the young girl and the woman are one, and what was done to her by her mother she in turn does to her daughter." * Or to her son, whichever the case may be. Rheingold sees this destructiveness as a reaction to the mother's fear of being a woman. This fear causes her to reject her femininity (femaleness is more appropriate) and to reject her child, who is its manifestation. The rejection occurs despite conscious intentions to love and accept the child. She will become openly hostile whenever the child makes a demand on her that she cannot fulfill and which, therefore, arouses her guilt. His crying may drive her to distraction and may even lead to murderous feelings: The remark "I could strangle that baby if he doesn't stop crying" is not infrequently heard.

Thus, added to all the other factors determining the depressive reaction, there is the child's fear of his mother's destructive potential. The giver of life can also take away life, and every infant is acutely aware that his survival depends on retaining some positive connection with his mother. To the degree, therefore, that he senses the mother's hostility, he will react with assertions of love. The hate will be there, but it will be suppressed as too threatening. It is the only explanation I have for the repeated observation that the child who is most rejected and abused in a family becomes the adult who is most devoted to the mother. This is the child who also feels the most unworthy, most guilty, and most filled with self-hate.

In every mother there is a seed of love which may either

* Joseph C. Rheingold, *The Fear of Being a Woman* (New York, Grune & Stratton, 1964), p. 141.

germinate and blossom or lie sterile. In every newborn infant the love for his mother (seen as a desire for closeness) is full blown, but in the face of rejection and hostility, this love will wither. However it will never die. It cannot, for this would also mean the death of the child. We are not dealing therefore with absolutes but with ambivalences in which the relative proportion of love and hate is a measure of the amount of pleasure or pain in a relationship. In a similar way the anger arising from the loss of pleasure in the mother is mixed with fear. And the sorrow associated with the loss is streaked with hope. The loss is never experienced as absolute, the child feels that there is always the possibility his mother will come to her senses and realize she loves him and that her pleasure is biologically tied to his pleasure. No child can survive without some faith in human nature.

Also, no child can accept and mourn a loss that is equivalent to his own demise. His sanity and survival require that he see his mother in a positive light. This can be done by dissociating her clearly destructive behavior from her personality, which is then projected on a "bad mother." Later, when reality proves that there are not two mothers, the child absorbs the mother's negative aspect into himself. The child sees himself as the villain or monster who by some twist of fate behaves so as to merit the pain he experienced. It can be stated as a general rule that the unloved child feels unlovable. But no child can consciously make this connection. He cannot comprehend the insane state of affairs in which a mother turns against her own child by denying him pleasure or causing him pain. He can only reason, that the fault must be his own and so must be the blame and the guilt.

Every depressed person carries an enormous burden of guilt. *Mea culpa* is his constant refrain. He feels guilty because he is depressed. He cannot function effectively, he is a burden to others and a damper on their spirits. So he seems to have every reason to feel guilty. His depression is the sign of his ultimate failure. He does not realize that his depression resulted from his guilt when the burden became too great to carry. By feeling guilty over his depression, he digs the hole in which he lies a little deeper and makes his recovery more difficult. But every depressed person is blind to the psychological dynamics of his condition, and it requires some therapeutic intervention to free him from the vicious circle which entraps him.

The circle can be temporarily broken by any form of psychotherapy. Viewing the depressive reaction as an illness removes the stigma of failure and releases the patient from his superficial guilt about the depression. The interest and encouragement of the therapist temporarily acts as a substitute for the loss of affection that undermined his will to live. With this new lifeline to the world the patient can slowly pull himself out of the darkness and into the light. An analytic therapy also offers the patient an opportunity to become aware of some of the suppressed emotions associated with the many losses he had experienced in his life. In these people the original loss is always compounded by later disappointments in love. If the therapy is effective, it may enable him to reexperience the original loss and now, as an adult, to abreact its pain by a proper mourning.

A Proper Mourning

In the preceding section it was pointed out that a young child reacts to the loss of his mother with angry and violent outbursts, with screaming and crying. The loss is not accepted quietly.

Among primitive people mourning is also a violent affair. If the love object is important, its loss is not accepted without a show of anger and protest. Elias Canetti * quotes a report of a mourning among the bushmen of Central Australia. It reveals several unusual features. As soon as news that a man is dying reaches a village, men and women rush to the dying man and fling themselves on him, forming a heap. At the same time they fill the air with loud lamentations and inflict wounds on their bodies. Finally, when death ends the man's suffering, they withdraw and continue their lamentations in a new locale. The significance of the heap for Canetti is that the natives do not accept the loss, "he still belongs to them; they hold him back amongst themselves." Self-mutilation in mourning is well known among primitive people. Canetti sees it as an expression of anger. "There is much anger in this self-mutilation, anger at impotence in the face of death."

Sometimes the anger is directed outward. Esther Warner † described the reaction of native women to the death of a young woman who died in childbirth. One of the native boys told her, "Just before the sun gets up, the women of the town will hold a Cursing of Men. If they catch one, they will lack small (take little) to beat him to death. The women will take revenge because it is woman that has hurt and dies from pickin (baby)." The author continued, "The women did not hold off until dawn for their cursing. We soon heard them, whacking on doors with clubs, shouting in the hoarse and helpless voices of anger." The next morning, the women were subdued and quiet. "Their fury at pain and death having been spent; they were again ready to meekly accept the endless chores attendant on living."

If no anger is felt at a loss, no real grief can be experienced

* Elias Canetti, *Crowds & Power* (New York, Viking Press, 1963), pp. 103–7.
† Esther Warner, *Seven Days to Lomaland* (New York, Pyramid Publications, 1967), pp. 156, 158.

and a proper mourning will not take place. It is the nature of human beings to protest their pain and not to choke the protest off masochistically. It seems strange, then, that our culture so admires the individual who can bear a loss stoically, without showing any emotion. What great virtue is there in the suppression of feeling? Such behavior may reveal that a person's ego dominates and controls his body, but it also indicates that some important aspect of his humanity is missing.

The depressed person has lost his ability to protest his fate. I have found in treating these patients that they cannot say "Why" in a loud and convincing voice. The inability is easily rationalized. *"What's the use of saying why? Nothing will change."* True, nothing will change on the outside. Every mourning primitive knows, I am sure, that his wails and lamentations will not bring back the dead. Mourning has no such purpose. It is an expression of feeling and it enables life to go on. When the expression is inhibited, the flow of life is restricted. This will eventually lead to further suppression of feeling and ultimately to death in life. Depression is a living death.

The etiology of depression is twofold: First, there is a significant loss of pleasure, as an infant and child, in relation to the mother. If we can accept the hypothesis that full oral gratification requires approximately three years of satisfactory nursing at the breast, it is easy to see why a vulnerability to depression is widespread. Second, the right of the child to protest his deprivation is denied and his expression of rage and anger is punished. The result is a serious loss in the ability to reach out and fight for what one wants. One has only to observe the sheeplike behavior of the mass of people to realize that the tendency to depression is endemic to our culture.

On the other hand, the mass protests which are becoming

part of our national scene are a reaction against an emotional submissiveness that harnessed man to the industrial machine. Actually the two tendencies, one to depression and the other to protest, belong to the same picture. As the meaning of life is constantly eroded by the loss of pleasure in living, people will become increasingly depressed. At the same time they will engage in more frequent and larger protests, hoping to find in social action the meaning that escapes them on the personal level. As a momentary release, participation in a mass protest serves to prevent one from becoming depressed. This means, however, that the person, the militant student, for example, must live in a state of continual protest to avoid depression. Since this is an impossible way of life, we can anticipate that more and more people will become depressed and suicidal.

I am not against social protest for a legitimate cause. The basic problem, however, is the loss of pleasure. Most protesters do not seek to restore their capacity for pleasure but aim, rather, at gaining power. If they do gain power, they will find it has no value in terms of pleasure. The antithesis between power and pleasure is fully discussed in *Pleasure: A Creative Approach to Life*. If they fail to achieve their aim, which is the more likely alternative, since the forces that shape the social situation are often beyond the control of individuals, the road to depression is wide open.

A protest, to be effective for the individual, must express his personal sense of loss. When a person asks, "Why did this happen to me?" he implies that he is aware of a personal loss. When patients say "Why" with feeling, they often burst into sobbing as a sense of loss and a feeling of sadness sweep over them. I recall an example from a bioenergetic workshop for Esalen residents at Big Sur, California. A young woman had been doing the breathing exercises described in the previous chapter. Then she lay down on a bed and I asked her to kick her legs into the bed and yell "Why." She started easily, but in a moment she was possessed by feeling. Her kicking became stronger, her yelling louder when suddenly she broke down crying. When her crying subsided, she turned to me and asked, "How did you know that was what I wanted to say?" Apart from the fact that I had an intuitive sense of her need, I could only answer, "It is something everyone wants to say, but some dare not and others cannot." We all have suffered losses and hurts that our minds may accept but our bodies do not. The body cannot release its pain except through a violent catharsis.

Among the many techniques used to bring a depressed patient to the point where he can feel his loss as an immediate experience and vent the rage associated with it is a simple exercise involving the use of a rolled-up Turkish towel. The patient takes the towel in his hands and twists it with all his strength. This is generally done while he is lying on a bed. Then with jaw thrust forward and teeth showing, he screams, "Give it to me." If the grip is not relaxed and the screaming continues, the patient's arms will begin to shake and he will find himself acting as if he were trying to tear the towel away from someone. This same exercise can also be done with the expressions "Damn you," "I hate you," "I'll kill you." Often they turn into intense emotional experiences.

I said in the previous section that the depressive tendency is overcome when a patient gains the ability to reach out for pleasure. This involves more than a psychological attitude. The muscles of the throat, jaw and mouth must be relaxed if a meaningful movement is to be made. The arms must be free and not restricted by chronic muscular tensions. These tensions develop out of fear of expressing the anger and rage a loss provokes. Therefore, not until the anger and rage are released are the muscles free to open the person to love.

Bioenergetic therapy does not aim to help a patient adjust to a life-crippling loss. Rather, it helps him overcome the effect of the loss by restoring his body to its natural state of loveliness. In the process of therapy he will reexperience the deprivations and pains of his childhood and youth. To these he will react with rage and sorrow. He will protest the inequities of his life. But he will also gain the courage and the ability to reach out anew for life, unafraid of the pain that may attend the opening of one's being to love.

You may ask: Where does a person who has been badly hurt as a child get the courage to risk additional hurt? My answer is that life is courageous. A person's courage is a measure of his life force. As long as a person's body is frozen or locked in the pain of his loss, his breathing is restricted, his motility is diminished, and his life force is reduced. A proper mourning, with all that is entailed in that term, is nature's way of overcoming the shock and freeing the spirit. It is the therapeutic task to provide the patient with the understanding and the means to accomplish his liberation.

6. Deception and Self-Deception

Playing the Game

Most adult patients who suffer depression have not actually experienced the loss of a mother. What they *did* experience were disturbances and conflicts in the mother-child relationship, which, however, seem to have no bearing in the patient's mind on the cause of his illness. These conflicts are so much taken for granted as being part of the normal pattern of child rearing that the patient does not feel that he was deprived of normal mother love. We must remember, too, that the depressive reaction in an adult is separated from the infantile or childhood experience by a relatively long period of apparently normal behavior. This was not healthy functioning, as I pointed out earlier, or the patient would not have become depressed. But the patient isn't aware of the difference between seemingly normal and healthy functioning any more than he is aware of the connection between his illness and the events of his childhood.

This lack of awareness amounts to a naïveté which characterizes the attitude of the depressed person and constitutes his predisposition to the illness. Naïveté stems from an unconscious denial of the facts of life, particularly, the facts of one's own life, of one's deprivations and disappointments.

The effect of the denial is to leave the individual open to similar disappointments in adult life. Naïveté does not preclude the person from displaying a certain shrewdness in life. In fact, the two are often found together; naïveté being revealed in those areas where the denial is operative while shrewdness is seen in other areas of life.

Naïveté is not to be confused with innocence. An innocent person lacks the experience by which to judge attitudes or actions. He is open to deception, but he will learn quickly from his deception. The naïve individual has had the experience of being hurt by a deception but denies its significance. He, too, is open to deception because he is unable to recognize its nature. Naïveté is a form of self-deception into which a person is forced when he is being deceived and cannot or dare not acknowledge the truth. In such a situation one may be forced to play the game because one has no alternative. But playing the game can often lead to a belief that the game is life, that the rules of the game are the rules of life, and that winning or losing provides the meaning of one's existence.

The game I am interested in here is called "Bringing up baby." Some readers may object to my qualifying such a serious undertaking as a game. However, the seriousness with which one engages in an activity is no criterion of whether or not it is a game. People take a game seriously when the stakes are high. What makes child rearing a game is the contest that develops between a parent and child. In this contest the child fights to retain his animal nature while the parents fight to civilize him. It is a game in which no holds are barred.

Let me say at the outset of this discussion that not all parents make a game out of child rearing. It becomes a game when the outcome is judged in terms of winning or losing.

The goal of this game is to rear a child who is socially acceptable. In the modern world this outcome is uncertain, it contains an element of chance. Parents who play bring all their wits to bear on the situation, hoping that they can "play their cards right" and win. There are stakes here that have nothing to do with the real situation. Winning, for the parent who plays the game, means the achievement of some extraneous gain, some reward or acclaim that would acknowledge his winning. Or when a parent feels that losing would lower his self-esteem, he is treating the child-rearing process as a game.

The full name of the game that parents play is "How to bring up baby without spoiling him." The prizes seem high. The parent who succeeds in rearing the good, obedient, well-behaved child is praised and recognized by friends, teachers and other representatives of society. The parent who fails is regarded as a weakling, a person without standing or authority in his own home. "You let your child walk all over you" reveals contempt for the poor parent, who in the eyes of many people is like a poor, powerless fish. There is another unspoken and often unacknowledged reward the parent hopes to gain: namely, that the good child will be devoted to the parent especially in his declining years. He will feel obliged to take care of the parent in his illness and infirmity.

The game is played with the infant or child being at first entirely unaware of what is going on. Nevertheless it is a game, like others, in which the child has to be outmaneuvered if the desired result is to be obtained. The parent assumes, quite rightly, that the child will resist and that by the proper use of rewards and punishments his resistance can be overcome. The rewards used are approval, toys, indulgences and so forth. The punishments are threats to withdraw love, disapproval, restrictions, castigations, and physical abuse.

A parent who uses these tactics doesn't think he is playing a game. To him or her the issues are real and serious indeed. The child who is allowed to have his own way will be a failure in life, a rebel and a misfit. And the parent who is afraid this can happen feels he has a moral responsibility to prevent it. He feels justified in his attitude and may even identify it with love. He would certainly resist any suggestion that it betrays a lack of love for the child. By the same token he would regard the obedient child as a loving child and the rebellious one as hostile.

Playing this game denotes a lack of faith in human nature and in one's own child. If we believe that a child is inherently a monster, a wild animal that must be tamed and whipped into line to become a civilized being, then we must put our trust in authority and discipline as the only forces that can ensure orderly living. If we believe that human beings are naturally greedy, selfish, dishonest and destructive creatures, then our only recourse is to the power of the police or the army to control behavior. These attitudes may seem extreme, but we can be driven to them if we have no faith in life. Faith implies a trust in one's own nature and, by extension, trust in the nature of others. A person with faith trusts himself to do what is right and he trusts others, including his children, to do the same. A person without faith trusts no one.

If a parent has no faith in a child, it is difficult to see how the child can develop faith in himself or in his parent. The relation between parent and child degenerates from one of love and mutual respect to one of conflict and tension. Each views the other as an adversary to whom one is, nevertheless, bound. Resentments arise, which further alienate two people whose interests should be common. A parent wants to see his child joyful and content and the child wants his parent to feel pleasure in his joy. These feelings pervade many parent-child relationships that are based on love and faith. They are unfortunately absent from those relationships in which parents play games with children's attitudes.

Without faith there is no true love. In the absence of faith the love parents hold out to children is conditioned on their behavior. Conditional love, implied in the remark *"Mother loves you when you are a good child,"* not only carries the threat of loss of love but actually amounts to a rejection of the child. In effect, the mother is saying that she cannot love the child as he is but only if and when he surrenders his spontaneous responsiveness and becomes a submissive, obedient person. Since healthy children normally display a certain amount of willfulness and assertiveness as part of their growing self-awareness, such an attitude on the mother's part constitutes a withholding of love. But there are many cases where love is actually withdrawn from a child, when a mother turns cold or hostile as a means of curbing a child's assertiveness. The game is not one that can be played easily or lightly, it is always dead serious.

Everyday observation shows that there are few parents who do not use these methods to bring their children into line—into line with their own upbringing—and there are few parents who do not justify their actions by the necessities of their own lives. A parent cannot constantly give in to a child. A parent cannot let a child run the home. Parents are people, too, who have needs that must be fulfilled. Unfortunately these often seem to conflict with the needs or desires of the child, and in this conflict the child's needs manage to get reduced to a minimum. Then when the child cries, is restless, or has a temper tantrum, the parents feel put upon and react with anger and hostility.

Parents who play the game always see the issue as one of

principle not circumstance. It is a matter of principle not to let the child have his own way. A child can sense this antagonism and reacts to it with overaggressiveness. Once the lines of conflict are drawn, the outcome of the struggle can only be disastrous. If the parents yield out of guilt or simply to quiet the child, they will spoil him. Sensing their weakness, they will attempt to be firmer on the next occasion. But the child, having learned he can get his way by creating a disturbance, will fight back with more vigor. In these situations the battle is a never-ending one, with the parents overcoming the child's resistance at times and giving in at others. For the child, too, the issue becomes one of principle—on principle he will oppose his parents' every demand.

A child growing up in such a home never develops a faith in life. He has learned that he can get what he wants only by outmaneuvering and outyelling the opposition. His opponents, however, are those whose love he needs and they will include all the people with whom he desires intimacy. He has also learned how to manipulate people by playing on their guilt, and he will use this tactic when his bullying fails to achieve its end. The character one develops from these experiences has a strong sadomasochistic streak, which turns every effort to gain love into defeat. Each defeat will end in a depressive reaction from which the individual will rouse himself when his determination to fight back and win returns. The depressive reactions of this personality are not generally as severe as those described in the two preceding chapters. They have an intermittent quality which masks the chronic nature of the problem.

Strictness is the only way to have an effective discipline. But one may ask to what extent discipline is necessary with children. The concept of discipline as used in this respect involves punishment if the authority of the parent is defied.

When we think of discipline as self-discipline, it lacks this connotation. There is an important difference between the two. The study of any branch of knowledge is a discipline because the person who commits himself to its study submits to the authority of his teacher. He becomes a disciple—that is, one who will follow and learn from the master. But the disciple is not punished if he challenges his master's author ity. He may be dismissed or simply rebuked. Punishment must be used when one is trying to train an animal or a person to obey commands. Training and learning are two very different procedures. We train rather than educate when we have no faith that what we offer is in accord with the nature of the student and desired by him.

A child will naturally follow the way of his parents if it is a way of love, acceptance, and pleasure. He will respect their values and consciously identify with them. But he will also assert his individuality and demand the freedom to find out things for himself. Thus he will learn about life and grow up to be a mature, independent person who can stand on his own feet. His way will not be very different from the way of his parents. Why should it? Since their way was a source of pleasure to him, he has no motivation to make any radical changes in it. This is the way faith works.

A child can also be trained through an effective discipline to adhere to the way of his parents. Through the proper combination of force and seduction his personality can be structured to the model they want. Of course, if the rewards are insufficient or the punishment too severe, the scheme may fail. It often succeeds, however, and the child learns to play the game. He knows what behavior will win his parents' approval and what will evoke their displeasure. He will make every conscious effort, therefore, to be what they want. Unconsciously, he will deeply resent their lack of faith in him and their lack of acceptance, but these resentments must remain unconscious if he is to play the game. He will have to suppress any feeling of hostility or rebellion.

The child who learns to play this game will appear well adjusted to the average observer who has learned to look at the superficial aspects of behavior and not to see the quality of the bodily response supporting it. He will not be aware if a person is grounded in his legs or in his body. He will notice only that the child or young person seems to get along well with his parents and other authority figures, that his school work is of high caliber, and that he doesn't question the direction of his life.

This apparently well-adjusted child may go on for years playing the game of being and doing what is expected of him. His conduct will gain the approval of most people, which he will value as a sign of love. Sooner or later, however, some event will bring about his disillusionment. The game will suddenly become meaningless, although he may not be aware of this. He will sense he has lost the interest and motivation to continue the play. He will become depressed but he will not know why. This fairly common experience is illustrated by the case of Marta.

Woman on a Pedestal

I first saw Marta at a training workshop for bioenergetic analysis. She had come with her husband, who was a clinical psychologist, to see what help she could get from this new approach. At these training workshops for professional people, my associates and I explain the connection between body attitude and personality. We point out how a diagnosis of personality problems can be made from the way a person holds and moves his body. Then we put the participants through some of the bioenergetic exercises described in the preceding chapters to show them how their problems can be worked out by releasing the chronic muscular tensions that are the physical counterpart of these problems.

What impressed me most about Marta's body was the way she held herself. She had pulled the upper half of her body up, as if by conscious effort; her shoulders were raised, her chest was high and inflated, while the abdominal and pelvic areas of her body were tight and also drawn up. Her legs were rigid and thin, the leg muscles so contracted that her legs looked like sticks. I could sense that she wasn't in her legs and that they were functioning like mechanical supports. The lower part (from her hips down) struck me as resembling a pedestal on which the upper half rested.

The accompanying figure illustrates the idea of the pedestal in the human body. It is, of course, schematic.

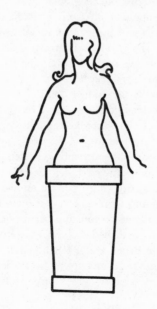

When I pointed this out to Marta, it struck a responsive chord. She felt she had always been placed on a pedestal, first by her parents then by her husband. The latter agreed, saying that he had idealized Marta as the perfect wife. Both were highly impressed that I was able to see this in the body. Marta's participation in the exercises designed to deepen breathing and ground the individual in the legs, made her realize that her problem should be treated both from the physical and the psychological sides.

The story Marta told me on the occasion of our first private session was that she had functioned well as wife and mother until the preceding ten years. Then she became depressed and was unable to keep up with her housework. "Before that," she said, "I remember people saying that I always seemed happy. Up to that time I always felt cheerful, though I had occasional depressed feelings.

"It happened one day when my husband came home and I had a problem about my parents. I wanted to talk to him about it, but he was involved in his own affairs. We had an understanding that we would be there for each other. I always used to listen to his difficulties. So I kept asking him to listen to me. Finally, he said, 'I don't want to listen to you.' I answered that I couldn't be what he wanted me to be. I had to be myself. To which he replied, 'Where is my wife? You're not the wife I know.'

"Up to that time my husband idealized me, believing I was perfect. He felt betrayed and I felt betrayed. He became angry, so I started to withdraw more and more into myself. He felt disappointed in me because I wasn't taking care of the house. I wasn't the responsible person he admired. I was angry and furious with bad feelings that I couldn't express. My depression deepened and I felt hopeless. The first break came a few months ago at another workshop. My husband

and I were encouraged to fight, which we did. After that experience I felt freed for a little while and it gave me a ray of hope."

It was obvious from her body that Marta could not easily get off the pedestal. For one thing she had no feeling of being able to stand on her own feet. For another, she was consciously committed to the role she was playing. This became evident through an incident which occurred shortly after we began the therapy. Marta told me what had happened.

"Yesterday I was at a workshop and the leader kept picking on me and criticizing me for no reason I could see. I began to get depressed. I felt hurt and on the verge of tears, but I couldn't get angry. Even today I can't get angry about it. I realized that this is what my mother did to me all my life. At the same workshop another participant was putting me on a pedestal. She pointed to me again and again as her ideal. It irritated and saddened me, but it also pleased me. I saw that I liked being looked up to, although I felt that I didn't really deserve it."

To release Marta from the pedestal, the proper therapeutic procedure would be to evoke feeling in the lower part of her body, which was relatively immobile as befitted a pedestal. This could be done by deepening Marta's breathing, which was severely blocked at the diaphragmatic level, and by having her use her legs in expressive movements like kicking to protest what had been done to her. It would also be necessary that she become acutely aware of the trauma she had experienced. She had to sense the loss of that part of her personality which was represented by the immobility of the lower half of her body and face the pain and sorrow of this loss.

Personality disturbances are characterized not only by some

loss of function but also by a loss of the awareness associated with the function. For example, a person with myopia not only is handicapped visually, but also has difficulty seeing relationships. The visual function and the perceptual function cannot be dissociated.

Marta presented another aspect of this phenomenon. Being on a pedestal, she lacked standing. It can be inferred from this that she would lack understanding of her problem. Understanding implies a sensing from the core or from the roots of one's being. It means knowing a thing from the ground up. On the other hand, one can have a fairly sound intellectual grasp of the psychological factors involved in the depressive reaction by rising above the situation and seeing it objectively. Unfortunately, knowing a thing with one's head is not the same as "knowing" it in one's guts. Marta was caught by this split in her personality. She might know why she became depressed, but she could not emotionally experience her condition.

To gain a true understanding of her problem Marta would have to get into or to get in touch with the lower half of her body. If she did this, she would experience or understand her animal nature. She would come into contact with her passions, feel her sexuality, and sense her womanhood. All this was lost to her when she was placed on a pedestal. She became a model person (the perfect child, the perfect wife, and the perfect mother), but she was forced to sacrifice her humanity and her reality. This is a big price to pay for "social acceptability." Joan, who was forced to adopt the role of a statue, had suppressed even more of herself in the so-called civilizing process.

In Chapter 2 I pointed out that the upper half of the body is identified with consciousness and the ego, the lower half with the unconscious and sexuality. In mythology * the diaphragm is equated with the surface of the earth. Below the diaphragm are the nether regions, the abode of the dark forces, the passions that are not fully subject to the rational control of the mind. The feelings of the upper half of the body are closer to consciousness and therefore more subject to ego authority. These mythological or primitive ideas may seem strange to modern sophisticated thinking, but we must recognize that they were based on subjective data—that is, feeling and self-perception. In discarding such data, science has fostered a split between thinking and feeling, the ego and the body, man and nature.

A holistic view of life demands the integration of objective and subjective data, of both conscious and unconscious phenomena, of knowledge and understanding. A comprehensive therapy deals simultaneously with both the psyche and the soma. To encompass the individual, it proceeds in two directions: from the ground up and from the head above, analysis from above and analysis from below, as Sandor Ferenczi described it. Let us look now at the facts of Marta's life as they came to light in therapy.

Marta was an only child, which raised the specter in her mother's eyes of a spoiled child. Her mother often said she would not have a spoiled child and prided herself on the fact that Marta was not. Marta told me that her mother made it perfectly plain that her love and approval were conditioned on Marta's being and behaving the way she wanted and that she wouldn't tolerate any other behavior.

Several early memories tell us how the mother's attitude was implemented. Marta recalled: "My earliest memory involves a doll to which something happened. Its face got soft

* Erich Neumann, *The Origins and History of Consciousness* (New York, The Bollingen Foundation, 1954).

and when it fell into the sand, the sand stuck to it. My mother threw it away. I recall the scene where I was crying for the doll but my mother was firm. Even when my grandmother offered to go to the dump to retrieve it, my mother wouldn't let her.

"Another memory also involved a doll which had been sent to a doll hospital when its face became damaged. After it was returned, the doll was placed on top of the refrigerator and I was told that I couldn't have it until I ate my eggs. I couldn't eat the eggs and I don't remember ever getting the doll. My father backed my mother in this. My mother always believed she could control my father surreptitiously. I remember feeling stubborn and not crying. This memory is later than the first one."

One wonders how a child would be spoiled by sparing her the pain of such losses. There was not even a real issue until the parents created one by forcing the child into a position of defiance or rebellion. Once the issue was raised, however, it became a contest of wills. Before that it was simply a question of how much pleasure the parents could afford to allow the child and how much pain they would necessarily cause her. It seems to me that the first consideration of unneurotic parents is to see a child happy. This wasn't the view of Marta's mother, who played the game early in Marta's life.

Marta tells a revealing story of the time when she was two months old: "I heard that they [mother and grandmother] would rock me and nurse me until I fell asleep. One time when I was about two months old, my mother decided to let me cry myself out. I cried for hours—my grandmother was going crazy, but my mother refused to let her go into my room. Finally I stopped crying and my mother said, 'See.' They opened the door and saw. I was blue. I had vomited and was choking on the vomitus. My mother also says that she put bitter aloes on my fingers to prevent me from sucking them or biting my nails, and I heard the story, too, from her that she would put a spoon of oatmeal in my mouth, and before I could spit it out, she put her breast in to stop me. My mother tells these stories with pride."

Marta's early years were full of conflict and torment. She threw up a lot as a child and was intensely carsick. She had temper tantrums, screamed and tore her hair. She said, "I was regarded as crazy. I was punished by being shut in my room, having things taken away, or being kept from dinner. My mother simply wasn't going to have any spoiled brats in her family."

Her mother tried to control every aspect of Marta's life, always with the delusion that she was doing it for Marta. Even the child's excretory functions did not escape her attention. "If I had a bowel movement, I had to call my mother to come see. If I didn't call her, I was scolded. I remember one enema when I was about five or six. I had to be held down by three adults. I fought, scratched and screamed. I was placed across my father's knee and I got the enema, but it was the only one."

Sometime after six years of age Marta's resistance to her parents collapsed. The change coincided with the beginning of the latency period, when the tide of infantile sexuality retreats. It had something to do with her inability to resolve the Oedipal conflict. Her recourse was to cut off the sexual feelings (not genital feelings) she had for her father, which immobilized the lower part of her body. Another factor in her submission was starting school, which introduced Marta to a new world with new demands. Marta became an obedient child; she then tried to be and do what her parents wanted. She was, for example, the smartest one in her class. "It was expected of me," she said. "I recall getting 99½ on a test in high school and my mother saying that if I could do that well, I should be able to get 100."

One would think that, knowing these traumas, Marta would react emotionally to them and free herself from her depressive state. But we must remember that she was depressed because the ability to react emotionally was blocked. During the early sessions of therapy our efforts were directed toward the mobilization of feeling through the breathing exercises, the induction of vibrations in the legs, kicking, yelling "No," and so on. Although Marta tried hard, progress was very slow. On one occasion I used a little shock therapy to shake her up. This consisted of drumming on her upper back lightly with my two fists. Her breathing became spasmodic, but no reaction occurred. I repeated the drumming and Marta broke into sobs.

After sobbing for a while, Marta moved to the bed. She kicked her legs into the bed and screamed "Why." She felt, "Why did you hurt me? Why do I have to be hurt?" But this was the first time Marta's voice rose to a scream. However, when I asked her to hit the bed with a tennis racket, she could not evoke any feeling of anger at having been hurt. I then applied some pressure on the anterior scalene muscles at the sides of her neck. Marta began to scream again and continued after the pressure was removed. She said she could sense the terror in her body but was detached from it in her head. So overwhelming was the terror that she could not let herself perceive it subjectively. However, at the end of the session, she felt clear and somewhat grounded. Her whole body was in a state of vibration.

In the next few sessions Marta became aware that she was in a strong conflict between letting down or giving in, which she regarded as self-indulgence, and doing what she was supposed to do, namely, hold herself up. She was able to relate the feeling of self-indulgence to her father, who "is self-indulgent, goes to bed with the slightest illness and gets depressed. My mother," she said, "believes that you don't give in to anything. She could be dying but she would continue to go to work." I pointed out to Marta that the upper half of her body represented her mother's values—control, achievement and pride—while the lower half, with its sexual orientation, was equated with her father. Just as her mother surreptitiously dominated her father, Marta's ego, associated with the upper half of her body, negated and controlled her sexuality.

An indication of the intensity of this conflict can be gauged from the following remarks: "I have the feeling I want to give up, but I am afraid it's all I would ever do—I would become a vegetable. I need an excuse like being sick to rest in bed, otherwise I feel guilty. I'm afraid that if I let myself withdraw, I'd become a catatonic. I have to fight that tendency." Giving up referred to her mother's values. She saw no alternative between her mother's aggressive ego drive and her father's sexual passivity.

Following these sessions Marta became depressed again. She said, "I feel in a state of collapse. Everything seems a great burden, but I have no excuse not to do my chores. I feel I am in a state of suspended animation—without thoughts. I can push myself but it's depressing." Marta was physically tired; her body needed to rest, to recuperate its energy, and to restore its strength. Most patients are unwilling, however, to accept this realistic bodily need. They expect that therapy will magically release an untapped reserve of energy. They do not realize that they have been pushing themselves along on their reserves for years and that depression ensued when these reserves were exhausted. Marta had to give in to her body if she wanted to get well.

In the next session Marta was able to get some vibrations into her legs through deep breathing. Then, when I again applied some pressure to her neck muscles, she began to cry and scream "Mama." The screaming ended in a feeling of frustration and hopelessness. "It doesn't do any good," she said. "Mama will never come. You can scream your head off, it doesn't make any difference. In fact it might be the other way around. She would stay away the more. She wasn't going to have a spoiled brat, though I was an only child. My mother used to say, 'You don't give a child something because they want it. They have to earn it.' No matter how hard I try, I never seem to get what I want." What she really wanted was love and acceptance and one cannot get them by trying.

Marta then began to say "I hate you." Saying this, she remarked, "I felt terror at first, but it changed within me to a feeling of fury." We can surmise that Marta was terrified of her mother and furious at her, too. The blocking off of these feelings was part of her predisposition to depression.

Some sessions later, Marta said, "All the wanting is bottled up inside me. I am unable to reach out and ask or take. My mother said I mustn't be selfish like a friend of mine who wanted and demanded things. I only got things if I deserved them.

"My mother's way of rejecting is to get calm and icy-cold, distant. I remember being frightened by it, wondering what would happen. Once when I was little and wanted to run away, my mother said, 'Good, I'll help you pack.' I went out and sat on the stoop, feeling lost, as if I couldn't come back. 'If you're going to be a stupid child, we don't want you,' my mother told me."

For two months Marta struggled with a sense of futility. She couldn't be an ideal figure any longer—in fact, she didn't really want that anymore—but neither could she assert her wishes. We worked steadily with her breathing, kicking, hitting and screaming. Despite the feeling of futility, the life forces in her body were being mobilized to free her from the deadlock.

"For two weeks," Marta said, "I've been feeling miserable. I've had an upset stomach, diarrhea, and nausea. Then my throat got sore and my chest congested. Two days ago I felt a surge of fury. I wanted to scratch, twist someone's neck, bite, and so on, but I couldn't give in to it. It had to go somewhere, so I got depressed. I feel swollen and achy in my body. I feel lethargic." The physical symptoms indicated that Marta's body was beginning to react, although her head was still detached.

In the sessions I had noticed that her breathing when she was over the stool was better. The respiratory wave was able to go down into her belly a little, causing a small involuntary vibration in her pelvis. This was the beginning of sexual feeling as distinguished from genital sensation. She also developed stronger vibrations in her legs. At one session she sat down on the floor and remarked, "What keeps going through my mind is: I don't want to."

She didn't want to make any effort. She was tired of trying. This is what her depression was saying in body language, but she didn't know it because she was out of touch with her body. She wanted to be held, to be helped, even to be taken care of, but she still couldn't bring herself to ask for it. And she couldn't get angry at her mother because she thought she still needed her mother's approval. Disapproval meant death.

The themes of death, terror and sexuality were contained in a recurrent dream. "I was about fourteen and asleep on a studio couch from where I could look down a long corridor. In the dream I heard a tapping coming down the corridor. It came closer and closer till I saw it was an old man with a long coat and a beard. I became very frightened. When he got to my doorway, I realized that there was no escape and that the only thing I could do was lie still as death, hoping I would not be seen. I was paralyzed by terror." She associated the figure of the old man with the long coat and beard with the orthodox Jews one sees at cemeteries who, for a fee, intone a prayer for the dead.

The sexual significance of the dream can be inferred from the fact that it occurred at fourteen years of age in a situation where she could have indulged any feeling or desire to masturbate. It is significant that her terror was so great she could not make a sound. While the fear is projected on a male figure, it stems from her mother, for she remarked, "My mother would let me die before she'd give in to my need." Her need was to get close to her father.

Always after the release of fear patients respond with good feelings. Shortly after Marta recalled this dream, she reported, "I've been feeling agitated, not depressed. My legs have been hurting to the point where I've been taking aspirin.

"One day I had a great feeling, such as I haven't had in years. I identified with a patient in a group who said, 'I want to be a two-month-old baby who doesn't have to give but is taken care of and loved.' When I told this to my husband, he assured me it would be all right and that he would love me. This time I believed him and it felt so good. I also had strong feelings of wanting to destroy things—smash a door, break some furniture. Hitting the bed with the racket didn't seem to help."

In the course of the next two months Marta made signifi cant progress. Her breathing was becoming deeper and easier. She became aware then that fear inhibited a full respiration. She said, "I sense now that I am stopped by fear, a fear so great I don't want to get into it. But I also feel restless, wanting to do something but unable to do it myself."

Marta had a severe constriction in her throat just below the angle of the jaw. It reminded me of a rubber band wound tightly around the neck of an inflated balloon. It was responsible for her inability to scream and for the difficulty she had in releasing crying. It also represented a strong inhibition of sucking actions. In past sessions pressure on the scalene muscles, which in their contracted state contributed to this constriction, led to crying and screaming. Under a steady pressure a contracted muscle will often let go. The tension becomes unbearable and the muscle relaxes. This time, as I applied pressure under the angle of the jaw, sucking movements and sounds emerged with her breathing.

Following this lead, I asked Marta to reach out with lips and arms. She was able to do this with some feeling, and I saw her body begin to come alive. "It was good," she said, "and I wanted to go further, but I relaxed and the feeling went away. Was I afraid," she asked "to go deeper into it? I sense that I am like a two-month-old baby who wants to be taken care of."

One week later the terror broke through again. She was able with my help to open her throat, and as she did so, she exploded into loud and frightful screams. Following this her breathing became deep and strong. "When I was screaming and feeling the terror, I could hear the sound of footsteps," she told me. "I associated them with the recurrent dream I related to you sometime ago." But this time she was able to react to the terror. Her legs, however, felt paralyzed, so I had her kick and scream again. The terror left her and she reported feeling tingling sensations going all through her body.

These sessions marked a definite turning point in Marta's

therapy. Her mood ameliorated rapidly and her depression lifted. The therapy continued for another six months on an average of once a week. Achieving the previous breakthroughs had taken about sixty sessions. During these six months we worked to increase her ability to reach out, to say "No," and to become angry. I spent more time on her relation to her father, which opened up a well of hidden sexual feeling. At each session she got over the stool to deepen her breathing, then bent forward to bring the charge down into her legs and feet. She was becoming more firmly grounded all the time.

One can get some idea of how inhibited Marta was about sexual feeling from the fact that throughout her marriage she had never allowed herself to be sexually excited by another man. If she found herself drawn sexually to another man, she withdrew from any social contact with him. Truly, Marta was a woman on a pedestal.

Before I conclude the account of her case, I would like to describe one of the exercises that had a dramatic effect on her mood. This exercise is a rocking of the pelvis. It is done in a standing position, with the knees in a bent position and the hands on the hips. The pelvis is rocked back and forth by a movement which begins in the feet and flows upward through the legs. When done correctly, the body arches slightly backward as the pelvis swings forward. It is important that the movement should come from the action of the feet and not involve a deliberate pushing of the pelvis or bending of the body.* Marta had done a number of other exercises designed to achieve the same sexual movement, but the feeling never came through. When she did the exercise described above, she was able to do it correctly and to feel her feet in the process.

* A fuller discussion of the natural sexual movements can be found in *Love and Orgasm* (New York, Macmillan, 1965).

The result was dramatic but not immediate. She left the session feeling in contact with her feet. But when I saw her the following week, she told me that after she got home, she felt very alert and bright but not elated. This beautiful feeling, the exact opposite of her depressed state, lasted all day. She tried the same exercise herself at home and got the same bright, alert feeling but for a shorter duration. Of course we repeated the exercise in my office, but the result was not the same. When she first did this exercise, she released a depth of sexual feeling she had not known before. She was, however, unprepared without further analysis to integrate this feeling into her daily life.

When the therapy ended, Marta was no longer a girl on a pedestal. Not that her problem had been completely resolved. These personality problems never are. The lower half of her body still showed a degree of rigidity and tension, which suggested a pedestal. But the overall change was such that one would not get this impression from her. Her shoulders had dropped considerably, her chest had come down, her belly and pelvis were fuller and more relaxed, and her legs were softer. There was a brightness about her that reflected her new enthusiasm for life. She knew, however, that she wasn't finished. We ended the therapy because she wanted to carry on for herself. She had done many of the exercises at home and was going to continue with them. She knew she had to stay grounded and that she could do this only if she kept in touch with her body, her legs, and her sexuality.

Marta's therapy ended several years ago. I saw her a number of times since to discuss some aspect of her life. She never fell back into a deep depression again, although there were times when she would become tired and want to give up. When that happened, she let herself cry, feeling again the sadness of the child who wanted to be taken care of but

DEPRESSION AND THE BODY

wasn't. She will never fully lose this sadness, which is part of her life, but she will know the deep pleasure of being fully alive in her body.

Love Versus Discipline

I presented Marta's case in some detail because it illustrates the problems that result when parents play the game of trying to rear an unspoiled child. Marta was unspoiled but also unripened; she had not matured emotionally and was naïve about the sexual aspects of life. Marta's mother believed she loved her daughter and was devoted to her, although she caused her much pain and suffering in her attempts to discipline and control the girl. Portnoy's mother also believed that she loved and was devoted to her son, but the consequences were equally disastrous. I don't doubt that these mothers loved their children in their hearts, and I am sure that the children knew this. Unfortunately, their actions do not express their love but their hostility. In pretending that their disciplining and controlling actions represent loving concern, they deceive themselves and their children.

Love cannot be separated from freedom and pleasure. No one truly loves another if he limits the loved person's freedom to be himself, to express himself, and to act for himself. By the same token, one shouldn't talk of love and cause pain. The two are irreconcilable. If we love someone, we want to see him happy and joyful, not miserable and suffering. Another important point is that loving actions are dictated by the heart, not the head.

It is difficult to see how love and discipline can be combined. I know this sounds like a radical idea. Discipline is so much a part of our way of life and thinking that we fail to see its dangers. Spare the rod and spoil the child is an old

182]

tradition in Western culture, one that also equates obedience and duty with love. Part of this tradition sees pleasure as sinful while work and productivity are the cardinal virtues. Another part of this tradition regards the body as an inferior aspect of man's nature. In *The Betrayal of the Body* I have shown that this tradition, when carried too far, ends in a schizoid condition.

My main argument against discipline at home stems from the relation it imposes on parents and children. A discipline without punishment would be meaningless, so it is really the question of punishment that concerns us. When a parent assumes the right to punish, he puts himself in the seat of judgment. He must judge his child's behavior to decide whether it merits punishment and how much. The very act of judging disrupts a relationship based on love. Love demands understanding, whereas judging requires omniscience. The judge is not on a par with the person judged. He occupies a superior position, the person judged an inferior one. The latter cannot help but feel resentful at this denial of his status as an equal in the family.

Is the child an equal to his parents? In wisdom, maturity, responsibility, obviously he is not. But in the sense that his feelings are as important as those of the adults, he is an equal. It is characteristic of a love relationship that the feelings of the loved person are as important to us as they are to him. If the feeling of equality is not present, the relationship becomes one of master and servant. Such relationships may contain strong feelings of love, but they are not love relationships.

Another relationship that has degenerated into a superior-inferior status situation is that between teacher and pupil. By definition, education means to lead or guide someone. A teacher should lead his pupils into the paths of learning and knowledge, not push them or drive them by threats and punishment. Since we have no real faith in our educational system, we must rely on a system of rewards and punishments to motivate students. This places the teacher in the position of having to judge a pupil's responses and subverts a relationship that should be one of friendship into one of power. We need not look far to find why students almost universally hate school.

We are beginning to learn that schools need not be run like modified penal institutions. Following the lead of England, we are exploring the possibility of the open classroom, where children are free to wander from one activity or table to another according to their interest. Since there is no rigid curriculum, there is no necessity for discipline. And since children who are free are eager to learn what they want to know, the whole system of rewards and punishments is unnecessary. Studies have clearly shown that the open classroom is a more effective teaching device than the rigid, controlled and disciplined classroom situation. But of equal importance is the fact that this new procedure reestablishes the natural relationship of teacher and student as equals and friends in the shared adventure of learning.

If the act of judging alienates the person being judged, it has a similar effect on the judge. A judge must set aside his empathic understanding, which would identify him with the person being judged, if he is to make a ruling. He must rely on formulated laws to make his decision. Theoretically he should not allow his personal feelings to affect that decision. We would like to think that a judge in a court of law could take such an objective attitude; such objectivity is not to be expected, however, from a parent. An objective parent is impersonal and detached, he is no longer a true parent. The child, as Marta observed, feels lost. On the other hand, if one's personal feelings enter into his judgments, the proceeding is a sham and a deception.

The big deception in the game parents play with children is the pretense that they can be loving and objective or involved and detached at the same time. This pretense permits them to deny their own feelings when it might be inconvenient to admit them. Thus they can accuse a child of being unruly when the child's actions are a response to the parents' hostility. Or they can be stubborn and unyielding to a child's crying because it annoys them and justify their behavior as discipline and firmness. They will deny a child pleasure out of envy (they were denied it as children) and pride themselves on not spoiling the child.

Parents deceive themselves in this game, for many actually believe that what they are doing is best for the child. They believe in discipline and punishment as the only way to rear a child, although they may have some doubts about their value. Yet to think that administering a painful punishment to the child will have a positive effect on his personality is a form of self-delusion. An effective punishment produces fear, which may make a child more submissive but never more loving. Parents were children once and they were subjected to this manipulation. Why have they forgotten? To answer this question we must see what happens to the child under this treatment.

Children have no choice about accepting or rejecting the deceptions parents employ. They are not independent agents. The love and approval of their parents is a matter of life or death to them. Most children will go through a period of rebellion, as Marta did, fighting for the understanding they so desperately need. Unfortunately, their struggle serves only to further alienate their parents. They are viewed as monsters or crazy or wild ones. They are forced to accede, which means that they will finally accept the idea that one must deserve love and one must earn pleasure. They will come to believe that they weren't loved because they didn't deserve it.

"If that is the way the game of life is played," the child thinks, *"I will abide by the rules and play the game."* Observation informs the child that the same game is played in other families. Children even adopt their parents' language as part of their own play. One can often hear one child say to another, "You are a bad girl. Mama doesn't love you." Or "You are naughty and have to be punished." Once the decision is made to play the game, the child must suppress his hostile and negative feelings. The suppression is never 100 percent effective, and even in the most obedient child there are occasional outbursts of resentment. These support the parent's view that every child has a nasty streak which must be curbed.

The child who has been forced to give up his birthright and play the game has been driven into a bad bargain. No matter what he does, he can't win. No matter how hard he tries, he can never get the love and approval he needs. We may remember that Marta's mother was not satisfied when her daughter received a mark of 99½. She demanded perfection. Parents who play the game demand the impossible. Their unconscious motivation is to transfer the guilt they have for not being a loving parent to the child. And the child will accept the guilt in order to feed the illusion that the parent's love is still obtainable.

Every depressed person is caught on the horns of a dilemma. Part of him says, "Fight, hang on, it's your only chance." The other says, "Give up, you don't have a chance." Yet how can he give up when the outcome seems to mean desertion and death? But if he doesn't give up, he expends his energy in a struggle that was lost before it began and the inevitable outcome of this direction is depression and death.

The opposite of discipline is not permissiveness. That word when applied to the bringing up of children is abhorrent to me. A permissive parent is a confused parent, one who has doubts about the use of discipline but has nothing to replace it with. He still holds himself out as the authority figure, since he is being permissive. If the stern disciplinarian can be viewed as a tyrant, the permissive parent is a benevolent despot. He may actually be a weak ruler whose permissiveness is a reflection of his incompetence. His child will know the true state of affairs and react accordingly. The confused or the weak parent will be tested and defied, for the child must know exactly where he stands.

Permissiveness denies the basic truth that a child is born with certain natural or God-given birthrights: the right to be loved for what and who he is, the right to seek his pleasure where he can find it, since pleasure is the spark that keeps the motor of life running, and the right to express his feelings. We all want the same rights for ourselves, but if we deny them to ourselves, we will deny them to our children. These rights are not within the province of a parent to give or withhold. Permitting a child to be himself and to express himself implies that one can withhold this permission. One can deprive a child of these rights, but it can be done only by using the power a parent has by virtue of a baby's helplessness or a young child's dependency.

Permissiveness is not the equivalent of love. A child brought up in a permissive home may be as love-deprived as the child in an authoritative, disciplining home. He can suffer the same insecurities and struggle with the same lack of understanding in his parents. He will, however, have much greater difficulty in playing the game, since its rules have become vague and confused. Despite the liberalism expressed by his parents, he is still expected to perform well at school, to behave properly, and to listen. He will not make as much of an effort to meet these objectives as the disciplined child and his failure will evoke his parents' disapproval, spoken or unspoken. It can be anticipated that he will take advantage of the permissive attitude in his home to join the movement of protest and rebellion. He may easily be drawn to drugs. This path, too, leads nowhere, and he will become depressed, not finding anywhere the faith he needs to live by.

The trouble with permissiveness is that it is not a positive but a negative attitude. The permissive parent and the permissive teacher have rejected the strictly disciplined approach both in their personal lives and in their relation to others, but they have not replaced it with an inner morality that would provide the security and order necessary for true freedom. They have adopted the philosophy of "anything goes," which in practice turns out to be "nothing works." The permissive parent is as confused about himself as he is about his relationship to his children. In his rebellion against the rigidity of Victorian moralism, with its acceptance of a double standard, he has abandoned all morality. Small wonder, then, that his world collapses about his ears.

Neither permissiveness nor a rigid discipline is the answer to our difficult times. Since the emphasis in modern psychology is on the individual, the responsibility for order and morality must also rest with each individual. A self-discipline must replace an outmoded authoritarian discipline. This is in line with self-awareness and self-expression, which necessarily include such concepts as self-possession and self-restraint. The parent who exercises self-discipline will encourage his child to develop the same function by allowing the child to take increasing responsibility for the satisfaction of his needs. The underlying concept is self-regulation, which starts in the earliest infancy with what is called demand feeding. The child who is self-regulating will gain faith in his own body and in his bodily functions. He will become a person who is inner-directed and capable of self-discipline.

Self-regulation differs from permissiveness in important respects. It does not represent an abandonment of parental responsibility, which is often true of permissive parents. Rather, the parent who believes in self-regulation has the responsibility of being "there" for the child whenever the child needs him or her. This is especially true where the mother breast-feeds the child. Such responsible behavior is fulfillment not permissiveness. Another difference is in the nature of the functions involved. Self-regulation is primarily concerned with body functions: The child is allowed to determine when and what he will eat within the limits of the food available, he determines when and how much he will be held within the limits of the mother's available time, he is not forced to develop sphincter control over his excretory functions until he is physically and psychologically ready, which in the average child occurs between two and a half and three years of age. Self-regulation accepts a child as he is, a new-animal organism; it allows him to be who he is, a unique individual; it does not approve of the "anything goes" philosophy.

Self-regulation does not mean that a parent should not lay down any rules or set any limits on a child's actions. Such a position would lead to chaos. A child looks to his parents for guidance and leadership. Rules and limits are needed if a child is to know where he stands. But the rules should not be rigid nor the limits inflexible, since they are designed to further the child's security and not to deny his freedom.

Above all the rules cannot be arbitrary; they must have a direct relationship to the way the parents live—that is, the parents should abide by the same basic rules they impose on their children. It should not be a matter of one rule for the parents, who have power, and another for their children, who lack it.

If parents have faith in their way of life and if their way is a life of faith, their rules and limits will reflect that faith. This statement raises the question: What is faith? which I shall discuss in the following chapter. Here I can simply say that every act based on faith is a manifestation of love and that every act of love is an expression of faith. Children are aware of these important values and respect them, since they are essential to their emotional growth.

A loving parent is neither permissive nor disciplining. He may be described as an understanding parent. He understands the child's need for unconditional love and acceptance. He also understands that it is not a question of words but of feelings expressed in action. A child needs physical intimacy with both parents. He needs body contact, especially during his infancy—he needs to be held, to be cuddled, and to be played with. This need should be fulfilled primarily by the mother, but the father's part in providing body contact, if secondary, is not negligible.

A loving mother is one who gives of herself, her time, her attention, her interest. Because of her love she doesn't begrudge the time spent with her child or resent the child's demands for her attention. When a patient says, "What's the use of reaching for Mama? She was never there," he means that she wasn't there for him. Her attention and her interest lay elsewhere. To know how much love a mother has for her child, one need only know how much time she spends with him and how much pleasure he gives her. The pleasure a mother has with her child is exactly equal to the pleasure the child has with his mother. This principle of reciprocity underlies all true love relationships. Love is based on pleasures shared. The pleasure of each person increases the pleasure of the other until the feeling between lovers is one of joy. This is how a mother-child relationship should be. It lacks this joyfulness when a mother manipulates a child for her own selfish or egotistic ends.

Loving parents want to see their child happy This is their main concern. They want their child to enjoy his life, and to the best of their ability they will try to provide him with the pleasures he seeks. This attitude and the feelings that accompany it give a child faith in life—first faith in his parents, then faith in himself, and finally faith in the world. Parents can do this for a child if they, themselves, have faith. But so few people do. Our culture mitigates it. We talk of love but we worship power. We even lack faith in the power of love itself.

7. Faith

The Importance of Faith

How important is faith? Can man live without it? Can he even survive without faith? These are questions that merit serious attention, since man's survival is not free from doubt and his life is not free from despair. But what is faith? Like all words it can be lightly used. It is so easy to say, "You must have faith." It is like saying, "You must love." Yet a moment's reflection will make us realize that neither the words nor the statements can add these essential qualities to a person's life.

On a number of occasions I have told patients they had no faith. It was an impulsive remark, generally made when the patient's response to the therapeutic effort seemed unreasonably negative. But having made the remark, I immediately distrusted it. What did I mean? Faith in me? Faith in my ability to help? Faith that the therapeutic work would succeed? That, I knew, I had no right to expect. Then, faith in what? I had no answer. Psychiatrists do not usually think in religious terms and I especially was very reluctant to do so. I would have avoided the word had it not spontaneously emerged in the course of my study of the nature of depression.

My ideas about depression grew out of my work with depressed patients. Their main interest, of course, is to overcome the problem that has brought their lives to a virtual standstill. In helping them regain a capacity for pleasure, which is severely diminished in the depressive state, the question of faith or its lack seemed irrelevant. I had to understand and the patient had to gain insight into the emotional conflicts blocking the flow of his feelings. He had to sense and release the chronic muscular tensions in his body that restricted his breathing and limited his motility. Generally, consistent therapeutic work along these lines which reached in and opened up the emotional wellsprings of life brought the patient out of his depressed condition. And in most cases, it also created a fairly stable bulwark against the common tendency to relapse. My recovered patients never spoke of having found a faith they could live by. In retrospect, however, it was rather clear that they had done so.

The more I thought about the problem of depression, the more convinced I became that the question of faith was important to its understanding. In the beginning I had no definite conception of what faith is. People seem to have so many different faiths; yet, regardless of the differences, the person with faith doesn't become depressed. As long as a person's faith is strong and active, it will keep him moving forward in life, which is what the depressed individual is unable to do. I was forced to the conclusion that the depressed patient is a person without faith. He doesn't think of himself in that way and I do not see him in that light. As a psychiatrist I see him as an ill person, one whose functioning as a human being is disturbed on both the psychological and physical levels. Nevertheless, it remains true that there is an intimate connection between his illness and the loss of faith.

The importance of this connection becomes evident when

we realize that we are currently witnessing an increasing incidence of depression on one hand and a corresponding disillusionment and loss of faith on the other. I don't believe it necessary to document the rising tide of depressive illness. Every psychiatrist, physician, and person in a counseling position knows how common it is. When we realize that anxiety and depression form part of a single syndrome and when we think of the drugs used so widely to counteract these states (tranquilizers, antidepressants, sedatives and sleeping pills), we can gain some idea of their ubiquity. The frenetic pursuit of fun and the continuous demand for stimulation by the mass of the people support this observation.

As to disillusionment and loss of faith one has only to speak to people to realize how widespread is our disenchantment with the world today. The most outspoken are the young people. In their writings, in their protests, and in their use of drugs they tell us how little faith they have in the future of this culture. But their elders share many similar misgivings. They see a constant deterioration of moral values, a progressive weakening of the religious and community ties that bound one man to the welfare of another, a decline in spirituality that accompanies an increasing emphasis on money or power, and they ask themselves: "What is this world coming to?" A consensus of opinion would show that most people feel that these are depressing times. And, indeed, they are.

They are depressing not because they are difficult but because our faith is progressively being undermined. People have lived through more difficult times without becoming depressed. The Pilgrims who landed on the bleak New England shores more than three centuries ago faced hardships far greater than ours, but they did not get depressed. If you say, "Their faith sustained them," that's my point.

The pioneers who crossed the country in covered wagons did not get depressed. The Jews who struggled and survived in the ghettos of Eastern Europe had a faith that sustained them through pogrom and persecution. The Greeks under the rule of the Turks were oppressed but not depressed. They, too, had not lost their faith in their future.

When a loss of faith occurs, people also seem to lose the desire and the impulse to reach out, to extend themselves, and to fight. They feel there is nothing to reach out to, nothing to fight for. And like my depressed patients, their ultimate attitude is, "What's the use?" This loss has been experienced by many primitive peoples whose culture was undermined by white civilization. As their faith in their way of life weakened, they seemed to give up, withdraw into themselves, and, not infrequently, to become addicted to alcohol. A feeling of excitement went out of their lives, the vital flame in their bodies dimmed. To survive, they had to find a new faith, which many did. In a sense it was fortunate, therefore, that the conquerors brought their missionaries with them. For those without faith were doomed.

I believe that it matters little what gods people worship, what beliefs they hold as long as their faith is deep. The sustaining power of a faith does not lie in its content but in the nature of faith itself. This becomes clear if we examine some simple examples.

A common game played by fathers and young children involves the issue of faith or trust. The young child is placed by the father on a high pedestal and told to jump into his outstretched arms. The child jumps and is caught, then squeals with delight and asks to play the game again. If the game is played long enough, it will lose some of its excitement for the child, who will then know that the father will be there to catch him. In the beginning, however, there is no sure knowledge and the child leaps on faith. There is an obvious moment of panic when he lets go of his security and feels himself falling. The fear of falling is one of humanity's deepest anxieties. But the panic is momentary, for the child soon finds himself safe and secure in his parent's arms. The release from panic is a feeling of joy. It is also a confirmation that one's faith is justified, which then strengthens the feeling of faith. Imagine the catastrophic consequences to the child if the father deliberately let him fall and get hurt!

A similar game is played in encounter groups, where it has the obvious purpose of teaching one person to trust others. Each participant is asked, in turn, to close his eyes and fall backward on the assurance that the person standing behind him will catch him as he falls. This of course happens and many people gain some reassurance from the experience. I doubt, however, that it has any real value in promoting one's faith. The participants know that they will be caught, since the rule of the game is that no one is to be allowed to fall. In this exercise knowledge precedes the event and thus robs the exercise of much of its value as a test of faith. What one learns to trust is not the sincerity of the other person but the rule of the game. Following rules is a fairly certain way to avoid getting hurt; it is not, however, the way to pleasure or faith in life.

Psychiatrists would find it easier to accept a word like "trust" to describe the relationship of one person to another in these games rather than "faith." Although the two words are often used interchangeably as synonyms, the word "faith" has a religious implication which does not attach to the concept of trust. For the average psychiatrist this religious implication seems to introduce a mystical factor which cannot be studied or controlled by objective means or explained by rational, scientific principles. Their reluctance to employ the term is therefore understandable. But this reluctance, which is so evident in Freud and other psychoanalytic writers, should not stop us from examining the role faith plays in human lives.

If we attempt to understand the human condition in terms of objective, scientific concepts, we leave out of our consideration a whole realm of human experience which, because of its subjective significance, profoundly affects human behavior. The relationship of one man to another, of man to his environment, and of man to the universe belongs to this realm. Religion developed out of man's need to comprehend these relationships, and we cannot afford to ignore them because they carry a religious connotation. We need not be afraid of this religious connotation, if we do not bind ourselves to accept the tenets of a specific religious belief. In trying to understand man's relationship to himself and his world we cannot dismiss the concept of faith.

Faith belongs to a different order of experience than knowledge. It is deeper than knowledge, since it often precedes it as a basis for action and will continue to affect behavior even when its content is denied by objective knowledge. Prayer is a good example. Many people have prayed for the quick ending of the war in Vietnam or for the safe return of a loved one or his recovery from illness. Now, most of those praying knew the prayer would be ineffectual in producing its desired objective. However this knowledge did not stop them, for their prayer was an expression of their faith. They sensed that its expression had a positive effect and that through it they were better able to go on. To pray it is not necessary to believe in an omnipotent deity. The power of prayer lies in the faith of the person uttering it. It is said that faith can accomplish wonders. We shall see that there are good reasons for this belief.

Prayer is not the only way to express faith. An act of love is an expression of faith, perhaps the most sincere that one can make. In the act of loving one opens his heart to another and to the world. Such an action, filling a person with inexpressible joy, also leaves him vulnerable to a deep hurt. It can be done, therefore, only if he has faith in the common humanity of man and in the common nature of all living things. The person who has no faith cannot love and the person who cannot love has no faith.

Actually when we examine the condition of living, it can be seen that faith is involved in almost all our daily actions. Take the case of a farmer who cultivates his land and sows his seed. He has no certain knowledge that it will produce a crop. Often an entire sowing is lost. He functions as much on faith as he does on knowledge, and this was even more true of primitive man, whose command of agriculture was extremely limited. It can be said his faith was based on experience, his personal experience, plus that of other farmers over the ages. Experience is an important factor; it can increase or diminish one's faith. I don't believe, however, that it explains the nature of faith unless one thinks of experience in terms that transcend individual existence.

When we contemplate the complexities of social living and the interdependence of people, we must come to the conclusion that social order would be impossible without faith. A mother has faith that the milk will be delivered to her door, a workingman has faith that the money he earns will buy the goods he needs, a patient has faith that a doctor will do his best for him. On occasion when this doesn't happen, we are deeply shocked. Human beings have lived in social communities for millennia, and out of this long racial experience they have gained faith in the cooperative effort. If this faith goes, we will be in for chaos. Despite these troubled times, most people have an inner faith that things will work out all right. I believe that it is this faith in the orderly process of life that sustains people in their daily activities.

Without some faith that one's effort will be rewarded, the motivation to extend oneself would be lacking. Necessity is not a sufficient incentive. My depressed patients are under the same necessity to function as everyone else, but it fails to move them. They have given up; in effect, they have lost their faith and have resigned themselves to die.

The intimate connection between loss of faith and death becomes clear in situations of crisis. In matters of life and death the strength of one's faith may be the deciding factor that enables one man to survive while another dies. One such extraordinary test of faith was the concentration camps of Nazi Germany. To those on the outside it seemed a miracle that anyone survived their horror. Yet many did and among them was Victor Frankel, an Austrian psychiatrist. His observation of the inmates led him to the conclusion that the only ones who survived were persons for whom life had some meaning. Those who lacked this belief gave up and died. They lacked the will to fight on in the face of torture, cruelty, betrayal, deprivation and degradation.

When I first read Frankel's book, I thought his explanation insufficient. It can easily be argued that the stronger ones survived while the weaker died. Were they stronger because they felt life held some meaning for them or did they find meaning *because* they were strong? I believe now that it is unnecessary to argue this point. Both positions are equally valid. Strong people have faith and people who have faith are strong. The pair cannot be split, for each is a reflection of the other. A person's faith is an expression of his inherent vitality as a living being just as his vitality is a measure of his faith in life. Both depend on the operation of biological processes within the organism. Antoine de Saint-Exupéry described a similar situation of crisis in his delightful book, *Wind, Sand and Stars.** His plane had crashed in the desert during a night flight in which he had been blown off course. He and his mechanic were lost and the crash destroyed almost all their food and water. They had between them half a pint of wine, a pint of coffee, some grapes and two oranges. For three days they explored the desert around the plane while hoping for rescue. On the fourth day, "scourged by thirst," they abandoned the plane and struck out, knowing that at most they could last nineteen hours in the desert without water.

They left without hope, and, in fact, they had no reason to hope for rescue. But during the next two days, despite the fact that they were burned out by the sun, they covered 124 miles on foot. What sustained them, Saint-Exupéry said, was the thought that their loved ones at home were suffering more pain than they felt. Much of the time they were too numb to feel anything, but some force from a source deeper than they could fathom made them go on as long as they could take a breath and make a step. I would describe this source as faith in life. As long as this faith persists, one doesn't give up. Reading Saint-Exupéry's story, I could sense that such a faith characterized the man. It pervades his writing.

Both for the individual and for society faith is the force that sustains life and keeps it moving onward and upward. It is therefore the force that relates man to the future. When one has faith, one can place some trust in the future, even though at the time it seems to hold no promise that one's aspirations, hopes or dreams will be realized. However, it is not the tie to a personal future that is essential to faith.

* Antoine de Saint-Exupéry, *Wind, Sand and Stars* (New York, Reynal and Hitchcock, 1939).

History is replete with examples of people who have sacrificed their individual futures to support their faith. Men have died rather than surrender their faith. This can indicate only that for them survival in a life without faith was not worthwhile.

Power Versus Faith

How can faith seem to have a value greater than life? This apparent contradiction can be resolved only if we accept the idea that an individual life is not the issue. A person may choose to sacrifice his life for the sake of other lives or for humanity. If we have faith, it is life in general that we hold precious. Because of this reverence for life we will strive to the utmost to save an individual life, including in that category an animal life. If we lose the sense that all life is precious, we surrender our humanity, with the inevitable result that our own lives become empty and devoid of meaning.

Yet in the name of faith (religious faith, national faith or political faith) people have made war on others, destroyed life, and violated nature. Such strange behavior requires an explanation which we must seek in the nature of faith itself. The fact is that faith has a dual aspect, one conscious and the other unconscious. The conscious aspect is conceptualized in a set of beliefs or dogma. The unconscious aspect is a sense of trust or faith in life which underlies the dogma, infusing the image with vitality and meaning. Unaware of this relationship, people regard the dogma as the source of their faith. They feel impelled to uphold it against any challenge to its validity.

All dogmas have a parochial character, that is, they develop out of a particular people's historical experience. They represent the attempt by man's inquiring mind to give meaning to his experience and in the process to structure the future experience of the people in accordance with that meaning. Since the historical development of all people in their evolution from the animal state to the human state of culture, regardless of its level, has followed a similar course —namely, the elaboration of language, the use of fire in cooking, the employment of tools and weapons, and so on— we find that their dogmas, their myths and their beliefs have much in common. They also have many points of difference reflecting the particular history of the group and its stage of cultural development. Unfortunately, each people identifies its faith with its particular dogma, often overemphasizing the differences. Those with another dogma are regarded as being without a true faith and looked upon therefore as less than human. Such an attitude seems to justify some people in being destructive to others.

But while differences in faith can be used as a justification and a rationalization for wars and conquests, I don't believe it is the real motivation. This must be sought in the struggle for power. Few people place all their reliance on faith as, for example, an animal does. Every wild animal lives in the faith that tomorrow will provide the necessities for its survival. It goes to sleep each night with no anxiety about its future. Of course an animal doesn't know that the future can bring disaster. It lives mainly in present time. Its consciousness does not embrace the past or the future except to a very limited extent. Its faith is not conscious either, it is an expression of its life force. We human beings, with our awareness of time, mortality, illness and insecurity, cannot fully depend on faith alone to ensure our survival. We must make provision for the future. Not for us are Jesus' words: "The lilies of the field work not, yet I provide for them." We demand the assurance of security, which we believe can be found in power. The more power we have, the more secure we seem to feel.

People who put their trust in power never seem to have enough to provide complete security. This is because there *is* no such thing as complete security. And our power over nature or our own bodies is strictly limited. Hitler sought to dominate the world through power and to create a Third Reich that would last a thousand years. His dream collapsed in ruins in twelve years. The trust in power to guarantee security is an illusion which undermines true faith in life and leads inevitably to destruction. Besides the fact that one can never have enough power, there is also the possibility of its loss. Unlike faith, power is an impersonal force and not a part of a person's being. It is liable to be appropriated by another person or another nation. Since people covet power, the man who possesses it is an object of envy. If anything, he cannot rest secure, since he knows that others are eternally scheming or manipulating to wrest his power from him. Thus power creates a strange contradiction: While it seems to provide a degree of external security, it also creates a state of insecurity both within the individual and in his relation to others.

As one examines the course of human history, the obvious development of a people or nation is from faith to power to decline. Take the case of the ancient Hebrews, for example. When they left Egypt they were a poor, powerless people who were rich in faith. This faith gave them a strength that sustained them through their wanderings and in their fights with the tribes they encountered in the desert. They wanted the power and glory of nationhood and their faith enabled them to obtain it. Their history after they settled in Palestine was one of conflict between the appeals to faith and the lust for power. As their power increased, their faith was slowly eroded. They quarreled among themselves and with their more or less powerful neighbors. These neighbors were equally power-hungry. It was inevitable, therefore, that sooner or later they would be overcome by a new rising power based on a young and stronger faith. The surprising ending of the Hebrew story is that when they became powerless again and were scattered over the earth, their faith gained renewed vigor and sustained them once again, in the face of all adversity, for the next two thousand years.

The story of the early Greeks is no different. The city-states grew out of the faith the Greeks had in themselves and in their destiny—a faith clearly reflected in their mythology and in the Homeric legends. As they grew, they gained power which enabled them to grow even more. But where faith unites, power divides. The struggle for power between the great cities of Athens and Sparta, which marked the more than forty-year Peloponnesian War, destroyed a faith that had previously bound Greek to Greek in mutual aid. Their fate was similar to that of other powers, to be overthrown by a younger people, younger in that they had a faith uncontaminated by the long exercise of power.

Arnold Toynbee has made a comprehensive study of the rise and fall of civilizations with proper regard for the complicated forces at work in these great adventures of the human spirit. As one reads Toynbee, one is continually impressed with his emphasis on the role of spiritual factors in the growth and decline of civilizations. In D. C. Somervell's abridgment one can find the following remarks: "They have lost faith in the traditions of their own civilization." And, speaking of our own civilization, he says: "The decline is not technical but spiritual." At the same time one senses

Toynbee's implicit recognition that power contributes to the loss of creative potential in a people. Such an interpretation is possible of the following quotation: "We have seen, in fact, that when, in the history of any society, a creative minority degenerates into a dominant minority which attempts to retain by force a position that it has ceased to merit, this change in the character of the ruling element provokes, on the other side, the secession of a proletariat which no longer admires and imitates its rulers and revolts against its servitude."

Toynbee is clearly aware that history cannot be divorced from the study of human beings, whose history one reviews. It is human nature that determines history and not the reverse. If it is true that an arrogant pride goes before an individual's fall, it is similarly true, as Toynbee points out, that self-idolatry in a people is one of the causes of their common spiritual collapse. In psychological terms this means that an inflated ego, either personal or national, precedes and may be held responsible for the breakdown of the social structure as well as of the individual personality. One can look at human beings from the point of view of their history as a people, or one can look at history from the point of view of individual psychology.

In my previous book I showed that the pursuit of power limits the experience of pleasure, which "provides the energy and the motivation for the creative process." Power expands the ego since it enhances the sense of control, which is a normal ego function. But in weaker individuals the sense of power may easily overinflate the ego, producing a dissociation of the ego from the spiritual values inherent in the body. These include the sense of unity with one's fellow man and with nature, the pleasure of spontaneous responsiveness, which is the basis of creative activity, and faith in oneself and in life. Since these values are inherent in the living process, they belong to the sphere of the body not to that of the ego. There is an antithesis between these values and those belonging to ego functions. The ego values are individuality, control, and knowledge. Through knowledge we gain more control and become more individual. But when these values become allied with power and dominate the personality, they become dissociated from the spiritual values of the body. This changes what was a healthy ego position into a pathological one.

The antithesis between ego values and body values need not become an antagonism that culminates in a split in the personality. By virtue of their polar relationship, the two sets of values can stimulate and enrich the personality. Thus the man who is truly an individual can be keenly aware of his brotherhood with other men and his dependence on nature and the universe. His control will reflect his self-possession. He possesses self-control, it does not possess him as it does the neurotically controlled individual. And his knowledge serves to strengthen his faith in life, not to undermine or deny it.

The true individual, in contact with his body and secure in his faith, can be trusted with power. It will not go to his head because it does not play a significant role in his personal life. He can take it or leave it. He will use it but not abuse it. On the other hand, the person who believes in power and relies on it will become a demagogue (or demigod) who can only act destructively, not creatively.

The world is in a dangerous and desperate state today because we have too much power and too little faith. Such a situation can have only two possible outcomes. Many people will get depressed because they feel powerless to fulfill their dreams. Others will become rebels and revolutionaries seeking through violence to gain more power and redress what they consider social injustices. Their violence is an antidote to their depressive tendencies. They would become depressed if they eschewed the violent way. Violence and depression are two reactions to the sense of powerlessness. A third is the turning to drugs and alcohol. The drug user also counteracts the feeling of being powerless through their narcotic or hallucinatory effect. None of these ways will work, though. Our only salvation lies in faith.

The Psychology of Faith

Man has been termed a history-making animal. This means he is conscious of his past and concerned about his future. He knows he is mortal (no other animal carries this burden), but he also knows his personal roots go deep into the heritage of his people. He is also tied to the future, which is his immortality, by the knowledge that through him this heritage will be transmitted onward. No man can live only for himself. He must feel that whatever he does, no matter how little it is, contributes in some measure to the future of his people.

All studies of primitive people show that they are extremely conscious of being links in the great chain of tribal life. The knowledge and skills of the tribe, which provide the tools for its survival, and its traditions and myths, which determine its place in the scheme of things, are solemnly passed from generation to generation. Each member is a living bridge that connects the past to the future. As long as both anchorages are secure, life flows easily through and over the bridge, endowing each individual with a faith that gives meaning to his existence. When a people's vital connections to the past and the future are severed, they lose faith, faith in themselves and in their destiny. We have seen that primitive people become depressed when their culture is disrupted.

Like any other depressed person, the primitive may then take to drink or he may lose his interest and desire to carry on.

Many aspects of our culture today suggest a parallel with this phenomenon. The traditions and customs by which Western man has lived for centuries are losing their influence. In almost every area of life changes are occurring which make the past seem irrelevant. No one can live his life today as his grandparents did. With the facility of motorcars and the ease of jet travel it is physically impossible. But the change has also affected human relations. There is a loosening of family bonds and a radically new sexual morality. Even the ways of earning a living are different; for example, there has been a large decrease in the number of people directly engaged in agriculture, there are more people working in service-type industries than in manufacturing, and new professions such as social work, psychological counseling and computer programming have developed. Thus the problems that arise for the new generation are different from those their forebears faced, and as a result the wisdom of the past painstakingly gathered through years of struggle seems or is inapplicable.

And what of the future? Obviously in a world where change is the order of the day, the future is more uncertain than it has ever been. Scientists even talk of the question of man's survival. René Dubos of the Rockefeller Institute believes we may not have much more than one hundred years before man's time runs out. This possibility is apart from the danger of nuclear warfare, which poses the threat that the earth may become uninhabitable even sooner.

The surprising thing in this situation is that more people are *not* depressed. One reason is that many people, especially older ones, have a strong personal faith derived from personal experiences with the mother and the family. Others are sustained by an optimism based on a belief in the power and technological capacity of modern society. It would seem logical to think that if we can send a man to the moon, we can do anything. Future events will determine whether or not such optimism is justified. I pointed out that a trust in power is not the equivalent of a faith in life. The danger in the present situation is that we are losing our faith.

The very process that has plunged our culture into turmoil and has corroded every past faith has also given modern man a new vision of himself. This is the idea of his own omnipotence. Until the twentieth century man had always felt himself subject to a higher power, be it one God or many. He never had the audacity or the means to challenge the superior authority of a divine Providence. That is changing or has changed for many people. Whether or not God is dead is not the issue; he is dead in modern thinking. Modern man no longer recognizes a supreme authority. He believes nature is governed by physical laws, that if he can decipher those laws, then he can control nature. It is an audacious vision, and science seems to continue to provide man with the means to achieve it. This vision is not limited to scientists in laboratories. The mass media feed it to the public with news of each advance in our quest for knowledge. And the thought has entered many minds that we may be on our way to eliminating old age and death.

Can it be said, then, that man has gained a new faith, faith in science or in the ability of the reasoning and inquiring mind to unravel all mysteries, to overcome all obstacles? The fact is that many people really believe in science and in this possibility. But belief is not faith; a belief is subject to some verification, faith has no need of verification. A belief is a product of the conscious mind, true faith is an affair of the heart. One can argue about a man's beliefs, one cannot argue with faith. Beliefs may constitute the content of faith, they are not its essence. One can have faith against all belief and this faith will sustain a person in his times of crisis.

Another aspect of our changing culture is the increasing individualization and isolation of the average man. Individualization and isolation are not the same thing, but they have moved along parallel paths. In proportion, as man has become more conscious of himself as a unique being, he has cut the ties that bound him to his community. He has been able to do this by having more power at his command; power to move about more freely, to communicate over greater distances, to command services or to buy necessities, and so forth. He still remains as dependent on his community as primitive man was, but he doesn't feel his dependence. He doesn't think of himself as being part of a larger order upon which his survival depends. He knows the community is there, but he sees it only as a matrix for his personal self-realization. We are taught not to destroy the goose that lays the golden eggs, but we are told that the eggs themselves are up for the grabbing. In a society that promotes the philosophy of each man for himself, the sense of community does not exist as a potent force.

If each man is a world unto himself, then he has the right to believe that within this personal world he is god. No one can tell him what to think or believe. But such personal worlds have very little contact with one another. They communicate formalities and trivia but no real feelings. Like chickens being incubated in a hatchery, each person lives within his own shell, subject to common dangers and sharing similar concerns but unrelated to each other. There is no greater isolation than that produced by a mass society with its reliance on technology.

The conditions of modern living create a mass culture, a mass society and the mass individual.* People in a mass society are like beans in a sack; they count only as a quantity. And although each person in a mass society is different from every other person (as is each bean in a sack), he is not a true individual because he has no voice in his destiny and can take no responsibility for his fate. From the moment of birth in a mass hospital, one's life is processed by a system structured in the facilities of mass education, mass communication, mass travel, and so on. The mechanics of this system do not allow for the exercise of personal taste or judgment. Even the choice of the mass-produced goods we buy is conditioned by massive advertising.

Individuality is a function of self-expression; that is, it depends on the ability to respond to the challenges of life freely and fully. Among human beings self-expression doesn't operate in a vacuum. Each act of self-expression aims at creating an impression and evoking a response. But true responsiveness and personal responsibility have no place in mass society. A newborn infant crying in a hospital nursery gets no response from his mother isolated in another room. A student struggling with a curriculum that is personally meaningless gets little response from the educational systems. Systems lack the ability to respond to human needs, and it is this lack of responsiveness that forces people to engage in mass protests. Every mass rally or demonstration, regardless of its stated objective, is really a protest against the conditions of mass living. It is the only form of expression open to a mass individual in a mass society.

True individuality can exist only in a community where each member is responsible for the group's welfare and where

* I have contrasted the mass individual with the true individua' in my previous book, *Pleasure: A Creative Approach 'o Life,* pp. 89 ff.

the group is responsive to the needs of each member. In a community a man's individuality is determined by his personal value to the group. In a mass society it is determined by the power of his position. Thus true individuality is a measure of one's participation and not a reflection of one's isolation. In a mass society only the system is important, since any one person can be replaced by another. And the mass individual, whether he is at the bottom or top of the heap, is important only to himself. This system forces people to become egotists, whose main effort is directed toward gaining recognition.

I have said that through faith the past is linked to the future. Through faith the individual is linked to the community. Communities have been formed by people with a common faith and they disintegrated when it was lost. Can you imagine a group of egotists trying to establish a community, with each person interested solely in his own importance and his own image? No community was ever founded on the principle that its only function was the promotion of the individual's well-being. The force that binds people to each other cannot be a selfish interest. To be effective it must be a force that transcends the self or at least that narrow aspect of the self that is called the ego.

The appeal of every religion is the feeling of community it engenders. A religious person feels himself part of a community of man, to belong to the community of nature, and to participate in the community of God or the universe. And every person who feels this way is a religious person, whether or not he is a member of a religious group. The strength of every religion lies in the degree to which it fosters a sense of responsiveness and responsibility in its adherents. All religions have emphasized this personal factor in man's relationship to other men, to nature and to God. The effect is that the spirit of community is furthered at the same time as the sense of individuality is enhanced. By the same token, every individual who has a sense of his personal responsiveness and responsibility can be said to be religious.

Religious institutions lose their effectiveness when they fail to meet man's needs to belong and to express himself. In this situation new systems of thinking will develop that aim to satisfy these needs. They may not be called religions, but they will have a religious flavor for those who find a feeling of community and a sense of responsiveness and responsibility in them. For many people the group experience in therapy, especially bioenergetic analysis, which promotes the spiritual values of the body, satisfies these needs. At a recent professional workshop in bioenergetic analysis one participant said he thought therapy was the religion of the future. What he meant was that therapy and religion have in common the aim to give a person the sense of belonging, identity, the ability to express himself, and a faith in life.

Egotism and faith are diametrically opposed. An egotist is concerned only with his image; a man of faith is concerned with life. An egotist is oriented toward the pursuit of power, for the more power he has, the larger the image he can project. A man of faith is oriented toward the enjoyment of life, and the pleasure he gets from living is shared with those about him. Egotism is a belief in the magic of the image, especially the word. To an egotist the image is everything, his only reality. He believes fully in the power of the conscious mind and he identifies his own being with its processes. True faith is a commitment to the life of the spirit—the spirit that resides in the body of a person, manifesting itself in feeling and expressing itself in the movements of his body.

Few people can be characterized as being total egotists, but in our society more people can be found on the side of the ego than on that of faith. Our culture, our education, and our social institutions favor the ego position. The pitch behind most advertising is an appeal to the ego. Education promotes the ego position by its great (and I believe) exaggerated emphasis on abstract thinking. Abstract thought tends to dissociate the individual from his environment, both human and natural. It has, of course, given man the immense power he possesses, but it has done so at the cost of his faith.

The dangers we face in this insidious reduction of our faith are twofold: For the individual it poses the threat of depression; for society it leads to the disintegration of those spiritual and communal forces that imbue social institutions with meaning and relevance for human lives. Both are real dangers in our present time, and the likelihood is that the situation will grow worse.

We cannot legislate faith, we cannot manufacture it, and we cannot teach it. Fiats and laws backed by the police power of a state can force submission to dogmas, but every act of submission feeds the inner fires of rebellion, which will inevitably erupt in a cataclysm. That we cannot manufacture faith needs little comment, since no one expects it from a machine. My statement that it cannot be taught may be shocking. We seem to believe strongly in the power of education. But education was not designed to reach a person's heart. It aims to instruct the mind, and so it may alter one's beliefs without in any way affecting one's faith.

Despite the difference between belief and faith, the two can be and often are related. Although beliefs are a product of one's thinking and faith is a feeling closely akin to love, head and heart need not be disconnected. What one thinks can directly reflect what one feels, but it is not necessarily so. We can be objective in our thinking by deliberately dissociating it from what we feel. Similarly, our beliefs can express our faith, but they need not do so. A man who proclaims his belief in God may have little faith, witnessed, for example, by the fact that he becomes depressed. On the other hand, an atheist may be a man of tremendous faith. He may not believe in a superhuman God of destiny, but his faith will be related to his identity with and love for his fellow man and life. People of faith can have different beliefs and people with similar beliefs may vary greatly in their faith. All too often beliefs are inculcated by a process of education which mistakenly assumes that it is teaching faith. When, however, a belief arises from one's personal experience uninfluenced by any dogma, it does have an impact on one's faith. The effect of the experience on faith may be positive or negative. It will be positive if it opens one's heart and negative if it closes it.

The Growth of Faith

Faith arises and grows out of one's positive personal experiences. Every time one is loved, it increases one's faith, provided that one responds to the love. This is what I learned from my depressed patients whose personal history showed a lack of love, especially in childhood. Many believed they were loved, but such beliefs were often indoctrinated into the child and did not correspond to his feeling. A belief based on feeling has the quality of true faith.

I have described faith earlier as a bridge linking the past and the future. For each individual the past represents his forebears, the future his children and their children. It is the bridge across which life flows from ancestor to descendant in an orderly fashion. This analogy reminds me of the runners in a strawberry plant. When a strawberry plant is mature, it sends out strands which at points along the ground root into the earth to start new ones. Actually, new leaves develop before the rooting is secure. The daughter plant is nourished by the mother plant through the runner until the young plant is firmly established. After this happens, the runner withers away like an umbilical cord after a child starts his own independent respiration.

Faith begins in the process of conception. A spark from the father lights up the fire of life in an egg, which is subsequently nourished by the mother's blood. If we think metaphorically, we can say that the flame of life is passed from one generation to the other with the hope (consciously in humans) that it will be everlasting and will grow brighter with each successive passage. When the flame burns brightly in an organism, it radiates a feeling of joy.

But life is not an ordinary fire, which must be fed from without to sustain its flame. It is a self-sustaining fire, once it has become fully established—a fire conscious of its existence, proud of the light it casts, and, most mysteriously, desirous and able to seek its own renewal. Faith is the aspect of this vital flame that keeps a man's spirit warm and alive against the cold winds of adversity that threaten his existence. Love is another aspect of this same flame. Its warmth draws us close to people, whereas a cold person or a person with a cold heart is a misanthrope.

All warm-blooded animals need the care and protection of their parents so that the tentative fire of young life may burn strong and hot in their young bodies. This is not just a metaphor. An infant needs the warmth and closeness of his mother's body to excite and deepen his respiratory movements. In babies who lack this contact, breathing tends to become shallow and irregular. Good breathing provides a strong draft for the fire and ensures an adequate supply of oxygen for the metabolic processes of combustion.

Biologically the faith of a child is kindled and nourished by the love and devotion of his parents. This loving devotion confirms the child's feeling that the world is a place for men to live in with joy and satisfaction. As the child's developing consciousness expands, he returns his parents' devotion with his own devotion to the ways of life and to the values they represent. Then, in his proper time, the child as a grown adult will pass this devotion on to his own children, instilling in them a reverence for the past and a hope for the future.

The reciprocity of love demands a reverence for the past to balance the concern for the future. We cannot look only ahead but must also look back from whence we came. Every organism starts its individual existence by retracing the evolutionary steps that brought its species into being. That is the meaning of the phrase "ontogeny recapitulates philogeny." Thus the devotion of parents to children is naturally matched by filial respect. The interest of a community in the welfare of its young is normally returned by the respect of the young for their elders. This is the basic law of tribal life without which true community living becomes impossible. In such communities it is the role of the wise elders to act as guides. Esther Warner writes, "One of the most desirable aspects of tribal life is that older people are not neglected. They are the revered, the sought-after persons in each town." * In their respect for the elders the young people of a tribe honor the source of their being and thereby affirm their faith and confirm their identity.

I am sure that at this point many parents will question my hypothesis. Are we not witnessing a situation where children are consciously rejecting their parents' values despite the love and devotion given them? I would say rather that the

* Esther Warner, *The Crossing Fee* (Boston, Houghton Mifflin Co., 1968), p. 215.

present situation has arisen because parents have *failed* to transmit a sustaining faith to their children. I have known parents who were more devoted to their way of life than to their children. But the basic reason for this failure is that the parents themselves lacked faith. Without faith, their love was an image not a reality, a statement of words not an expression of feeling.

Faith is a quality of being: of being in touch with oneself, with life, and with the universe. It is a sense of belonging to one's community, to one's country, and to the earth. Above all it is the feeling of being grounded in one's body, in one's humanity, and in one's animal nature. It can be all these things because it is a manifestation of life, an expression of the living force that unites all beings. It is a biological phenomenon and not a psychic creation.

In his new book, *Touching*, Ashley Montagu develops the thesis that skin contact of a pleasurable kind between mother and child is essential to the development of the child's personality. Body contact reaffirms the mother's tangible presence. It provides the security on which the child can build stable object-relationships. The mother's tangibility, which the child experiences as he touches her with hands, mouth and body, is the "absolute reassurance." And Montagu remarks, "Even faith rests ultimately upon a belief in the *substance* of things to come or of past events experienced." * The touchstone of faith is touch itself.

Superimposed on this biological basis are the psychological concomitants of faith, the specific beliefs that are the heritage of people who have tried to comprehend their human destiny. These are like the clothes we wear. They may distinguish one group of people from another, but they are not

* Ashley Montagu, *Touching: The Human Significance of the Skin* (New York, Columbia University Press, 1971), p. 106.

the essence of the people. We can easily lose sight of the essence and think that people of different colors and with different beliefs and ways lack dignity, grace and faith. We do this when we have lost sight of the basis for our own faith, believing mistakenly that our faith comes from what we are taught and is identical with our beliefs. We fail to recognize, too, that our beliefs can become instruments in our struggle for power both personal and political. Beliefs can be easily manipulated to serve the ego's desires.

When a belief is not rooted in a true faith, it cannot be a genuine belief. It is not a lie, the person may actually hold the belief. In that case it becomes an illusion. In earlier chapters I gave some illustrations of the illusions my depressed patients have clung to with all the power of their minds. However their hearts weren't in these beliefs, and despite all the hot air (words) blown into the bubbles to keep them aloft, the bubbles burst. The illusions collapsed, as all illusions will, and my patients became depressed.

One can't take away a person's illusions by offering him another belief. This in turn will become an illusion unless it is imbued with faith. To take a mundane example, consider the reactions to all the diets that are constantly proposed. Each new diet evokes a wave of enthusiasm and belief that lasts until the next one arrives on the scene. Then it fades out and the crowd surges to hop onto the new bandwagon. While the enthusiasm lasts, the diet seems to work wonders. It is strange that people do not perceive that the true miracle-working ingredient is enthusiasm. Unfortunately such enthusiasms are short-lived like the last flickers of a dying fire. A consistent and enduring enthusiasm takes on the character of faith. And faith can work wonders because life does.

The central issue, then, is how to restore an individual's or a people's lost faith. This is not easily done and I have no facile answers to this question. One cannot preach faith. This is like preaching love, which sounds great but is really only a rustle in the wind. One cannot give another person faith; one can share one's faith with another in the hope that the spark will ignite the embers in the other's soul. And one can as a psychiatrist help another person recover his faith by finding out how he lost it. This, of course, is what I have done with my depressed patients. In sharing my experiences with you, I hope also to share with you my faith in life.

8. The Loss of Faith

The Erosion of Our Roots

We have so far been following two parallel lines of investigation. The first related the problem of personal depression to the loss of loving contact with the mother and the resulting inability of the person to reach out to the world for the satisfaction of his needs. The second dealt with the importance of faith as a cohesive and life-promoting force in society and showed that in the absence of faith a society stagnates. It is necessary now to bring these two lines of thought together and to show that both phenomena, the personal and the social, reflect the operation of the same forces. These may be described as technology, power, egotism, and objectivity. Their effect has been to alienate man from his fellow man, from nature and from his body—an alienation that begins early in life in the relationship of mother to child. Let us return to the problem of depression.

Depression is not a new phenomenon in human history. Freud, as we noted, studied the problem of melancholia, a severe form of depression, before the turn of the century. And we can be certain that some individuals suffered from depression in past ages. The conditions which predispose an individual to it are not unique to our time. Children have suffered a loss of mother love before, although it was much less common. The main reason is that almost all children were breast-fed in those days, and if a baby lost his mother, his chances for survival were slim unless a wet nurse was found or a new mother could be brought in who would rear the child as her own. In addition, there was also more body contact between mother and child. Babies were regularly carried by their mothers or, if she was occupied, by an older sibling. The rocking chair and the cradle required a more active commitment than the crib or the playpen.

Montagu makes the same point in *Touching:* "The impersonal child-rearing practices which have long been the mode in the United States, with the early severance of the mother-child tie, and the separation of mothers and children by the interposition of bottles, blankets, clothes, carriages, cribs, and other physical objects, will produce individuals who are able to lead lonely, isolated lives in the crowded urban world with its materialistic values and its addiction to things." * Unfortunately, these practices are becoming established procedures in other countries as they seek to emulate the American way of life.

We must face the fact that there has been a radical change in child-rearing practices in the course of the twentieth century. The most important aspect of this change is the decline in the frequency and duration of breast feeding. As a direct result, the amount of skin contact between mother and infant, which serves the important function of stimulating the child's energy system, has been reduced. Other values are also lost. Breast feeding deepens the child's respiration and increases his metabolism. In addition, it fulfills the child's oral erotic needs by providing a deeply sensuous pleasure extending from the lips and mouth to the whole body. A mother who

* Montagu, *op. cit.*, p. 287.

breast-feeds has to be there for her child; it is not a function that can be relegated to baby-sitters or others. Thus by this single act a mother affirms both the child's developing faith in his world, which at this stage of life is the mother, and in his own natural functions.

Here is what Erik H. Erikson says about breast feeding: "The mouth and the nipple seem to be mere centers of a general aura of warmth and mutuality which are enjoyed and responded to with relaxation not only by these focal organs, but by both total organisms. The mutuality of relaxation thus developed is of prime importance for the first experience of friendly otherness." * Erikson recognizes as I do that breast feeding may not always provide the full pleasure and satisfaction it promises. "The mother may try to force matters by urging the nipple into the baby's mouth, by nervously changing hours and formulas, or by being unable to relax during the initially painful procedure of suckling." † But the value of breast feeding leads him to conclude that "if we expend a fraction of our curative energy on preventive action"— namely, promoting breast feeding—we can avoid much of the misery and many of the problems that stem from emotional disorders.

The basic issue in the mother-child relationship is not breast feeding but faith and trust, although the three are closely related. Through this relationship the child either gains a basic sense of trust in his world or he must struggle with doubts, anxieties and guilts about his right to get what he wants or needs. Implied in the term "to get" is the right to receive and the right to reach out and take. When a person is unsure that he has this right, his reach-

* Erik H. Erikson, *Childhood and Society* (New York, W. W. Norton, 1950), p. 71.
† *Ibid.*, p. 72.

ing out to the world is hesitant, hedged with caution, and never a total commitment. Ambivalence pervades his actions; he reaches out and holds back at the same time. Such behavior poses a problem for others, for one cannot fully respond to an ambivalent attitude. Unfortunately the individual is aware neither of his ambivalence nor of his distrust. His holding back has become structured in chronic muscular tensions that have long since become unconscious patterns of movement. His conscious mind senses the impulse to reach out. What he doesn't sense is his restraining this impulse on the body level.

When a child loses faith in his mother through the experience that she is not always there for him, he begins to lose faith in himself. He starts to distrust his feelings, his impulses and his body. Sensing that something is amiss, he can no longer trust his natural functions to provide that rapport and harmony with his world that will ensure the continued fulfillment of his needs and desires. But this is what our Western civilization seems to demand as it imposes a fairly rigorous artificial regulation of bodily functions on the young child. Again I will quote Erikson: "The dominant classes in Western civilization . . . have been guided by the conviction that a systematic regulation of functions and impulses in earliest childhood is the surest safeguard for later effective functioning in society. They implant the never-silent metronome of routine into the impressionable baby and young child to regulate his first experiences with his body and with his immediate physical surroundings. Only after such mechanical socialization is he encouraged to proceed to develop into a rugged individualist. He pursues ambitions, strivings, but compulsively remains within standardized careers which, as the economy becomes more and more complicated, tend to replace more general responsibilities. The specialization thus developed has led Western civilization to the mastery of machinery, but also to an undercurrent of boundless discontent and of individual disorientation." *

The Western attitude toward bodily functions grows out of and parallels Western man's attitude toward life in general and toward his environment in particular. This can best be described as one of dominance and control as opposed to an attitude of reverence and respect that is typical of more primitive people. And, unfortunately, we have been able to achieve dominance and control because we have power, an amount inconceivable to primitive people or even to our forefathers two hundred years ago. I say unfortunately because the effects on the individual have been less than desirable, while the effect on our environment, as we are beginning to discover, has been disastrous.

Power has blinded us to the realities of our existence. We see the world as subject to our will and our conscious effort, completely ignoring the fact that we are dependent on this earth for our well-being and our very existence. And we have adopted the same attitude to our bodies. We regard the body as subject to the will and the mind, again ignoring the reality that our will and our minds are completely dependent on the healthy and natural functioning of the body for their operation. When these illusions collapse, as they do in depressed persons, the impotence of the will and the dependence on the body becomes a shocking reality.

Power derives from knowledge, which is always an incomplete understanding of the natural order. It is incomplete because we are always gaining new knowledge that necessarily changes or may even contradict our previous ideas. Nowhere is this truism more evident than in theories of child rearing. Do you recall the time, a generation ago, when be-

* *Ibid.*, p. 139.

haviorism was in vogue and pediatricians advised mothers not to pick up their crying babies lest they spoil them? Now permissiveness seems to be the fashion, but this concept, too, is under attack. I believe that we can anticipate a new formulation with each generation designed to meet the problems of the preceding generation but inadequate to the unforeseen problems that it will inevitably produce. Do you remember when tonsilectomies were routinely prescribed just as circumcision now is for young boys? One shudders to think of the traumas that an incomplete knowledge can so easily produce especially when propounded by authorities.

On more than one occasion I have been asked to write a book on how to rear a child. How flattering to think that I know! But how arrogant it would be for me to believe it. Working with my patients, I can tell what went wrong in their own lives. Hindsight may be achieved by an inquiring mind, but foresight is not within the province of man unless he attempts to regulate and control the natural flow of life's forces. By this very process he risks exerting a destructive influence on them. On the other hand, we are by our very nature in tune with these forces. If we cannot predict their operation, we can at least understand them and, with faith, go along with them.

No one can understand a child as well as his own mother. Prior to his birth he was part of her body, nourished by her blood and subject to the streamings and charges that flowed through her body. She can understand him as well as she understands her own body. Not know him but understand him. She can sense his feelings almost as acutely as she can her own. A real problem arises, therefore, when a mother is out of touch with her own body and her feelings. This becomes a tragic situation for the child. If a woman is not "there" for herself, she cannot be "there" for her child—and no amount of knowledge or information can remedy this lack. I can say this in different words. If a mother has no faith in her own feelings, she will have no faith in her child's responses. Or, not having faith in herself, she has no faith to transmit to her child.

Where did the break in the transmission of faith occur? From time immemorial women have reared children and the human race grew and prospered. We are still growing but not prospering. In the past the link between mother and child was immediate, body to body. Giving birth and nursing were holy activities in the sense that they commanded universal awe and respect. In discharging these functions a woman fulfilled her need to be responsive and responsible to another. Her ego was only minimally involved in these activities; her body sensed what had to be done and she did it. Her love for her child poured out in her milk. A woman was bound to her nature but also realized within it. How true this is was shown in a study made by Dr. Niles Newton,* associate professor of psychiatry at Northwestern University Medical School. "Women who breast feed may also tend to be responsive in other sexual areas. Sears and his colleagues found that mothers who had breast-fed were significantly more tolerant of sexual matters such as masturbation and social sex play. Masters and Johnson note that for the first three months after delivery, the highest level of sexual interest was reported by the nursing mothers." According to Dr. Newton, a "mother-child relationship without enjoyable lactation is in a similar psycho-physiological position as a marriage without

* Niles Newton, "Interrelationship Between Various Aspects of the Female Reproductive Role: A Review." Talk given at the American Psychopathological Association, February 5, 1971.

enjoyable coitus." This means that a woman cannot be fully "there" for herself unless she is also fully "there" for her child.

The main harmful effects of technology, power, egotism and objectivity lie in their disturbance of the normal mother-child relationship. As these forces enter the social scene, women are seduced away from nursing. Formerly only women in high social and economic positions could make this move, since only they could command the services of a wet nurse. Today, with pediatric formulas, bottles, and sterilizing equipment, most women seek to free themselves from what they regard as subservience to the child. But we should not underestimate the role of egotism in this change. In Japan, where despite the fact that pasteurized milk is not readily available, women are refusing to breast-feed their children because they regard it as a sign of social inferiority. Their ideal is the liberated American woman.

The woman who doesn't breast-feed must rely on her pediatrician's knowledge in finding the proper formula. By this very act she has surrendered her faith in herself. Having transferred the responsibility to the doctor, she must depend on his knowledge and not her innate responsiveness to rear her child. This places a barrier between mother and child, for it inhibits her spontaneous reaction by forcing her to consider whether her actions are approved and right. Following her doctor's advice may give her the illusion that she knows what to do, but that is no substitute for a loving response that is an expression of faith and understanding.

I have long been impressed with the observation that most mothers really "know" their children. Talking with mothers, I have been astonished at how well each knew her child's weaknesses, his failures, and his problems. Perhaps this shouldn't be surprising in view of the long and intimate association between them. But while they knew their children's difficulties, they rarely understood them. Many a mother could not fathom why her child should feel and act the way he did. It may have occurred to her that in some way she had conditioned his attitude and behavior, but not understanding herself, she had no insight into her child. It may even be said that she knew her child's problems because she had unwittingly created them.

I draw a sharp distinction between knowing and understanding, which I explained earlier. Let me say simply, therefore, that no one fully knows a child or how to rear a child. One can understand a child. One can understand his desire to be accepted for what he is, loved for his very being, and respected for his individuality. We can understand this because we all have the same desire. We can understand his need to be free, we all want to be free. We can understand his insistence on self-regulation. Every one of us resents being told what to do, what to eat, when to go to the bathroom, what to wear, and so on. We can understand a child when we understand that we, too, are children at heart, on the outside a little older, perhaps a little wiser, but on the inside no different in any significant way.

Does this mean that books about child development are unnecessary and perhaps dangerous? They are dangerous if they are used as rule books. There are no rules for the rearing of healthy children. When we follow a rule, we ignore the child's individuality and the uniqueness of his life situation. On the other hand, a good book on child development may serve as a guide to a confused parent. It should not, of course, tell him what to do, but it can, by explaining the range of normal behavior, alleviate much anxiety. Above all, it should emphasize that the pleasure a parent has with a child gives the child the feeling that his existence is meaningful to the people in his world. It is also true that the pleasure a child has with his parent can do the same for the parent.

It can be argued of course that every culture places some controls on human behavior and institutes them in childhood. Children have to be taught the ways of a culture if they are to adapt to it. But, and Erikson makes this point too, this cannot be done at the expense of body aliveness and feeling. Writing of the Sioux, he says, "Only when strong in body and sure of self is he asked to bow to a tradition of unrelenting shaming by public opinion which focuses on his actual social behavior rather than on his bodily functions or his fantasies." * He is not asked to turn against his body, his feelings or his impulses. These are the sources of his strength, the basis of his identity, and the roots of his faith. The Sioux assume society has a need to impose some restraint on individual actions but this is to be conscious and its voluntary exercise is an expression of a man's pride in belonging to his tribe. Among the Sioux, training in such restraint doesn't begin before the fifth year and is not associated with punishment.

There is an antithesis between knowledge or information and understanding, just as there is between power and pleasure, between the ego and the body, and between culture and nature. These antithetical relationships do not necessarily produce a conflict. It need not follow that because one has knowledge, one must lack understanding. It is not necessarily true that power destroys pleasure or that the ego must deny the body its proper role. Not every culture has been at odds with nature as ours is. When these opposing forces are harmoniously balanced, they form a polarity rather than an antagonism. In a polar relationship each opposite force supports and enhances the other. An ego rooted in the body

* Erikson, *op. cit.,* p. 138.

gains strength from the body and in turn supports and furthers the body's interests. The most evident polarity in our lives is consciousness and unconsciousness or wakefulness and sleep. We are well aware that a good night's sleep promotes one's daytime functioning and that a satisfactory day's work (pleasurable, of course) facilitates sleep and the pleasure of sleeping.

But these polarities break down when the relationship becomes too heavily weighted on one side or the other. If we become excessively tired during the day or too consciously preoccupied with our problems, sleep sometimes becomes difficult. An overemphasis on the artifacts of culture, such as every person having his own automobile, can have a deleterious effect on nature. The price of our highly technical civilization is the erosion of our natural resources and the destruction of our natural environment. Similarly, too much power reduces our capacity for pleasure. We become power-oriented and lose sight of the simple delight in using our bodies. Too strong an involvement with one's ego always results in a denial of the body and its values. I have emphasized these dangers in previous books. However I have not previously expressed my concern over what is happening.

I feel that the balance has shifted strongly against the natural life forces: understanding, pleasure, body, nature, and the unconscious. We are committed to more information without any safeguards that would protect our understanding. Doing research that is merely a gathering of information together with its statistical juggling has become the supreme goal of our higher educational programs. Fortunately most of the PhD theses that are written are never looked at. Yet the insidious effect of this focus on data is a progressive loss of faith in the natural capacity of the human being to understand himself, his fellow man, and his world. We don't need statistics to tell us things are not right. We can feel the misery about us, we can smell the foulness of the air, we can see the filth and disintegration of our large cities. We can and we must rely on our senses if we are to make sense out of the confusion of our existence.

Yet we are committed to more power. Studies clearly show that the power demands of our technological civilization will double in the next decade. People will have more power to move faster, go further, and do more things. The tempo of life will quicken despite the fact that the pace is already too frantic. We can anticipate that the opportunities and the capacity for pleasure will progressively diminish. We are becoming more ego-oriented, not less so, as the individual suffers a continuing loss of identity in a mechanized culture. Mechanization operates to dissociate the ego from the body, reducing body awareness and weakening the feeling of identity based on this awareness.

As the simple life disappears, so do the natural functions that are part of this way of life. Home baking and home cooking are replaced by commercially prepared foods and meals. Entering a home, one no longer smells the rich aromas of bread baking or food cooking. Splitting and stacking wood for the fire, knitting and sewing clothes, or feeding the chickens and pigs are activities few of our children ever witness. But the most important loss is the function of mothering—the transmission of faith and feeling through breast feeding, rocking, and cradling. The cradle has become an antique, the rocking chair a relic, and the breast has been transformed into a sexual symbol.

The natural function of mothering is being replaced by the mother as manager. Under the advice of a pediatrician, with formulas and rules, her role has changed from being the soil in which her baby establishes his first roots (rooting describes the head movements of an infant as he reaches for the breast) to being an organizer and administrator. In a sense, she is there for her child but not in her essential nature as a woman. All her activities could just as easily be performed by a man: preparing the bottle, feeding the baby, changing his diapers, or giving him a bath. It is not surprising that she resents being saddled with chores which do not fulfill her nature. And even if she proves to be a most efficient manager, she will not receive from her children the appreciation and love that a mother wants and should get.

Managing a home reduces children to the level of objects. All my depressed patients have the feeling, sometimes deeply buried, that they were objects to be cared for and brought up in such a way that they would reflect pride on their parents or at least create no problems for them. Very early in life they learned they were there to fulfill their parents' emotional needs and that their own desires had to be subordinated to those needs. And this became the pattern of their lives, resulting in a basic passivity of behavior and a need to please. Not one of my depressed patients felt he had the right to make demands, to assert his desires, and to reach out and take the pleasure he wanted. As soon as these patterns became structured in the body, the actual physical ability to reach out was limited.

We have been described as an alienated and uprooted people. The erosion of our roots begins early in life. At birth the infant is separated from his mother and placed in a nursery. At home the infant is fed on schedule, held on occasion, and responded to at the parents' convenience. His treatment is comparable to that of a hothouse plant. No matter how much he seems to bloom, his roots do not go deep into the soil of life.

Many young people have become aware of the situation

I describe. They understand that more power and more material goods, a greater urbanization and mechanization of life threaten the very meaning of existence. And they are moving spontaneously to communal and simpler forms of living—a renewal of interest in handcrafts, home baking, breast feeding, and nature. In the broader sense of seeking to reestablish our roots in nature and the natural order, this movement is not limited to young people, although they are in its forefront. However, it will not succeed as a "return to nature" in the Rousseauan sense of that phrase. We cannot go backward. We must go forward to a deeper understanding of human nature and to a new faith based on an appreciation of the divine force within the living body.

An Epidemic of Depression

In a recent article John J. Schwab noted that "epidemi-ological evidence points to the probability that depression will be epidemic in the next decade as our population reacts to the prevailing social forces and the social climate molds those reactions into forms which are as adaptive and as socially acceptable as possible." * Schwab sees an increasing incidence of depressive reactions in young people where formerly such reactions were "considered to be an emotional illness of the middle-aged or the elderly" as a result of the accumulation of losses and disappointments. He relates this phenomenon to the collapse of the Protestant ethic, with its emphasis on property, productivity, and power and to the absence of a philosophy of values that would appeal to the young. He also believes that the aspirations of young people are "too high, they want to do too much, and subsequent dis-

* John J. Schwab, "A Rising Incidence of Depression," *Attitude*, Vol. 1, No. 2 (Jan./Feb., 1970), p. 2.

appointment at the lack of achievement nourishes the soil in which depressive illness flourishes." *

But are the aspirations of young people too high? Are they, in effect, different from the aspirations of any young generation which is by nature idealistic and wants a world in which peace, justice, self-fulfillment and pleasure are possible? Every new generation has tried to make a better world, and each one has suffered its share of disappointment at its failure to achieve its goals. Disappointments in achievement are not the predisposing conditions for depression, although they may be the exciting or triggering cause. A person with faith can tolerate disappointment; the individual without faith is vulnerable.

We must ask, therefore, how the faith of our young people has been corroded, and we must look for the answer to this question in the family as well as in society. Society directly influences an individual only in his later or mature years. In his earliest years this influence operates through the family, the immediate unit of society. Precisely because modern society has had such a disintegrating effect on the family, it has contributed greatly to the loss of faith in young people.

Family and home were equivalent values in past generations. As the French say, to be home is to be *en famille*. The family home has always represented stability, security, and a sense of permanence. It was a retreat from the pressures of the world and a haven against the storms that often ravaged the world. It was the one place where the current of life flowed relatively smoothly and quietly, undisturbed by the political or religious conflicts that raged outside. Of course, not every home had this quality and not every family was a cohesive unit. There were conflicts, but despite the

* *Ibid.*, p. 6.

arguing and fighting the home and the family seemed indestructible.

How many of these attributes of the good home or the united family exist today? It can be argued that I am describing an ideal family, that the patriarchal family of Western culture has been responsible for neuroses and unhappiness in its members. I do not wish to minimize the problems of the patriarchal family, but depression among young people was not typical of them. Perhaps their security was obtained at the expense of the individuality of its members, but we must also recognize that security is essential to proper family functioning. It will be my thesis in this section that an exaggerated emphasis on individuality, especially on the ego aspects of individuality, is responsible for the inability of the modern family to provide the stability and security children need.

The single factor most responsible for the disruption of the family is the automobile. Its full effect cannot be assessed. Modern life, as we know, would be impossible without the ubiquitous motorcar. It broke up the old family and community groupings and promoted the nuclear family—two parents and their children without grandparents and relatives. The nuclear family is an isolated unit, removed from the direct influence of grandparents, who would normally promote the traditional ways of living and child rearing. Grandparents may have old-fashioned ideas, which are certainly not ideal, but when young couples take off on their own to rear a family, they assume a big responsibility. They have to provide a setting that relates the past to the present and looks forward to the future. The weakness of the nuclear family is its isolation, not only spatially but in time. It lives solely in terms of its own existence, which, given the frequency of divorce, is relatively unstable.

The appeal of the nuclear family with its mobility and

its motorcars lies in the opportunity it offers for individual expression. Each parent in a nuclear family believes that he will do it differently and probably better than his parents. For a woman a new home is a challenge to creativity. It can become a unique expression of her individuality. For a man it is an expression of his status and position. All this may be well, but the tremendous investment of time and energy in the material aspects of home life often leaves little for its more human aspects. With so much to be bought and so much to be done to furnish a modern home, it loses its character as a retreat from the world and becomes, instead, part of the world.

The character of retreat is further forfeit by the intrusion of the world into the home through radio and television. These constitute a stimulation of the ego functions by forcing the individual to cope mentally with the stress and conflict newscasters report. I shall discuss their effect on the young child later. The point I want to make here is simply that the modern home is rarely a place for quiet living and contentment. It is constantly subject to change with a view toward improvement that doesn't really improve the *quality* of living.

A basic proposition of modern living is that we express ourselves through doing. One can contrast this view with a style of life that sees self-expression as a way of being. We express ourselves by being warm, understanding, sympathetic, alive, vibrant, joyful or sad, angry, and so forth. We also express ourselves by being a devoted mother, a devout believer in a religion, or a dependable worker in a trade. These basic forms of self-expression, which also include those associated with being a woman or a man, normally provide life's deeper satisfactions. Superimposed on these satisfactions are the ego satisfactions that come from doing. But when we attempt to derive the meaning of life from the ego satisfaction of doing alone, we are in trouble.

Satisfaction from doing is the gravy on the meat of the satisfaction of being. Meat without gravy can satisfy one's hunger; gravy without meat doesn't provide any fulfillment. And because it doesn't, one is tempted to more doing, to greater activity and to a deeper involvement in the world. The demand of our times is that *we must do more*. It is a demand that ignores the simple truth that *only by being fully what one is can one fulfill his existence*.

The philosophy of doing is insidious and pernicious. It is insidious because it is couched in the rational terms of "one must do one's best," or "one must achieve one's potential." These demands allow no peace, for they force an individual to compete against himself. It is a pernicious philosophy because it is applied to young children before they have had the opportunity to savor the joy of just being themselves, free and innocent creatures who can play to their heart's content under the protection of home and parents.

Let us have no illusions about the predisposition to depression. It is not the aspirations of young people that prepare the ground for their subsequent illness, but the expectations and demands of parents. We expect them to grow up quickly, to become independent early, to learn rapidly, to be reasonable, responsible and cooperative adults while they are still only children. We demand that they go to bed alone, unsympathetic to their fear of being alone in the dark. We demand the recognition of our rights at an age when the child is only aware of his needs. We demand that the child adapt to adult conditions of living that are ages removed from his own state of being, which is close to the animal or primitive condition of life. Think how difficult it must be for a young child to feel at home in a modern house compared with the child who grew up in a thatched hut or shack.

These demands increase as the child becomes older. He is expected to do his best in school, to achieve recognition, and, if possible, to excel at some activity. His young mind is exposed early to the world and its crises. He rides with his mother in the family car, he watches television, he listens to adult talk and may even be an experienced airline traveler. We expect that with all this stimulation he should be a genius. Often at a still tender age he shows a grasp of adult reality that surprises us, sometimes even a maturity that delights us. But where is the baby and the child? And what happened to the innocence that was his precious gift?

It is an old adage that a tree is no stronger than its roots. A good nurseryman will retard the growth of a sapling to promote the development of its root system. We are doing just the opposite with our young children. We are over-stimulating them to grow fast while withholding the support and nourishment that would strengthen their roots. We push our children as we push ourselves, little realizing that this forcing them to grow and do undermines their faith and security.

The problems caused by overstimulation for children and adults have not, I believe, received the attention they deserve. A person is overstimulated when the number and kinds of impressions he receives from the world exceed his capacity to respond fully to them. The effect is to keep him in a state of excitation or charged up, from which he cannot easily come down and relax. He becomes hung up and his ability to discharge the excitation in pleasure is reduced. He feels frustrated, becomes irritable and restless. This combination leads him to seek further stimulation in the attempt to overcome his unpleasant state by getting out of himself. A vicious spiral is created, spinning the person higher and higher, with deleterious effects on his behavior. He may be forced into the use of drugs—the prescribed or illicit varieties—or of alcohol to deaden his sensitivities and diminish his frustration.

Overstimulation drives a person out of his body by disturbing his inner rhythms and harmony. Like a person who has diarrhea, his body has to keep running. It also seduces him away from his body by offering him a false excitement— that is, an excitement which provides no prospect of its release in pleasure. One can gauge the severity of this disturbance by a person's inability to sit quietly, to do nothing, or to be alone—in other words, to be in himself. It can also be gauged by the restlessness that drives people into constant activity, into continually doing something, and into ever new projects. It forces one into a position of having no time for oneself and, by extension, no time for easy personal relationships. Husbands have no time for wives, mothers have no time for children, and friends have no time to spend with each other. It's go, go and do, do, and it ends with most people having no time even to breathe.

A day in New York will give a clear idea of what I mean by overstimulation. The amount of noise, the pace of movement, the crowds of people are almost unbearable. To endure it one has to deaden oneself; close one's ears, shut one's eyes, and cut off one's feelings. But are the suburbs much different? The traffic is equally bad, the pace equally hurried. Inexorably, the phenomenon of overstimulation creeps into the home, too, through radio and television, through the continual changing and "improving," and through the myriad things—toys, gadgets, bottled drinks, prepared foods—that are constantly introduced to vary the routine. I have a personal bias against advertising, which I feel is partly responsible for this state of affairs. It is well known that advertising aims to encourage or create "wants" that often have no relation to a person's needs. But I place the real blame on a technological economy that equates the good life with material things.

Children are more easily overstimulated than adults because their sensitivity is keener and their ability to tolerate frustration is less. Thus a child who is overindulged with toys will incessantly demand new ones. If he is allowed to watch television, he will want to watch it all the time. If he is permitted to stay up late, it will be difficult to get him to bed. But a child is also overstimulated by the hyperactivity and restlessness of his parents. A mother's overcharged state communicates itself to her child. Unfortunately parents seem to think that the more activity a child is encouraged to do, the more he will learn and the quicker he will grow up. The intensity of this unconscious drive "upward," toward the head, toward the ego, and toward dominance is alarming. Being "down," quiet, with time to feel and to think, is almost an unknown way of life.

Every depressed patient I have treated was a person who had lost his childhood. He had forsaken the infantile position in an attempt to relieve his parents of the burden his care placed on them. He had grown up too fast in an effort to meet expectations that were coupled with approval and acceptance. He had become or he had tried to become a doer and an achiever only to find that his achievement was meaningless, since it was at the expense of his being; now unable to be and unable to do, he falls into a depressive reaction.

Depression will befall anyone who lacks faith in being and must compensate for it by doing. It matters little whether the doing is to achieve a personal ambition or to redress a social injustice. Thus the successful businessman is as vulnerable to depression as the militant who seeks the overthrow of the system. Both have come to my office with the same complaint. The issue is not whether one accepts the establishment or rebels against it. What *is* involved is something deeper than a system. It is a way of life in which the individual sees himself as part of a larger order and derives his individuality from his sense of belonging and participating in this larger order. This is in contrast to an individuality based on the ego and its image, which overemphasizes the I at the expense of the person's relationship to the great forces of life that have made his existence possible and continue to support it in the face of his avarice and greed.

If I have emphasized the importance of breast feeding, it is not because this act in itself determines a child's future well-being. Unfortunately it doesn't, though it has many positive benefits. The woman who nurses her baby as a doing perverts the natural relationship. Her ego or her "I" will get in the way of the baby's pleasure. He will be too conscious of her will to be freely and fully himself, his being will be disturbed. It is not the act of nursing that is so significant but what it implies. If it implies that the mother can find satisfaction and fulfillment in her natural function as a woman, then the infant can experience the same satisfaction in his own functions. If it means that a woman can accept herself as an animal mother who gives of herself and her body to her child, then the child can accept his basic animal nature. But if her ego will not allow her to recognize her common humanity with all women or her common mammalian nature with all mammals, it will prevent her from being there fully for her child and sharing with him the joy this intimate relationship offers. Whatever satisfaction she may gain by efficiently doing as a manager is more than offset by the loss of the inner satisfaction of being a woman.

The Demise of God

When a people believe and have faith in God, His will becomes the supreme authority in their lives, especially in situations where man's will is felt to be helpless or powerless. But as a people gain knowledge and power, their reliance on and respect for the deity declines. Situations which formerly called for divine intercession no longer require it. For example, where primitive man used magic and sacrifice to ensure the fertility of his fields, modern man does a soil analysis and employs chemical fertilizers to achieve the same end. In a similar way the use of magic and prayer to cure the ill has been supplanted by a medicine based on objective examination and empirical research. Many people still pray, but few believe that God intervenes directly in human affairs. The sophisticated view is that praying helps the person who prays feel better, though it has little or no impact on the course of human events.

Modern man seems to have no need of faith in a god. He has a degree of power that man never dreamed of before. Simply in terms of horsepower each individual in our Western countries can command an amount of power such as few kings possessed in times gone by. The motor of an average automobile has a rated capacity of more than 200 hp. If to this is added the power used in motorboats, airplanes, power tools, refrigerators, dishwashers, heating units, cooling units, radios, television and lighting fixtures, the sum total of available power for each person is tremendous. But it is not just the total power that interests us. The uses to which it can be put have also increased. In almost every area of life there are machines that can translate power into action. Man has not yet arrived at the position where he can lead a push-button existence, but he is steadily moving in that direction.

As man's power grew, God's declined. With the loss of His omnipotence the rational basis for a belief in God vanished. But only people who require a rational basis for their faith can dismiss God so lightly. His demise indicates, therefore, that we have become too rational and too objective to believe in a divine Providence that could protect and comfort us. If we need guidance, we turn to professional counselors or read books on psychology to discover the answers to our difficulties. Our assumption is that if we can just get the right answers, we can apply them to our lives. We have put our trust in the reasoning power of the human mind, confident it has the ability to resolve all man's problems. Modern man seems to believe that with enough knowledge and power he can become omnipotent.

Pride goes before a fall and we are witnessing the beginning of the fall. We are becoming aware that power is a mixed blessing, that it has its destructive as well as constructive aspects. We are realizing that man cannot alter the fine ecological balance of nature at his will without paying a price. It seems that the more power we produce, the more contaminants we create. Yet we are obsessed with power, for we believe that we must have still more in order to control the pollution. The reliance on power can create a downward spiral that will end in disaster for mankind.

If we wish to reverse this process, we must first understand how man got into this dilemma. At what point did he lose his faith? When and how did he abrogate to himself the right to control life? These are big questions which, unfortunately, I cannot attempt to answer here. However I would like to discuss the role psychoanalysis played in this development. It cannot be coincidental that psychoanalysis rose and flourished during the period that saw man's faith in God diminish.

We must start with the proposition that psychoanalysis made one of the most important contributions to our understanding of man. This was Freud's demonstration of how unconscious processes operate to influence and distort conscious thinking. He also developed a technique for making these unconscious processes conscious. Thus psychoanalysis provided us with the means to see the forces behind the façade of rationalization and socially approved behavior. It was like an X-ray machine of the mind. Through psychoanalysis Freud showed that the organism strives for pleasure by the satisfaction of its instinctual drives and that when these drives come into conflict with the reality of the social situation, they are either repressed or sublimated.

The repression of a drive leads to an internal conflict that handicaps the personality. The drive is turned against the self, and the energy of the drive is used to block its expression. In sublimation, however, the energy of the drive is supposed to be channeled into an acceptable mode of release which not only avoids the internal and external conflict but also becomes a creative expression that furthers the cultural process. Freud was most concerned with the sexual drive. He called the energy of this drive libido, which he first conceived as a physical force but in his later writings described as a psychic force.

Freud firmly believed that culture was impossible without sublimation. Since the gratification of all instinctual drives would, he thought, leave nothing to be desired, there would be no motivation for cultural growth. Necessity, we say, is the mother of invention. If all necessity were removed, there would be no reason to invent. This argument is valid, but it overlooks the fact that necessity is inherent in the natural order. The world has never been free from illness, famine or the threat of famine, natural catastrophe and death.

Instinctual gratification of oral needs and sexual satisfaction would not eliminate these threats to our security. Cultural development should not be seen, therefore, as the result of frustration and sublimation. For Freud, "Human progress necessarily leads to repression and neurosis. Man cannot have both happiness and progress." *

There are two basic reasons why Freud accepted the inevitability of conflict between instinctual gratification and culture. One is that he was bound to the ideological basis of his society. He was, as Fromm points out, "a critic of society. . . . But he was also deeply rooted in the prejudices and philosophy of his historical period and class." I believe that Fromm is right in saying that Freud "was impeded by an unquestioning belief that his society, although by no means satisfactory, was the ultimate form of human progress and could not be improved in any essential feature." †

Such an attitude on Freud's part indicates that he was a man of faith. A man of faith doesn't question the roots of his faith. It is significant that Freud never seriously analyzed his relationship to his mother. As Fromm says, "Freud could not conceive that the woman could be the main cause of fear. But clinical observation amply demonstrates that the most intense and pathogenic fears are indeed related to the mother, by comparison, the dread of the father is insignificant." ** Nevertheless Freud's faith in himself and in his mission was the source of his strength.

The other basic reason for Freud's position was his commitment to reason and rationality. This commitment, however, did not blind him to the irrational aspects of human

* Erich Fromm, *The Crisis of Psychoanalysis* (New York, Holt, Rinehart & Winston, 1970), p. 45.
† *Ibid.*, p. 6.
** *Ibid.*, p. 73.

behavior. Psychoanalysis claimed to be the science of the irrational or unconscious, since it clearly recognized that the unconscious exerts a strong determining influence on consciousness and behavior. But Freud accepted the thesis that there is an irreconcilable conflict between these two forces, rationality and irrationality, or the conscious and unconscious aspects of the human condition. And he also believed that some resolution of this conflict was possible through the analytic technique, which aimed to make the unconscious conscious. If this could be done, then man through the power of reason and the strength of his mature ego could "liberate himself from the dominance of unconscious strivings; instead of repressing them, he can negate them, that is, he can lessen their strength, and control them with his will." *

In this view of man the irrational is seen only in its negative aspects. The unconscious strivings from which one must liberate himself are seen as immature, selfish, destructive, and hostile impulses. My teacher, Wilhelm Reich, pointed out that for Freud, the id was a Pandora's box of negative feelings. Every therapist working with patients in an analytic way can confirm that the unconscious is indeed replete with negative and hostile impulses. If one could not get beyond this negative layer, one would have to agree with Freud that the only solution is to make them conscious and subject them to voluntary control. The failure of the psychoanalytic technique was that it never went deep enough. It operated only with the mind, ignoring the heart and the body. Starting from the premise that the id is not to be trusted, it ended with the dictum "Where id was, there ego shall be." Given its bias against the irrational, psychoanalysis could come to no other conclusion than that the child is an amoral, sinful

* *Ibid.,* p. 36.

and perverted creature who must be trained to become a cultured being.

If rationality has a positive value, then the irrational must be assigned a negative one. If reasoning and logic are superior ways of functioning, then emotional responsiveness is an inferior way. If mental functioning is the higher mode of being, then bodily functioning is a lower mode. These judgments are not unique to psychoanalysis, they pervade Western culture. A simple example will illustrate: A child tells his mother, "I don't want to eat my vegetables." Some mothers may insist, but many will reply, "Why don't you want to eat them?" If the child answers, "I don't feel like eating them," it may be met with the demand, "Give me a reason." We seem to need reasons to justify behavior. Feelings are not reasons and are therefore insufficient grounds for one's actions. But since feeling is the motivation for action, we are constantly forced to justify our feelings, which really means to justify our right to be. Reason takes precedence over feeling.

Freud's bias against the irrational (let me call it the non-rational to remove its negative value) came out strongly in his analysis of religion. In *The Future of an Illusion* Freud attacked the validity of religious beliefs. Now, Freud was a logical reasoner and it was not difficult for him to show that the specific dogmas of religion lacked an objective basis. He observed that "countless people have been tortured by the same doubts" * which he believed they dared not express out of fear or suppressed out of duty. But Freud overlooked the fact of faith, which is a state of feeling. A person with faith doesn't question its roots, for he knows that if he subjected it to the critical examination of his intellect, he would end up without faith. The same thing can be said of any

* S. Freud, *The Future of an Illusion* (New York, Liveright, 1953), p. 4.

feeling. You can analyze any feeling to death, but when you do that, you end up without feeling and without a meaningful life.

While we must recognize the very important contributions psychoanalysis has made to our understanding of the human condition, we should realize that it has also had some negative effects on that condition. It has tended to increase the split between the ego and the body or between culture and nature by emphasizing the antagonism between these polar aspects of life and ignoring their underlying unity. Also, by focusing almost exclusively on psychic processes, it tends to denigrate the role of somatic factors in emotional illness. Thus psychoanalysis tends to foster the illusion that the mind is the all-important aspect of human functioning. In practice this leads to a concentration on and absorption with words and mental images to the relative neglect of nonverbal modes of expression. It must end therefore as a system of intellectualizations that have lost their essential connection with the animal nature of man.

It is not my purpose to attack psychoanalysis. Every valid concept can be misused, and Freud would not have approved the misuse of his method described above. I do want to make the point that psychoanalysis has a very strong bias against feeling, against the body, and against the concept of faith. Freud's bias against faith is understandable when it is seen in the light of the misuse of faith by organized religion. Just as Freud opposed the claims of religion by an appeal to reason, so organized religion opposed the discoveries of psychoanalysis by an appeal to faith. The concept of faith can easily degenerate into a vague mysticism that would destroy its true character and value. Since people desperately need faith, one can easily seduce them into a surrender of their individuality by offering them a set of beliefs in the name of faith.

Freud finally placed his trust in science. He wrote, "We believe that it is possible for scientific work to discover something about the reality of the world through which we can increase our power and according to which we can regulate our lives." * Then Freud asked if this belief could be an illusion and immediately answered that the successes of science show that it is not. I agree it is not an illusion. Science *does* give us power and provides dicta to help us regulate our lives. My question is: Do the concepts and the power that science offers necessarily promote man's happiness and well-being? I would be loath to answer this question in the affirmative.

One need not take a stand between the arguments of religion and those of science. Neither religious nor scientific beliefs confront the basic issue of depression. Neither a belief in God nor a belief in science will prevent one from becoming depressed when the energetic charge in the body collapses as a result of the loss of feeling. And when this happens, the idea or belief loses its power to hold us up, since the strength of an idea derives from the amount of affect (feeling) or cathexis (change) invested in it. Freud, himself, had discovered this principle.

There is another bias in Freud which should be exposed. This is a false view of nature. He wrote of nature: "She has her peculiarly effective mode of restricting us: she destroys us, coldly, cruelly, callously, as it seems to us, and possibly just through what has caused our satisfaction." And later, "Indeed, it is the principal task of culture, its real *raison d'être,* to defend us against nature." † These are strongly

* *Ibid.,* p. 95.
† *Ibid,* p. 38.

negative statements, and in some cases they may be true, but they are unaccompanied by any remark about nature's positive side. Does she not also nourish us, support us, and make our lives possible? If she is indifferent to the fate of the individual, why call this cruelty? Freud really knew better. He actually delighted in nature. One of his great pleasures was hiking in the mountains. We can explain this contradiction in Freud's personality by interpreting it in terms of his relationship to his mother. Freud's feelings about his mother were also ambivalent, but in this case he suppressed the negative aspect, which he then projected on the universal mother—nature.

The effect of this bias was to blind Freud to those aspects of human life that deal with the relationship of a child to his mother or of man to nature, the great mother. It also blinded him to the important insights Carl Jung developed. It caused Freud to ignore the important discovery of Johann Bachofen and Louis Henry Morgen that matriarchy and matriarchal cultures had everywhere preceded the establishment of patriarchal society. In such cultures frustration, repression and neuroses were unknown. Yet these very early cultures were not without religion or without deities. The gods they worshiped were goddesses, mother figures or earth figures.

Erich Fromm makes an interesting comparison of the matriarchal versus the patriarchal principle. "The matriarchal principle is that of unconditional love, natural equality, emphasis on the bonds of blood and soil, compassion and mercy; the patriarchal principle is that of conditional love, hierarchical structure, abstract thought, man-made laws, the state and justice. In the last analysis, mercy and justice represent the two principles, respectively." *

* E. Fromm, *op. cit.*, p. 83.

These two principles can also be equated with the ego and the body respectively, or with reason and feeling. If we extend them, the patriarchal principle represents the ego, reason, belief and culture, whereas the matriarchal principle stands for the body, feeling, faith and nature. It is true that the patriarchal principle is today in a stage of crisis. It has become so overextended by science and technology that it may be on the verge of collapse. But until this happens and until the matriarchal principle is restored to its rightful place as an equal but polar value, we can anticipate that depression will become endemic in our culture.

9. Reality

Getting in Touch with Reality

I have used several phrases to describe the depressed patient: (1) he pursues unreal goals or he is hung up on an illusion, (2) he isn't grounded, and (3) he has lost his faith. At different points I have emphasized one or the other of these aspects of his problem. They are, however, only aspects, which means that we have been studying a single situation from three different points of view. The person who isn't grounded has no faith and pursues unreal goals. On the other hand, the person who is grounded has faith and is in touch with reality. Perhaps the best way to say this is that the person who is in touch with reality is grounded and has faith.

"Reality" is a word that can have different meanings for different people. Some may see it as the necessity to earn a living; others may equate it with the law of the jungle—the strong survive while the weak die off—and still others may regard it as a life free from the pressures of a competitive society. Although there is some validity to each of these world views, what we are concerned with here is the reality of the self or the inner world. When we say a person is out of touch with reality, we mean he is out of touch with the reality of his being. The best example is the schizophrenic who lives in a fantasy world and is unaware of the physical conditions of his existence.

For every person the basic reality of his being is his body. It is through his body that he experiences the world and by his body that he responds to it. If a person is out of touch with his body, he is out of touch with the reality of the world. This is a thesis I developed in *The Betrayal of the Body*.* I shall quote a passage from that book: "If the body is relatively unalive, a person's impressions and responses are diminished. The more alive the body is, the more vividly does he perceive reality and the more actively does he respond to it. We have all experienced the fact that when we feel particularly good and alive we perceive the world more sharply. In states of depression the world appears colorless."

The first step in the treatment of depression is to help the patient get in touch with the reality of his body. The degree of his depression is a measure of how much he has lost his self-awareness as a bodily person. In this respect he is like the schizoid individual, who however denies the reality of his body in contrast to the depressed person, who ignores it. The inescapable reality of life is that the person is the body or that the body is the person. When the body dies, the person dies. When the body goes "dead," that is, when there is no feeling, the person ceases to exist as an individual with a definable personality. Another quote from *The Betrayal of the Body* will make this clear: "It is the body that melts with love, freezes with fear, trembles in anger, and reaches for warmth and contact. Apart from the body these words are poetic images. Experienced in the body, they have a reality that gives meaning to existence. Based on the reality

* Alexander Lowen, *The Betrayal of the Body* (New York, Collier Books, 1968), p. 6.

of bodily feeling, an identity has substance and structure. Abstracted from this reality, identity is a social artifact, a skeleton without flesh." *

The problem of therapy is that the person who is out of touch with his body doesn't know what you are talking about. He may even make the statement, "What has my body to do with the way I feel?" The statement is absurd because what he feels *is* his body. Apart from the body there is no feeling. How can a person make such a statement unless he has been conditioned to believe that the body is only a mechanism which maintains his life but in no way determines it? But such conditioning is part of Western culture and rooted in the Judeo-Christian ethic, which regards the body as sinful, inferior, and the prison of the spirit. Man's mind, that glorious faculty that distinguishes him from all other animals, is regarded as the true mark of man's nature, the criterion of his humanity. Where primitive man worshiped the body and its vital functions as manifestations of a divine force, we have dissociated this force from the body and invested it in a disembodied spirit which we consider divine.

This denigration of the body in Western religion was an attempt to spiritualize man; to raise him above pure animal existence. And as long as man had an alive body and kept in touch with it by the physical necessities of daily living, this effort made sense. It makes no sense in our present situation. The overemphasis on the mind and spirit has resulted in disembodied spirits and despirited or disenchanted bodies. The final result is that religion has lost its efficacy as a bulwark of faith by undermining man's roots in his body and in his animal nature.

This process was abetted by a scientific position which ignored the validity of subjective experience in favor of an

* *Ibid.*, p. 6.

objective, emotionless attitude to life. By treating all vital functions as purely physicochemical mechanisms it reduced the body to an object—one of the many science sought to control and manipulate. Here, again, the objective made sense in the beginning, for it increased man's power and dominion and greatly augmented his external security. But this value was lost when the whole process of life faced the danger of being turned into a mechanical operation.

I have long regarded psychoanalysis as the final great effort to subdue and control man's basic animal nature. It belongs, therefore, with religion and science in the Western tradition of mind over matter and man over nature. Like the other attempts in this direction it made sense in the beginning. Man had to gain insight into his unconscious mental processes if he was to understand his behavior. But how could he develop the necessary understanding if the basic reality of his being, namely, his bodily functioning, was ignored? Yet it was through psychoanalysis that this flaw in man's approach to life was recognized. For it was Wilhelm Reich, the psychoanalyst, who discovered the obvious fact that an individual's psychological character is expressed in his body attitude.

How a person holds himself, moves, talks, and radiates feeling tells us who he is. We all know this instinctively, we knew it as children. How did we become so blind as not to recognize this truth? Such blindness in the face of the obvious could come only from a long conditioning which taught us to believe that the person is identified with his mind, not his body. We have become conditioned not to trust our eyes or our senses, since they only convey subjective information to the mind. But the person who doesn't trust his senses can have no faith in his perceptions or his responses. And, of course, he can have no certainty about reality.

The resistance to seeing the body as the person is deeply structured in most people. It is not an easy resistance to overcome, for few people are prepared to surrender the illusion that the mind of man, given enough information, is omnipotent. The following case is one more illustration of the unreality that pervades the depressive condition.

Some time ago I saw a man in his middle forties who complained of a depressive reaction that had begun a year earlier, some six months after he had sold his business to a large company for a considerable sum of money. The sale was made with the condition that he manage the business for five years, since he was outstanding in his field. What might have been a typical success story soon turned sour for my patient as he became restless and began to fret at the idea of working for someone. He grew impatient with his employees and began to scream and rage at them. These outbursts were short-lived and his general good nature soon restored the situation. But his depression deepened steadily. He then unfolded this story.

Ten years ago, just prior to the breakup of his marriage he had experienced attacks of dizziness and had had some difficulty in walking. He described this as a condition of agoraphobia, the fear of open space. These attacks led him to seek psychiatric help, and for five years he was in psychoanalytic treatment with sessions four to five times a week. As a result he was able to cope somewhat with his anxieties and phobias. Through the analytic treatment he also acquired the aggression that had enabled him to become a successful businessman. He had gained some meaningful insights into himself, but many problems were left unresolved. He knew that a major one was a need to be in control—of himself and others. The analytic treatment, however, offered him little help in learning how to let go of this need for control. This was evident in his sexual functioning. It required a long familiarity with a sexual partner before he could become erectively potent. Also he could not ejaculate without the use of fantasy. He could not give in or surrender his ego to a woman or to his own sexuality.

In view of the above I was surprised when he said, "In spite of all my problems, I enjoy my life. I am happy most of the time." When I pointed out the absurdity of this statement, he clarified it: "I play games and my big game is to outsmart my neurosis. I also play the game of being happy, successful, and having friends despite my neurosis." This was an admission that he kidded himself into believing he was happy, whereas he was really miserable. He also said that he always felt forced to do the things he never wanted to do. For example, he had wanted to be a writer, but he instead received a PhD in engineering.

Given the emotional frustrations of this patient's life, is it not natural for him to be depressed? The answer is no. The natural reaction to frustration is anger, to a loss it is sadness and grief. A depressive reaction indicates that the person has been functioning under an illusion. It is certainly self-deception to believe that one can outsmart one's neurosis. Such an attitude divides the personality into a rational part, the conscious mind, and an irrational part, the neurotic behavior. This division leads to the illusion that the conscious mind can and should be in control of the personality. Every time this control breaks down, the individual panics and becomes depressed, which furthers the seeming need for more control. The individual is thus trapped in a vicious circle from which there is no escape.

To break it, the patient must be brought into touch with reality—the reality of his life situation, the reality of his feelings, and the reality of his body. These three realities cannot be separated from one another. The person who is in touch with his feelings is also in touch with his body and his life situation. By the same logic, the person who is in touch with his body is in touch with all aspects of his reality. Getting in touch is, therefore, the first step toward the release from depression and the acquisition of faith. The most immediate way to accomplish this objective is to help a patient gain contact with his body.

My patient was vaguely aware he had some physical tensions, but he was out of touch with their severity and the degree to which they immobilized his movement and feeling. As we talked together, I observed that he sat slumped in his chair, his head pulled down between his shoulders. He sat "in himself," which means that he was held in and couldn't open up and let his feelings out. When I put him over the stool to breathe, I noticed that his breathing was shallow and he experienced the position as a severe stress which frightened him. To alleviate his anxiety, I went over the stool myself and showed him that, with a little relaxation, one's breathing deepened and one could tolerate the stress for a time without any hardship. My demonstration relieved his anxiety and he was able to let go a little more. Actually my patient was surprised that I, an older man, could do this exercise so much more easily, for he considered himself somewhat athletic, since he was a skier.

As he lay on the bed, I asked him to kick his legs into the bed and say no. His expression of this attitude was weak and unconvincing. But he told me, "At the office I am easily provoked and yell all the time." Yet he couldn't do it in my office, where such actions would be appropriate and serve to release his suppressed feelings. Many people suffer from the misconception that hysterical outbursts are valid forms of self-expression. They are, in fact, just the opposite, for they indicate a lack of self-possession and an inability to release feelings except through provocation. After this explanation the patient made a greater effort to get some feeling into his kicking, hitting, and yelling.

At the next session he reported a slight improvement. His anxieties had diminished and his depression had perceptibly lifted. He attributed the improvement to the release of anger, for he believed that its suppression was responsible for his depressive reaction. This is only partly true. The suppression of any feeling is associated with the suppression of all feeling—sadness, fear, love, and so on. Although my patient was more conscious of holding in his anger, he actually "held in" *all* his feelings. The term "held in" means that the mechanism of suppression is the closing off of all the outlets, genital, anal, and oral. In these individuals the main tension areas are in the muscles of the neck and throat and in those of the pelvis and buttocks. My patient had a short, thick neck. The muscles at the back of his neck were overdeveloped and severely contracted. A similar condition could be palpated in the muscles surrounding the lower outlets.

The character attitude of "holding in" can be contrasted with that of "holding back." In the latter case the main tensions are in the long muscles of the body, especially those along the spinal column. This tension pattern produces a rigidity of the body generally associated with a more compulsive and aggressive personality. "Holding in" is more typical of the masochistic character structure.*

After several weeks of continued improvement, the therapy was interrupted for two weeks by my absence from the city. When I saw the patient again, he was depressed and anxious

* A. Lowen, *The Physical Dynamics of Character Structure* and *The Language of the Body.*

I had warned him of the inevitability of relapse. During this session as he worked with breathing and movement, he suddenly became nauseated. At first he resisted the idea of throwing up. When I pointed out that this was his body's way of not holding in and getting it out, he agreed to try. He drank some water and, using his finger, threw up easily. The experience shook him, but he was pleasantly surprised to find that it immediately calmed his anxieties. I mention this incident to introduce the idea that the body, if allowed to come alive, will find its own way to release its tensions.*

This session was the last time I saw him. Why he didn't continue his therapy, I don't know. I can only guess that the idea of releasing feeling frightened him. He was unprepared to accept the pain and the physical work involved in freeing him from his muscular tensions. I surmise that he expected me to help him develop more control over his body so that he could overcome his depressive reaction by an effort of will. However this is *not* the way to handle a depressive problem, for it increases a patient's unreality by further dissociating him from his body.

This short case history serves to illustrate two basic points. One, all depressed persons are out of touch with the reality of their lives. I think this statement can be extended to include most people to a lesser degree. Two, they are out of touch with their bodies. They do not sense the muscular tensions that block and imprison them. If they feel tense, as so many people do, they attribute it to the immediate situation which they feel helpless to change. They turn, then, to a pill or a drug. They do not realize how much tension has become structured into their bodies or how these tensions contribute to their anxieties and their sense of helplessness.

* For the significance of spontaneous nausea and the role it plays in therapy I refer the reader to my previous book, *Pleasure*.

One of my depressed patients was a woman whose big complaint was that her husband was unresponsive to her. While there was some validity to this complaint, she was unaware of how her own problems contributed to the situation. During a session I asked her to reach up with her arms and say "I want you." She couldn't say it, not with any feeling. She wanted to, at least consciously, but her throat was too tight and her shoulders were too frozen to let the feeling through. She knew then that she could not reach out to her husband and that the problems of her marriage were not solely his fault.

I shall describe another case, that of a young man who through determination and will had been able to get most of the things he wanted. In order to do this he had cut off most of his feelings. Through therapy he recovered some of his capacity to express himself; he could cry and he could mobilize his anger. He had one problem however which became very clear when he reached up with his hands and said, "Give it to me." He made the demand strongly, and in response I gave him my hand, lightly curled into a fist. He took it, held it, and then became still. He didn't know what to do with it. Most patients in this situation bring my hand to their chest, their cheek, or their mouth. We repeated the maneuver with a rolled-up towel. He got a firm grip on it and held, but he was unable to move further. Then he said, "I can get what I want. I can even hold on so it won't be taken away. But I can't possess it. I can't make it part of me. I can't open up and take it into me."

To help my patients understand what opening up looks like, I describe the behavior of young fledgling birds when the mother bird appears with food. The little bird's beak opens wide, wider even, so it seems, than the sac of the body. It is a lovely sight and I have sketched it on the next page.

I am sure all of us have seen and have been impressed by the extent to which the baby bird opens its mouth and body to receive its mother's offering.

A nursing baby opens and reaches out in the same way to receive the breast. It is not just the mouth that opens but the throat and the body, not just the lips and hands that reach but the child's whole being. Opening and reaching starts as a wave of excitation in the center of the body that flows upward through the chest and outward through the arms, the throat, mouth and eyes. The accompanying feeling can be described as a reaching from the heart or an opening up that extends to and includes the heart. The infant opens and reaches with love, and so can take into his body the love that is offered him.

Opening the personality means opening the heart of a person so that he is capable of expressing and receiving love. This is not a metaphor but a physical reality. A heart is open when the feeling or excitation in the heart can flow freely into the arms or through the throat and into the mouth and lips or upward and into the eyes. Just as impulses flow outward along these pathways, impressions flow inward along them. An open person feels in his heart the affection that others have for him. Feeling flows from the heart upward and downward in the body, toward the head and also toward the genitals and legs. An open person is open at both ends of his body. His sexuality is imbued with love for his partner, and every step he takes is a loving contact with the earth.

When we say of a person that he has a closed heart, we mean that his heart can't be reached. If the heart itself should ever close down, the person would die. One can, however, narrow or restrict the approaches to the heart both from above and from below. And one can change the thoracic cage into a prison by muscular tensions that rigidify and immobilize the chest. The rigid, inflated chest says, in body language, "I won't let you get close to my heart." Such a body attitude develops as a result of a severe disappointment in an early love relationship, specifically, in the relationship of a child to his mother. Reich described such tension as a process of armoring designed to protect the person against being hurt again. It also serves to deaden the pain of the initial hurt and is therefore a defense against feeling.

My patients are blocked in their ability to open and reach out fully and freely. In most of them I find that the chest is tight and rigid like a vault to protect and guard the heart. Then there is a ring of muscular contraction about the root of the neck narrowing the opening into the chest cavity. In some the neck is short and thick, with strong muscles that effectively choke off any outgoing impulse. In others the neck is long and thin, with tight muscles that constrict any impulse. The jaw is locked to control the access to the interior or the egress to the exterior. Chronic jaw tensions are never absent, and in some cases the opening of the mouth is drastically reduced. Even the lips become paralyzed and are unable to move forward freely and easily. Muscular spasticities about the shoulder and scapula effectively limit the range of one's reach.

As I bring my patients into touch with their bodies, they can sense the frustrations and deprivations that produced these tensions. They recall their longing for a mother who was not "there" and they become aware how they suppressed the feeling to eliminate the pain. They feel how they choked off their crying when they found that it produced a hostile reaction in the parent. They learned the ways of a culture that believes in frustration. They learned to "keep a stiff upper lip," to bear up in the face of disappointment, "chin up, old man." It became second nature to be on guard, for they had long since lost faith in parental responses. They closed off and held in or held back their feelings. They stopped reaching out, since this only ended in their being hurt.

And they accepted the edict that love is to be earned by good deeds. This edict summarizes an attitude that regards the child as tainted with sin (the doctrine of original sin) or as a being whose rights are granted by the parents on condition that he adjust to parental demands. The child who submits to this attitude must suppress his own anger and hostility. This additional suppression further increases the state of being closed off.

The person who is out of touch with his body doesn't know that he is closed off. He will talk of love, he will even make some gestures of love, but since his heart isn't in either his words or his actions, they will fail to be convincing. He knows the importance of love and so will try through indirect ways to get the love he needs. He will try to help others without realizing he is projecting his own need on them. Being closed off to himself, he will place his problem in the external world, outside himself. For this reason, every effort he makes to gain approval (being good, getting rich, becoming successful) proves meaningless, since it doesn't affect his inner being. His achievements or accomplishments have no more than an ego value for him. He continues to feel frustrated without knowing why. Being closed off, he isn't touched by other people's response to him, which leaves him with the feeling they aren't doing enough.

When a person gets in touch with his body, he becomes aware of the restrictions and limitations of his being caused by his chronic muscular tensions. He gains insight into their origin and senses the impulses they block. With competent help he can release these impulses and diminish or eliminate the tensions. Step by step, he regains the ability to open up and reach out that he was endowed with at birth. This ability transforms the individual from a frustrated person into one who can participate emotionally in the give-and-take of life. Before that he was able neither to give nor to receive love, but only to do as a substitute for being.

This ability becomes the basis of a new faith in himself and in his feelings. Getting in touch with the body opens up a new mode of self-understanding, which becomes gradually transformed into self-acceptance. This change occurs as getting in touch gives way to being in touch. We shall see that loving is being in touch. I have defined love as the desire to be close to someone or something.* The sense of loving like the sense of touch is an intimate one. To touch one must be close and to be close one must love.

Being in Touch

We cannot expect people who are out of touch with reality, including the reality of their bodies, to be responsible adults. They cannot take a real responsibility for their lives or actions, since they are out of touch with the dynamic forces

* See Love and Orgasm.

that determine their behavior and responses. In past years such people could conform to established patterns of conduct secure in the knowledge that if they followed the forms, they were free from blame. But in a world that no longer recognizes or accepts formal patterns of relationship, the responsibility for meaningful emotional relationships weighs heavily on the individual. It is a responsibility one can discharge fully only if one is in touch with himself.

Being in touch means to be aware of one's body, of its expression, of its state of openness, and of its tension patterns. When one is in touch with the bodily self, one is not functioning solely on the basis of a mental image that may or may not correspond with this self. Being in touch also means that one has some understanding of the experiences that have shaped one's personality, particularly on the body level. I cannot overemphasize the fact that the body is the touchstone of one's reality. The person who thinks he knows himself but is out of touch with the quality and meaning of his physical responses is operating under an illusion. He mistakes the intention for the action. In his heart the person wants to reach out, but the impulse cannot flow freely through the muscular armoring. The action is hesitant, tentative and ambivalent. Naturally it evokes an equally tentative and ambivalent response. Such a situation could be very frustrating and could even lead to resentments unless the person is aware of his difficulty. In that case he could say, "I want to reach out to you, but I have been hurt so many times that I am hesitant and cautious about doing so." We can respond to this statement unhesitatingly with our sympathy and affection.

When the tensions in the body are more severe, the reaching out may be transformed into a cruel or sadistic act. I have seen this happen many times with patients when I gave them my hand. At first they took it gently, but as the feeling increased, their hands became claws and their grip intensified as if they would tear my fist from my arm. In a therapeutic situation this allows us to explore the patient's deeper feelings; in a love relationship it is disastrous. We can understand this phenomenon when we realize that the loving impulse becomes transformed into rage when it activates the negative feelings locked in the muscular armoring. This is schematically shown in the following diagram:

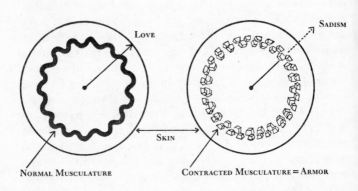

The combination of love and anger or rage directed at the same person is sadistic; that is, it is the need to hurt as an expression of love. As opposed to the hostile or hateful person, the sadistic person hurts the one he loves. Reich believed that the loving impulse was shredded by its passage through the constricted musculature and that the effort to unify it changed it into a hard and cruel action. In this situation, a person in touch would say, "I can't love. I am too full of hostility," instead of inflicting pain on the loved person.

Being in touch is not only the prerequisite for responsibility, but the essence of responsibility. An adult, in contrast to a child, is responsible for his own well-being. It is not a responsibility that is imposed from without but one that is inherent in the nature of an adult individual, man or beast. Yet it is common knowledge that many people, especially those who are depressed, are unable to assume this responsibility. They are troubled by feelings of deprivation stemming from childhood that undermine their self-possession and self-confidence. They seek approval and seem to need support and reassurance. Their behavior is described as immature. Their relationships are characterized by dependency. They are outer-directed individuals because they are out of touch with their feelings and their bodies.

In the course of therapy I often hear patients express a need to be taken care of, to be loved. I can very well understand why they feel this way, since these basic needs were not fulfilled in their earliest years. But what can be done? I have pointed out earlier that a therapist cannot take care of his patients or love them with the devotion their parents should have shown. He can be sympathetic, supportive, and understanding, but he cannot be a mother or father to his patients. Yet there is a reality to the patient's need for love. Through love, that is, through a mother's love expressed in holding, caring and responding, the child gains the feeling of and an identification with his body. In the absence of love the body is a source of pain; the need for contact becomes an agonized longing and the child rejects his body just as the mother had rejected him. The disastrous consequence of the loss of

[271

mother love is the loss of the body. Even for an adult the loss of a deeply loved person has a numbing effect on the body, one's feelings become meaningless, one's body goes dead.

Every patient needs to be touched and this is especially true of the depressed patient. By touching him, one evokes his feelings. By being in touch with him, one expresses one's sympathy and understanding to him. And by touching him physically with warmth and feeling, one extends one's love to him. Occasionally, as the need arises, this may require that the therapist hold the patient in his arms or embrace him. Such holding is not done with the feeling of a mother for a child or with that of a lover for his beloved but with the affection that a person who is not afraid to touch and love has for another human being. Physical contact between therapist and patient was and is taboo in traditional psychoanalytic procedure. This was done to avoid the implication of any sexual feeling between analyst and patient. It had the opposite effect. It heightened the sexual transference by driving it underground and made the patient afraid to reach out and touch the analyst. Since this is the patient's problem and the basic reason for his need of therapy, the taboo against touching handicapped the therapeutic intervention.

Important as being touched is, it is more important to be able to touch. Through touching we get in touch. By touching me a patient gets in touch not only with who I am but also with who he is. I will, therefore, suggest to a patient that he reach up and touch my face with his hands. The anxiety this prospect evokes is surprising. Some patients will touch me with their fingertips as if afraid to make a fuller contact. Others will scan my face with their fingers like little children trying to feel the human body. And still others will push against my face to guard against any real contact or touch between us. These responses allow me to analyze and work out the patient's anxieties about touching. If this is not done, how can one expect a patient to be in touch with life?

It is most important, however, for a patient to get in touch with himself, not through the intervention of another person, which would make him dependent on that person, but by his own means and from the inside of his being. This is done by having the patient do the various breathing and expressive exercises described earlier. He will first discover how much he is out of touch with himself, but this is a step toward being in touch. He will next discover that getting in touch is a painful procedure; it evokes feelings that were suppressed when they became unbearable. It is also physically painful, because the surge of blood, energy and feeling into contracted tissues often hurts. With some reassurance the patient can accept this pain as a positive phenomenon. The pain disappears as soon as the tissues relax, and the patient will finally discover that being in touch is the essence of pleasure.

As long as a person is out of touch with his body, he is bound to the loss that produced this state. His every effort has the unconscious motivation of reversing the loss. He will create illusions to deny the finality of his loss, but by the same maneuver he prevents the loss from taking its proper place in the past so that he can function as a responsible adult in the present. An illusion prevents the person from being in contact with reality, specifically, the reality of his present body, and thus perpetuates the sense of loss. I think this explains why so many people suffer the fear of abandonment or the anxiety of being alone.

If a therapist cannot give a patient the love he lost as a child, he can help him regain his body. This doesn't diminish the pain; it may in fact become temporarily more vivid, but it is no longer a pain that threatens the integrity of the individual. He accepts the loss and by doing so becomes free to live fully in the present. Instead of trying to reverse the loss by getting love, he directs his feelings to being loving or giving love. This change of attitude is not dictated by reason (we have been told about the importance of loving since we were children—generally to no avail) but by the needs of the body. A body seeks pleasure and it finds its greatest pleasure in self-expression. Of the many avenues of self-expression, love is the most significant and most pleasurably rewarding. Being in touch with the body is being in touch with the need to love.

One of the patients in bioenergetic therapy made a remark that I found very interesting. She said, "You gave me something to believe in." She said this as she was leaving my office, so I asked her if she would think about it and send me her ideas. I would like to quote some of her remarks that were made in several letters.

In the first, she wrote: "In you. In myself, my body—as an instrument, is the metaphor I thought. My rage, tears, pain and the other feelings—love, sexuality, fun, pleasure—cannot be 'heard' without the growing sense of my body. Mozart on paper without an orchestra would be nowhere. So I believe in the corporeal body. But I am afraid to be here, on earth, without a mother to love and care for me. So now, I face the fear believing that if I work with my body I will be my own good mother someday and not be afraid anymore."

Her second letter contained the following: "I trust this kind of work on myself with my body because it relieves the pain. I never enjoyed working so hard on anything before. It leads to real enjoyment of hard work on poems, in teaching, in cleaning my house, etc. It has changed my attitude to work.

"I no longer look to men so much to assure me of my body boundaries. I used relationships to find out through someone else's touching me that I was here and alive. But the dead feelings came back when I was alone. I now seem to feel my body in a newborn way. I wake up in the morning now and feel like playing like a baby in its crib—just being there in the world. This is a new feeling for me. It's always there when I think to notice it. Perhaps now it will be possible for me to love a man for my inner feelings."

In her third letter, she added a very significant note: "I feel more *belief*, can pick up more authentic responses when another human being is open and honest. I feel more compassion for others who are working and struggling. I believe in my contact with them; my general human identity. It gives me something to believe in, about my contact—no—my context in a world of others. I feel less lonely, less isolated. I am more human."

I have heard so many patients say that as they got in touch with their bodies they would then do the job their mothers failed to do. They are eager and willing to assume the responsibility for their own well-being. They do not look to others to give them a feeling of aliveness or a sense of self. But what is even more important is the fact that this new sense of responsibility is not limited to the self but extends to the world.

Responsibility is, as Fritz Perls observed, the ability to respond with feeling. It is not equivalent to duty or obligation, for it has a spontaneous quality that is directly related to the degree of aliveness or openness of the organism. It is a bodily function because it requires feeling, and in this respect it differs from duty, which is a mental construction independent of feeling and may often direct one to act contrary to his feelings. Thus responsibility is an attribute of a person as a body—as a somebody in contrast with the person who is a nobody. Being somebody—being in touch with the somebody one is—automatically makes one a responsible person.

Nothing brings forth the feeling of common human identity as being in touch with the body. It is always a tremendous experience to see this happen, and it occurs regularly at the bioenergetic training workshops that my associates and I run for professional people. They are attended by as many as thirty or forty people who come from different parts of the country to learn our concepts and techniques. In the introductory stage one senses that they are strangers to each other, but by the evening session of the first day the feeling of strangeness has disappeared. It is replaced by a sense of relatedness, of belonging, and of warmth that seem to arise out of nowhere.

A bioenergetic workshop is not like an encounter group. The participants are not there to learn about each other or to encounter the other. The aim of the workshop is to bring them into touch with themselves—that is, to encounter themselves on the bodily level. There are group exercises, but the emphasis is on each individual's experiencing his own body and the significant work is done on an individual basis. Yet by getting in touch with themselves as individuals they also get in touch with each other as individuals.

What we all have in common as human beings is the human body. Our backgrounds may differ and our ideas may conflict, but we all are alike in our bodily functioning. If we respect our bodies, we respect the body of another person. If we feel what goes on in our bodies, we also feel what goes on in the body of another being that we are close to. If we are in touch with the desires and needs of our bodies, we know the needs and wants of others. And conversely, if we are out of touch with our own bodies, we are out of touch with life.

Some measure of the degree to which we are out of touch

with life can be gained by the destruction we have caused our natural environment. Take the issue of air pollution. It has been going on for many years, and we have ignored it because we were so intent on producing that we didn't take time out to breathe. A person who is not conscious of breathing cannot be aware of air pollution—at least not until it becomes so bad that he cannot breathe. The same can be said about the eradication of the countryside, the elimination of wildlife, the trash and the littering rampant everywhere. Being out of touch with our bodies, we have been out of touch with the body's natural environment. A mind can seem to function adequately in an office or a library, but a body needs a natural environment if it is to be alive and responsive.

Without the body we are no-bodies, and we mean no more than a number to a mass civilization that ignores human values. We are part of a mass system, yet we feel lonely and isolated. We do not belong to life, for we belong to the world of machines; a dead world. And no words can change this situation, no amount of money can alter our condition. We can get back into life only by getting in touch with our bodies. When we do that, we will find that there is faith in life and that the body of man is the body of God and something to believe in.

10. A Faith in Life

Animism

The one positive feature of the ecological crisis that confronts man is his growing awareness of the interdependence of all forms of life. He is beginning to realize that the fine balance of nature cannot be tampered with lightly. This realization has had a sobering effect on those who believed in power and progress and saw no limitation to man's exploitation of the earth's resources. That there are limits is becoming clear as the world population continues to grow at an accelerated pace. It is also becoming evident that more power and further material progress may bring man closer to possible disaster. We are forced therefore to review and reformulate man's relationship to the world he lives in. He may be the dominant species, but he is still part of a larger order upon whose stability his own existence depends.

The story of man's changing relationship to his world is reflected in his religious beliefs. It is beyond the scope of this book to examine these in any detail. What we can do is to compare three widely different attitudes with a view to finding a basis for faith. These three attitudes may be described briefly as (1) animism, (2) a belief in a Godhead, either a single or multiple, and (3) a belief in the power of the rational mind—that is, in man as the supreme authority.

Animism, as defined by the dictionary, is "the belief that all objects possess a natural life or vitality or are endowed with indwelling souls." The term is "used to designate the most primitive form of religion," namely, that of Stone Age man. I prefer the word "spirit" to "soul," for primitives speak of spirits. This spirit or force, it was believed, resided in both animate and inanimate nature, in all living things as well as in rocks, tools, rivers, mountains and places. A special place was reserved in this view for the spirits of the dead, which were considered part of the living community. Esther Warner, in her sympathetic and delightful account of African life, wrote, "In African belief, it is the business of the dead to increase the life force and the welfare of the living. The deceased continue to participate in tribal affairs. The dead as well as the living make up the body of the people." *

The importance of animism for our discussion is that it represented a way of life based on a faith in and a respect for nature. Since Stone Age man had neither the means nor the power to control natural forces, his survival depended on his adaptation to them. This was achieved by an identification with the phenomena of nature; early man felt himself to be as much a part of the natural forces as they were part of his being. Thus he could not act destructively against nature any more than he could be self-destructive. If he expected nature to provide for him, he had to respect its integrity and avoid violating the spirits that resided in all natural phenomena. For example, he could not cut down a tree without making some gesture to appease the spirit of the tree. Esther Warner gives us an account of this mentality: "He explained that we must take rice and palm wine with us so we could make a

* Esther Warner, *The Crossing Fee*, p. 19.

sacrifice to the tree. We would be taking the life of the tree, we must beg it to forgive us and tell it why we needed it. The life force of the tree must join with the life force of Old One in the kingdom of the dead. And the tree must agree to place itself in my hands." *

From all recent accounts we learn that Stone Age man had achieved an admirable adaptation to the natural environment and lived in harmony with the natural forces to which he was subject. One of these accounts is Laurens Van Der Post's story of his visit to the wild Bushmen of Africa, a people still living a Stone Age existence. Despite their precarious condition he found them a joy and a delight—sensitive, imaginative and competent. He writes, "They were contained in a natural sense of discipline and proportion and curiously adjusted to the harsh desert reality." †

Their adjustment amounted to an intimate knowledge of the desert, a keen sensitivity to its signs and moods, an identification with its life, and an amazing bodily vitality and exuberance. I shall quote several comments from his book. "Whenever I accompanied them the intelligence, diligence and speed with which they harvested the earth never ceased to astonish me. A tiny leaf almost invisible in grass and turf just above the surface of the red sand, and to me indistinguishable from many others, would cause them to grub deftly with their wooden digging sticks to produce . . . wild carrots, potatoes, leeks, turnips, sweet potatoes, and artichokes." **
And again, "They were natural botanists and chemists and had an unbelievable knowledge of desert plants. A bulb gave them the acid to remove the hair from the skin [of animals]

* *Ibid.*, p. 29.
† Laurens Van Der Post, *The Lost World of the Kalahari* (New York, Pyramid Publications, 1968), p. 231.
** *Ibid.*, p. 232.

without damage, another softened it in a remarkably short time." * They had the physical grace of wild animals. In his first encounter with the wild Bushman, Van Der Post notes, "Then he walked away from us into the brown of evening, so supple in limb that I had only seen his equal in the wild hog whose inexhaustible capacity for movement carried him over land like a ripple over water." †

The Bushman was a hunter and food gatherer and so was completely dependent on the providence of nature. Yet without the security of agriculture or livestock, he had a serenity sadly lacking in most civilized people. Not that he was free from a deep unease or disquietude when drought threatened. However, the possibility of disaster did not throw him into panic or cause him to act self-destructively. Like Saint-Exupéry when he was lost in the desert, the Bushman was sustained by a deep faith in nature and in himself. Disaster or death was a cause for deep sorrow, but then providence and life were occasions for celebration and joyousness.

When the rain finally came after a long drought, the Bushman danced. He danced with a fervor that we would call religious because it was obsessional, but it was the fervor of life surging like a river after the spring thaw. First, "they danced their way into the life of their beloved eland and their mystical participation in his being." ** Then they danced the sacred Fire Dance, which continued throughout the night until the men fell from exhaustion. Thus in their bodies through music and dancing they renewed their spirits and strengthened their faith in the destiny of their people.

In some ways Stone Age man was like a child. He lived in terms of his body, he was immersed intensely in present time,

* *Ibid.*, p. 233.
† *Ibid.*, p. 221.
** *Ibid.*, p. 231.

and he was keenly sensitive to all nuances of feeling. His ego was still identified with his body and his feelings. The dissociation of the ego from the body, which characterizes the condition of modern man and forces him to be objective about all natural phenomena, including himself, had not yet occurred. The primitive lived on the subjective level much as a child does. Subjectivity leads to a belief in spirits and magic, which a sophisticated modern man can neither accept nor understand. He regards such thinking as unrealistic. He believes that an objective attitude based on detachment, employing logical thinking and relying on experiment and control, is the only valid approach to reality.

Is objectivity the only true approach to reality? Are we more realistic than Stone Age man? Does one aspect of reality necessarily preclude all others? Reality was limited for Stone Age man because he knew nothing of the laws of cause and effect that govern the interaction of material objects. It is similarly limited for us when we ignore the operation of forces that do not obey these laws. Emotions, for example, are such forces. Everyone knows that feelings and moods are contagious. A depressed person depresses the spirits of others without having to do anything to produce this effect. In the presence of a happy person we feel glad. He may be said to radiate good feelings. It cannot be denied that we are influenced by the spirit of another person. I have pointed out many examples of unreality in my depressed patients. But they are not unique. Too many people share the belief that raising the standard of material living is the answer to the personal unhappiness that is so common. To a primitive mind our emphasis on material goods and values would be regarded as unrealistic.

Stone Age cultures were gradually replaced in the major areas of the world by civilizations based on the use of metal as tools and weapons. Man slowly gained increasing power both over nature and over his fellow men. This power brought about a change in his thinking and in his relationship to the world. Seen from the point of view of the individual, the change represented growth: a growth in knowledge, control, and individuality. The main phase of this growth took place over the past five to ten thousand years of man's history. It is the story of civilization from its earliest beginnings to World War I. It is also the story of the rise of the great religions of the world.

The most significant aspect of this change was the gradual shift from subjective to objective thinking. To be objective, man had to detach himself from the natural order. He had to rise above the level of mystical participation in all natural events and become an observer of those events. From his superior position he could develop the concept and function of the will. The concept of will is alien to animistic thinking, according to which man's influence on natural phenomena can be exerted only indirectly through ritual and magic. The need for magic diminished and disappeared as one natural process after another was reduced to ascertainable laws of cause and effect. But in this period man had not yet arrived at a position where he felt himself master of the earth. His will was not supreme.

The more man detached himself from nature and became the dominant species on earth, the more he focused all spiritual feeling on himself. He did not deny his own spirituality, but he did deny any spirituality to other aspects of nature. The shift from animism to a belief in a single all-powerful God occurred gradually as the mystery was removed from those aspects of nature which had formerly filled man with awe because their mode of operation was incomprehensible to him. His earliest gods and goddesses took the form and assumed many of the functions of human beings, since they were projections of his own spiritual feelings. Then as these feelings became more abstract and more associated with his mind than with his body, his image of God took on an abstract quality.

The great religions of the Western world that grew out of this development picture a God whose primary concern is human affairs. In contrast with animism, which endowed all objects with a spirit or a soul, these religions credit man alone as having a soul. Of course this corresponds to the unique position of man in the world. He is supposed to be God's greatest creation, literally his greatest creature. Although it is stated that God is manifest in all other aspects of His creation, these aspects or creatures derive their spiritual significance only from their relation to man. The double order that emerges from this view is that of the spiritual versus the material. All that is denied spirituality becomes a lower order of things, a purely material order, without any rights. For example, no one today would offer a prayer before cutting down a tree or bulldozing some land. If one did say a prayer, it would be to God for having made the tree available but certainly not to the tree whose life is taken.

Yet the religious person is not unmindful of his relationship to the world. Since the world is God's creation, it is also under His wing. Animism is not completely dead. It has become transformed into the worship of the great spirit which still pervades all things. The religious person feels a kinship with all life, although he has lost his identification with that life. He believes that the spirit that moves him moves the world but it does so for his special benefit. Since God is the provider, the religious person has faith, but there is also room in this scheme for the operation of man's will. This creates a challenge for the individual; what to do when one's personal will conflicts with God's will. This issue never arose for Stone Age man. For the religious man it became a test of his spirituality.

The same forces that undermined animism are now undermining religion and the belief in a God. From the time of World War I and in some way related to that war, man's power and knowledge have increased enormously. But to the same degree he has become more detached and removed from the natural order. He has risen to undreamed-of heights in his technological progress, but his roots in the earth have correspondingly shrunk. He examined the heavens and discovered that God was not there. He examined his mind through psychoanalysis and found no trace of his supposed spirituality. It never occurred to him to look at his body for his spirituality, for the body had long been reduced to a material object along with the rest of the natural order. What could modern man conclude but that God was dead? It was a conclusion that he welcomed, for it freed him from the conflict of wills. Now his will could be supreme.

For a short time modern man believed he could do anything his mind conceived. We still hear such remarks as "Man now has the *power* to do anything he wants if he has the will." Presumably it means that man can eliminate all suffering, but, unfortunately, power doesn't make a distinction between good and evil, and the will sees only the self. If the judgment of right and wrong or good and evil rests with man, then for all practical purposes we become subject to the judgment of the men who wield the power, since theirs is the only judgment that counts. Man had never dared assume the full responsibility for that judgment before. It is a responsibility that only the most arrogant egos would willingly shoulder. And, today, with the development of the hydrogen bomb, with its power to destroy all life, the responsibility for the exercise of this power is greater than the human mind can encompass.

In placing our trust in knowledge and power we have betrayed our faith. We are beginning to discover that we have no faith to sustain us. We can talk of love, but love is a feeling that belongs to the realm of the body. And in our pursuit of power and control, we have lost touch with our bodies.

The Libido and Energy

Psychoanalysis ended as a system of metaphysical concepts. It did not begin that way. Freud was a physician and his early training was as a neurologist. Thus his initial attempts to comprehend neurotic functioning were made from the point of view of the physical sciences. When after many years he finally abandoned these attempts, he did so reluctantly, realizing that some day psychoanalysis would have to be grounded in biology. That grounding was finally achieved through the work of Wilhelm Reich, who took Freud's initial hypotheses as the starting point for his own investigations.

Freud realized very early that sexual disturbances were at the root of many of the problems he saw as a physician, namely neurasthenia, the anxiety neuroses and the hysterical reactions. At one point in his career Freud was very specific about the role of sexual disturbances. In 1892, he wrote, "No neurasthenia or analogous neurosis exists without a disturbance in the sexual function." * The disturbances that Freud mentioned were inadequate relief through masturbation (inhibiting the ejaculation, for example), coitus interruptus, and abstinence in situations of passion. Obviously Freud be-

* Quoted in Ernest Jones, *The Life and Work of Sigmund Freud*, Vol. 1 (New York, Basic Books, 1953), p. 256.

lieved that a failure or inability to discharge the sexual excitation transformed it into anxiety.

The question of how this occurred was never answered in
Freud's mind. He thought of sexual excitation as a physiological or chemical response of the body which was somehow
converted into a libidinal response in the psychic apparatus.
Freud was confused about the body-mind relationship. He
saw the two realms of functioning as separate and distinct
phenomena. His confusion is manifest in the following statement. "The mechanism of anxiety neurosis is to be sought in
the deflection of somatic sexual excitation from the psychical
field, and in an abnormal use of it." * I have studied this
statement many times without being able to understand it.
Freud finally relinquished the idea of correlating somatic and
psychic activity and confined himself almost exclusively to
the investigation of psychic processes. Yet reading Ernest
Jones' biography of Freud, from which the above quotes are
taken, it is apparent that Freud had not given up the hope
that this would be accomplished someday. Jones notes, "In a
letter a year later he [Freud] also remarked that anxiety being
the response to obstructions in breathing—an activity that has
no psychical elaboration—could become the expression of any
accumulation of tension." † Neither Freud nor the other
psychoanalysts followed up this lead, and it remained for
Wilhelm Reich to show the direct connection between restricted breathing, sexual inhibition and anxiety.

Freud belonged to the nineteenth century and his thinking
reflected the view that the body was a material object that
functioned according to physicochemical laws. He saw the
mind, on the other hand, as the spiritual aspect of man's
existence. Freud would disclaim the imputation of spirit-

* *Ibid.,* p. 258.
† *Ibid.,* p. 259.

uality to the mind, yet he assigned to this sphere the vital principle of man's being—the libido. The word is generally defined as sexual desire or lust. However, its root is related, according to *Webster's International Dictionary*, to a French word meaning "it pleases." "Love" also has the same derivation. In a broad sense, therefore, libido describes the force behind any striving for pleasure. According to Jung, "it is the energy or motive force or striving as derived from the primal or all-inclusive urge to live." In other words it is the force behind the spirit of man. Is it mental or physical?

Freud had defined libido as "that force by which the sexual instinct is represented in the mind." * But in another context he also described the libido as "the force by which the sexual instinct expresses itself." Thus on one hand the libido is seen as a pure mental force while on the other it is regarded as a physical one. However, Freud was unable to accept the idea of a physical force that could not be measured or objectified. He was too much the objective scientist and so he was forced into the metaphysical position of treating all vital phenomena, including sexuality, in abstract terms. It is interesting to note that Freud rejected Jung's equating the libido with life energy in general.

The question of anxiety was not disposed of by placing the libido in the mind. There remained the problem of the "actual neuroses," a set of anxiety symptoms that seemed to stem directly from a disturbed sexual function. These were so called to distinguish them from the psychoneuroses in which psychic factors could be shown to play an important role. Hysteria belonged to the latter classification, neurasthenia to the former. In the course of further analytic investigation it was discovered that psychic factors existed in

* *Ibid.*, Vol. II, p. 282.

every neurosis. This finding justified the psychoanalysts in ignoring the concept of the actual neuroses, although they never openly dismissed the idea of two different nosological categories. The consequence of this position was that anxiety, a somatic manifestation, was regarded as due solely to a psychic disturbance. The bodily response was discounted as a secondary phenomenon.

Wilhelm Reich took up the question of the actual neuroses at the point where Freud abandoned it. Knowing that anxiety was a somatic symptom, Reich realized that it could be caused only by a physical dysfunction, that is, by some disturbance of the sexual function on the body level. This meant that in every neurosis in which anxiety is present, as it is in all the psychoneuroses, there must *also* be some sexual disturbance. Thus where Freud and the other analysts emphasized only the psychic factors in the neurosis, Reich showed the importance of the somatic. If the sexual excitation is not fully discharged, whether for psychic or other reasons, there will be an "accumulation of tension" and the individual will experience anxiety. It followed logically that if full discharge occurred, there could be no anxiety. Since a neurosis without anxiety is meaningless, the neurosis itself would disappear in the presence of full sexual satisfaction.

Reich confirmed this hypothesis both in his work with patients and in his observations of people. Individuals who experienced full orgastic satisfaction showed no signs of neurotic behavior, and patients who gained this satisfaction as a result of their analysis lost all signs of their neurotic affliction. Reich also found that only those patients who were able to maintain this capacity for full orgastic discharge remained free from their neurotic disturbances. This insight led him to formulate the principle that the function of the orgasm * was to discharge all the excess energy or excitation in the organism, and thus maintain emotional health by preventing an accumulation of tensions.

With this principle, the breakthrough to the body was possible. Sexual excitation on the somatic level was no different from the same excitation in the psychic realm. Every psychic conflict had its counterpart in a corresponding physical disturbance, and the corollary of this was also true. Mind and body were not separate entities but two aspects of an individual's being. Their relationship to each other was expressed in the concept of psychosomatic identity and antithesis. They were both equally charged by the same excitation, yet each could influence the other. Space does not permit me to elaborate the thinking, the observations and the experimentation that led Reich to these great concepts. All the ideas expressed in the early parts of this book are derived from them.

They lead also to another very important conclusion, namely, that the libido or sexual excitation is not a mental phenomenon; it is a real physical force or energy. This conclusion is supported by a number of observations. First, we all know that there are different intensities of sexual excitation. These differences cannot be explained physiologically but only by the assumption that they represent different amounts of libidinal charge or catharsis of the genital apparatus. Second, the libidinal charge or energy can invest other organs and raise their level of excitation—the lips, the nipples and even the anus. Through this excitement these organs gain an erotic quality similar to that in the genitals. Third, any diminution of the energy level of the organism as in depression reduces the libidinal charge. Fourth, only

* Wilhelm Reich, *The Function of the Orgasm* (New York, Orgone Institute Press, 1944).

genital excitation gives the idea of sex its sense of tension or urgency. Without an accompanying genital charge the idea of sex is impotent.

Seen as a physical force or energy, the libido cannot be limited to sexuality. It must be conceived as a life energy in general, as Jung hypothesized. It is available for all the needs of the organism, libidinal or aggressive, motoric or sensory. Both the pathway and the outlet determine the nature of the drive and the feeling. When it flows upward toward the head end of the organism, it generally leads to actions whose function is to increase the energy charge of the organism. For example, the arms reach out to hold and take, the mouth reaches to suck and swallow. When the flow is downward, it leads to discharge activities of which sex is the best example.*

The body maintains a balance between energy intake and energy output. We expend energy in movement and discharge it in sex. The amount available for sexual discharge is the excess over what is used in maintaining the living process. Reich postulated that it was the function of the sexual orgasm to discharge this excess energy, which in its pathway to the genital outlet is experienced as sexual excitation.† The total discharge of this excitation or energy is experienced as a full orgasm, deeply satisfying and immensely pleasurable. A partial discharge like a partial bowel evacuation lacks this feeling of full satisfaction. The undischarged excitation or energy becomes a disturbing force in the body. It has no place to go and no means of getting out. It may even excite the heart, producing palpitations, or the belly, resulting in butterfly sensations. It is known as free-floating

---

* A fuller description of these pathways is presented in my first book, *The Physical Dynamics of Character Structure.*

† Wilhelm Reich, *op. cit.* See also A. Lowen, *Love and Orgasm.*

anxiety. It is also the basis for guilt feelings, since the lack of satisfaction leaves the individual feeling bad, which becomes translated into wrong or guilty.

This summary of the problems and thinking that led Freud and Reich in opposite directions is necessarily incomplete. I introduced it to lay a foundation for the concept that the body is an energetic system. One might ask what objective proof I have of this energy. Before I answer this question, let me say that objectivity is not the only criterion of reality. There is a subjective reality based on one's feelings, and this reality should not be ignored or denied. We don't question the reality of love, although it is incapable of objective measurement. We also know that neither physiology nor biochemistry can explain this feeling. Similarly when a person says, "I feel low in energy," this is a valid reality for that person, subjective though it may be.

Life may be viewed as an excitatory phenomenon. We are not ordinary pieces of clay but a substance that has been infused with spirit or charged with energy. When we become more excited, our energy level rises. When we become depressed, it falls. If we become highly excited, we light up or luminate and glow. These excitatory phenomena like sexual excitement are energetic processes. And the lumination or glow that they produce can be seen. Many others and I have seen it.

There is an energy field about the human body that has been variously described as an aura or glow. It has been observed and studied by many people, particularly by my associate, Dr. John C. Pierrakos. I shall quote some of his observations about the energy field. He writes: The "energies within the body also flow out of the body in the same manner as a heat wave travels out of an incandescent

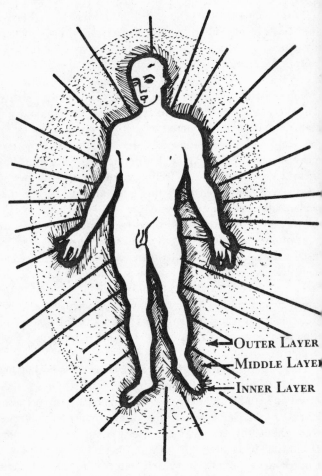

OUTER LAYER
MIDDLE LAYER
INNER LAYER

FIGURE A

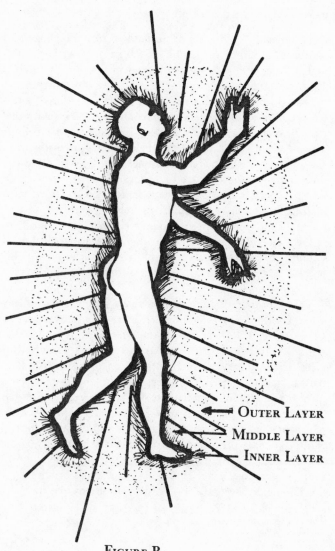

OUTER LAYER

MIDDLE LAYER

INNER LAYER

FIGURE B

metal object." * When a person stands against a homogenous background, either very light (sky) blue or very dark (midnight) blue, and with certain arrangements so that there is a softness and uniformity in the light, one can see with the naked eye or more clearly with the aid of colored filters (cobalt blue) a most thrilling phenomenon. "From the periphery of the body arises a cloud-like, blue-gray envelope which extends for 2 to 4 feet where it loses its distinctness and merges with the surrounding atmosphere. It swells slowly, for 1 or 2 seconds, away from the body until it forms a nearly perfect oval shape with fringed edges. It remains in full development for approximately $\frac{1}{4}$ of a second and then, abruptly, it disappears completely. It takes about $\frac{1}{5}$ to $\frac{1}{8}$ of a second to vanish. Then there is a pause of 1 to 3 seconds until it reappears again, to repeat the process. This process is repeated 15 to 25 times a minute in the average resting person." †

This rate of pulsation appears to be independent of any other known bodily rhythm such as respiration and heartbeat. It varies, however, with the overall degree of bodily excitation. When a patient strikes the couch repeatedly with a feeling of anger, the rate of pulsation of his energy field may increase to 40 per minute. Kicking the couch rhythmically will also increase the rate if it is done as an expression of feeling. Kicking, as an exercise without feeling, has no effect on the rate. When the body goes into vibration as a result of deeper breathing, the rate increases markedly, going as high as 45 to 50 pulsations. At the same time the width of the field extends farther and the color becomes brighter.

"The field reflects the level of excitation and the intensity

* John C. Pierrakos, "The Energy Field of Man," *Energy and Character, The Journal of Bioenergetic Research*, Vol. 1, No. 2 (May, 1970, Abbotsbury, England), p. 60.

† *Ibid.*, p. 66.

of feeling in the body. It seems to have some relation to the autonomic or involuntary responses of the body. One observes different color changes in the outer layers of the field that correspond to different emotions. Soft feelings of love produce a soft rose color. Sadness produces a dark blue hue in the field over the chest. Anger or rage results in a dark red color in the field over the back and shoulders. A golden glow may be seen over the head when the expression of feeling is forthright and sincere. There is a depression of the whole field phenomenon in states related to pain due probably to the action of the sympathetic adrenal system in withdrawing blood from the surface of the body." * The depression of the energy field is even more marked in people who are suffering from a depressive reaction.

Since the field reflects the energetic processes that are operative in the organism, it can be used to diagnose disturbances in body functioning. In the field of a schizophrenic person, for example, there are characteristic distortions such as interruptions of the field and color changes, which a trained observer can recognize. This aspect of the field phenomenon is more fully discussed in Dr. Pierrakos' articles. My purpose in this discussion is to establish the validity of the bioenergetic approach to the body and to life which, though independent of the field phenomenon, is strongly supported by the existence of this phenomenon.

The energy field is not a subjective fact like a body sensation. It has an objectivity in that different observers report the same visual phenomena. An individual in a state of intense pleasurable excitement may feel that he is glowing; he doesn't see the glow, but others can. If he feels radiant, the radiation from his body is observable. In fact under proper

* John C. Pierrakos, *The Rhythm of Life,* monograph (New York, The Institute for Bioenergetic Analysis, 1966), p. 32.

lighting conditions almost anyone can see the field phenomenon. One of the easiest ways to do this is to hold the hands about one foot from the eyes with the palms turned inward against a light-blue sky. If the hands are relaxed and the fingertips held about one inch apart, the pulsatory glow about the fingers is readily visible. For some people, however, it may take a little time until their eyes are relaxed enough to pick up the phenomenon.

The human being is not the only organism that has an energy field. All living organisms manifest this property. There is a visible energy field about trees,* which, I believe, is the basis for the animistic belief that a tree possesses a spirit. However the same phenomenon can be observed over mountains, ocean water, and crystals. Those who are familiar with Cézanne's paintings may be aware that they show a similar perception. The pictorial representation of his hills and mountains have a dark-blue border which can be interpreted as Cézanne's visual perception of the field.

The concept of an energy field is unknown to the primitive mind. A primitive, however, is in touch with the energetic phenomena in his own body and in the environment. He can feel the surge of excitement in his body that moves him to dance, for example, and knowing that this force is not the product of his conscious mind, he sees it as a spirit. Our word "spirited" derives from this feeling and we do not hesitate to apply this word to our mammalian relatives. We speak of a spirited horse when it holds its head high and shows an independence of character. The spirit of independence can also mean the independence of the spirit. If it is spirit that makes a man or an animal hold his head high, then, at least

* John C. Pierrakos, "The Energy Field of Plants and Crystals," *Energy and Character,* Vol. 1, No. 2 (1970), p. 21. Also, *The Energy Field in Man and Nature,* monograph (New York, The Institute for Bioenergetic Analysis, 1971).

in primitive thinking, it must be spirit that makes a tree grow tall and straight.

One can easily become mystical when dealing with vital phenomena. There are mysteries here which defy science. One reason for this is that man, himself, is part of the great mystery of life. If in order to observe life objectively he must detach himself and limit his participation, he will not understand what it means to be part of the larger order, to share its secrets, and to feel that one belongs fully to life and nature. But we need not be mystical about life or its processes. There is an alternative to the dichotomy of mystical versus mechanistic. The alternative is to recognize that there are energetic processes in life and nature which, if they cannot be explained mechanistically, need not be viewed as mystical.

In my years of psychiatric practice I have met very few patients who did not accept the bioenergetic view of the body. This acceptance developed when patients became more alive by breathing more deeply and feeling more fully. They felt the flow of life in their bodies. There is nothing mystical about this flow. We all have experienced the surge of anger, the melting sensation of love and the streaming of pleasure. These internal movements are neither mechanical nor mystical. They are the essence of life, manifested in all living processes: in the flow of sap in a tree, in the extension of a pseudopod in an amoeba, and in the reaction of a baby's arms to his mother. They reflect the energetic charge within the living organism.

The energy charge within the organism is responsible for its energy field. I have mentioned that these energy fields extend 2 to 4 feet from the body. That is not a fixed limit. In some cases they are seen to extend for many times that distance. Thus in many situations we are exposed to and in contact with the energy fields of other people. When the fields are in contact, they glow more strongly. People can excite each other, but they can also depress each other. A vibrant person with a strong field has a positive influence on other persons around him. Such a person is said to radiate good feeling. By the same token children growing up in a home that is charged with good feelings by the parents become more charged and more vibrant in their bodies. And people who live amid sparkling skies, in an atmosphere free from smog or other pollutants which deaden the aliveness of the air, feel and look better than those whose lives are passed in the life-negative atmosphere of a ghetto.

There is one further aspect to these energy phenomena that is relevant here. We have been told how important touch and skin contact is to children and adults. However we tend to think of touching in a mechanical way. The touch of a hand can be a positive or a negative experience. The touch of a warm hand feels different from a cold one. The touch of a dead hand is repulsive. We respond positively when the hand that touches us is alive and charged with energy and feeling. Touching is a two-way street. The hand that touches is also excited by the touch. Feeling is a state of increased excitation. We are in touch with another only when the energy of our organism is in contact with and excites the energy of the other organism. And we are in touch with life only when our energy or feeling goes out to the life around us. Then we feel the pleasure and joy which this contact gives us and we know the feeling of faith.

The Spirituality of the Body

Bioenergetic analysis is an approach to personality and human problems in terms of the body and its functions. This approach was necessitated by the tendency in Western culture to equate the body with the flesh and the mind with the spirit. As a result the mind was regarded as the superior aspect of man's existence while the body was relegated to an inferior and secondary role. One reason for this attitude may be man's erect posture, which elevated his head above the rest of the body. But there were other good reasons. The human brain is unique in the animal world. Man's ability to reason and to think abstractly still awes us. It would seem logical, therefore, for man to identify his mind with God. This idea is expressed in the Bible. Man was forbidden to eat the fruit of the tree of knowledge lest he become like God, knowing good from evil. As we all know, he ate the forbidden fruit.

Knowledge was so important to the development of civilization that it seemed justifiable to deny the body's claim to equality. We are beginning to discover that this was a serious error. Although man's body has the same basic structural plan as that of other mammals, it, too, is unique in important ways. Man is the only animal that is perfectly balanced when he stands erect due to the enlargement of his buttocks. Thus the advantages that accrued from this posture can be credited in part at least to his ass. The erect posture brought the most vulnerable side of the human body (the soft side) face-to-face with the world. So exposed, man would be more conscious of tender feelings and more capable of expressing and receiving love. The human hand is distinguished not only by its opposable thumb. Its sensitivity and flexibility are amazing. Watching a concert pianist play, one can almost get the impression that his hands have a life of their own. To his hands man owes his highly developed function of touch, which is so important to his grasp of reality.

We are witnessing the growth of a new respect for the body, and we are slowly moving away from the old dichotomy that saw mind and body as two separate and distinct entities. Body and mind go together, which we have really known deep within our beings. Is there a mind that exists apart from the body or a body that doesn't have a mind of its own? The answer is no. The Greeks had a phrase for it: *A healthy mind in a healthy body.* By the same token, a dull mind goes with a dull body, a spirited mind with a spirited body. A person's spirituality is not a function of his mind alone but of his whole being. The feeling of spirituality, like any other feeling, is a bodily phenomenon. The idea of spirituality is a mental phenomenon. This is the same distinction as the one I made earlier between belief and faith.

Nevertheless, we must recognize that idea and feeling do not always coincide, mind and body do not always go together on a superficial level. A person can engage his conscious mind in an activity that does not involve his body. Similarly he can perform a bodily movement without the conscious mind even being aware of it. We know that the conscious mind can act directly on the body and that the body can influence the mind. The reconciliation of these two views of the body-mind relation, the superficial duality and the underlying unity, was achieved by Reich through a dialectical concept that accounted for both the antithesis and unity of all psychosomatic phenomena. The following dialectic diagram shows this reconciliation:

This diagram shows that on the surface psyche and soma act on each other. The psyche influences the soma, and of course the soma can modify psychic phenomena. On a deeper level, however, there is neither psyche nor soma but only a unitary organism which has at its core a source of biological energy. The flow of this energy or excitation charges both the psyche and the soma at the same time, each in a different way. The soma responds to the excitation by some action or

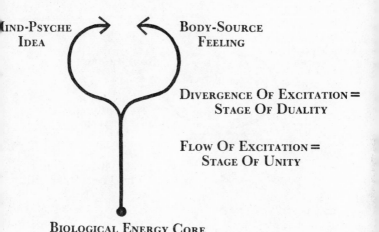

MIND-PSYCHE
IDEA

BODY-SOURCE
FEELING

DIVERGENCE OF EXCITATION =
STAGE OF DUALITY

FLOW OF EXCITATION =
STAGE OF UNITY

BIOLOGICAL ENERGY CORE

movement; the psyche responds by creating images which may be conscious or unconscious.

It is easy to see from this diagram what would happen if an individual were out of touch with the energetic processes of his body. He would be cut off from an awareness of the connection between the core of his being and the surface. I shall picture the cutoff as a block at the point where the stream of excitation diverges.

The block also operates to separate and isolate the psychic realm from the somatic realm. Our consciousness tells us that each acts upon the other, but because of the block it does not extend deep enough for us to sense the underlying unity. In effect the block creates a split in the unity of the personality. Not only does it dissociate the psyche from the soma, but it also separates surface phenomena from their

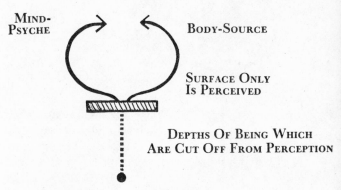

MIND-
PSYCHE   BODY-SOURCE

SURFACE ONLY
IS PERCEIVED

DEPTHS OF BEING WHICH
ARE CUT OFF FROM PERCEPTION

CORE OF BIOLOGICAL ENERGY

roots in the depths of the organism. And in terms of experience, it isolates the man from the child he once was; that is, it places a barrier between the present and the past.

This split cannot be overcome by a knowledge of the energetic processes in the body. Knowledge, itself, is a surface phenomenon and belongs to the realm of the ego. One has to feel the flow and sense the course of the excitation in the body. To do this, however, one must give up the rigidity of one's ego control so that the deep body sensations can reach the surface. This sounds easier than it is, for the control is established to prevent this from happening. Neither the neurotic nor the schizoid individual is prepared to let life take over. He is too frightened of the consequences, specifically, of the feeling of helplessness that develops when power and control are surrendered.

To surrender, one must have faith, but faith is the element that is lacking in these people. In the absence of faith one must have control. We must remember that all adults passed through a phase of helplessness in infancy and early childhood. If this helplessness had not been exploited and if their survival had not been threatened, they would not have set up the kind of ego control that blocks a person from feeling the depths of his being. Yet living on the surface only is relatively meaningless, and so all people want to break through the barrier. If no other way is available, they will use alcohol or drugs to gain some contact, even momentarily, with their inner being.

In addition to the fear of helplessness, there are other fears which fortify the barrier. People are afraid to feel the depths of their sadness, which in very many cases verges on despair. They are afraid of their suppressed rage and of their suppressed panic or terror. These suppressed emotions lurk like demons below the barrier and we are afraid to confront them. It is the task of therapy to help a patient confront these unknown terrors and so learn that they are not as threatening as they seem. He still sees them through the eyes of the child.

Letting go of ego control means giving in to the body in its involuntary aspect. It means letting the body take over. But this is what patients cannot do. *They feel the body will betray them.* They do not trust it and have no faith in it. They are afraid that if the body takes over, it will expose their weakness, demolish their pretentiousness, reveal their sadness, and vent their fury. Yes, it will do that. It will destroy the façades that people erect to hide their true selves from themselves and from the world. But it will also open a new depth of being and add a richness to life compared to which the wealth of the world is a mere trifle.

This richness is a fullness of the spirit, which only the body can offer. This is a new thought, for we are accustomed to think of the spirit as something apart from the body. The body is seen as a material object while the spirit is a living force that resides in and uses the body for its own ends. Here, too, we have the same dichotomy that plagued us when we attempted to comprehend the mind-body relationship. What strange malevolence forces man to turn against himself and split the unity of his being into dissociated aspects? I have suggested some of the factors responsible in my previous books. One of these is the lust for power, which is an attribute of Western man's personality. But this lust for power is inextricably bound to the quest of knowledge and few of us are prepared to give up this quest. Our only hope lies in tempering knowledge with understanding.

Carl Jung provides us with an understanding of the relationship between spirit and body that avoids the dichotomy. He says, "If we are still caught by the old idea of an antithesis between mind and matter, the present state of affairs means an unbearable contradiction, it may even divide us against ourselves. But if we can reconcile ourselves with the mysterious truth that spirit is the living body seen from within, and the body the outer manifestation of the living spirit—the two being really one—then we can understand why it is that the attempt to transcend the present level of consciousness must give its due to the body. We shall also see that belief in the body cannot tolerate an outlook that denies the body in the name of the spirit." *

It is apparent from this statement that what is called the spiritual life is really the inner life of the body as opposed to the material world, which is the outer life of the body. It

---

* Carl Jung, *Modern Man in Search of a Soul* (New York, Harcourt, Brace, 1933), p. 253.

is well known that people who wish to live more fully on the spiritual level cut themselves off to a large extent from contact with the outer world. By eschewing its pleasures they have been able to focus more intently on the inner life. Those people, on the other hand, who focus all their energy and feeling on the outer world lose much of their true spirituality. This was not a big problem in the past when man's spiritual needs were adequately met by the organized religions. It is a serious problem today not only because belief in religious dogmas has been undermined but also because people in our culture have become more deeply involved in the material world.

To fill the spiritual void in Western culture, people are turning more and more to the philosophies of the East. Writing in 1932, when this mass movement was little in evidence, Jung said, "But I forget that we do not yet realize that while we are tearing upside down the material world of the East with our technical proficiency, the East with its psychic proficiency is throwing our spiritual world into confusion. We have never yet hit upon the thought that while we are overpowering the Orient from without, it may be fastening its hold upon us from within." If this realization and thought were novel when Jung expressed them, they are hardly so today. The influence of Eastern thinking on our young people is widespread but equally so are the destructive effects which this thinking has produced, namely the widespread use of drugs.

In terms of inner and outer worlds, the East and the West have represented two different approaches to life. For reasons which cannot be fully elucidated owing to the complex nature of the situation but which most likely have to do with overpopulation and a rigid class or caste system that allowed no outward mobility, the East turned inward to explore the spiritual life of the person. The greater mobility in early Western culture, due in large part to an expanding frontier, allowed Western man to turn outward and explore space and nature. It was inevitable that when these two great cultures would meet, it would produce a cross-fertilization of ideas. We are witnessing that meeting today, but so far we have only an amalgam not a synthesis.

The East is hungry for the technological proficiency of the West. It is absorbing that know-how at a rate that surpasses the imagination. Japan today is the most advanced industrial country in the world. The speed with which the Chinese have mastered nuclear fission and nuclear fusion and gone on to develop intercontinental ballistic missiles has stunned Western scientists. But in Japan, where we can observe the effects, we see that their technological progress is made at the expense of the inner life. They are becoming Americanized, adopting our styles and our values and forsaking their traditional ways. The automobile is becoming in demand, rock music and hippie attitudes are intriguing the young people, and money or economic power has become the criterion of status. But are we different? It has become fashionable to do yoga exercises, to show one's familiarity with Zen concepts, or to follow a guru. While there is much of value in these practices, what we see is a mixture, not an integration of ideas and values.

Turning away from the outer world is not the true way to spirituality for Western man any more than abandoning his spirituality is the way to fulfillment for the Oriental. As long as the dichotomy persists between inner and outer, or between mind and body, man will be denied the full realization of his potential as a sentient being. Jung's statement that the reconciliation between the spirit and the body cannot be achieved by denying the body in the name of the spirit also means that it is equally damaging to deny the spirit in the name of the body. Actually we do both. In our athletic contests we pay homage to the despiritualized body, and in our classrooms and offices we revere the disembodied mind.

In the bioenergetic training workshops that are given on the West Coast I have had occasion to work with several Orientals. I observed that they had considerable difficulty in showing or expressing feeling, although their feelings were relatively closer to the surface than in most Americans. I was told that it was not the custom to show one's feelings and that as children they were shamed when they did so. My observations were limited to a few persons, but the impassivity of the Oriental countenance has long been known. Although the open display of feeling was discouraged in the home, there was no absence of affection, warmth and understanding among the members. In view of the overcrowding and close living in Oriental countries the inhibition of expression may be a necessary cultural adaptation to preserve privacy.

The Oriental is attracted to Western ways not only by his admiration for our technological proficiency but even more, I believe, by his desire to gain the sense of individuality and freedom of self-expression that Western culture offers. In the company of Occidentals he experiences his block in the expression of feeling as a handicap. He feels limited. Individuality means self-expression, which means the open expression of feeling. On the other hand freedom of self-expression is a relatively meaningless promise if one's feelings have been suppressed and are not available for expression. An individuality that is not imbued with deep feeling is only a façade, an ego image. We Americans are great on packaging, and if the East buys our product (mass individuality), they will make a bad bargain, having mistaken the display for the real goods. The Oriental must be careful that in his striving for individuality he does not sacrifice his feelings for an ego image.

Feeling is the inner life, expression is the outer life. Put in these simple terms, it is easy to see that a full life requires a rich inner life (rich in feeling) and a free outer life (freedom of expression). Neither alone can be fully satisfying. Take love, for example. The feeling of love is a rich feeling, but the expression of love in word or deed is a joy.

There is a big difference between the spirituality of the man who brings his warmth, understanding, and sympathy to people and the spirituality of an ascetic who lives in the desert or confines himself to a cell. A spirituality that is divorced from the body becomes an abstraction, just as a body denied its spirituality becomes an object.

When we talk about spirituality and the inner life, are we not talking about the feeling of love that relates man to his fellow man, to all life, to the universe and to God? Yet most people do not see it that way. They would regard the love of God as a spiritual feeling, whereas the love of woman would be a carnal feeling. In the former case the feeling of love is abstracted from an object while in the latter it is directly related to the object. An abstracted love may be pure love because it is uncontaminated by any carnal desire, but like a pure idea that has no emotional charge, it has no relevance to life. When the love of God is not also manifested in love for one's fellow man, including the opposite sex, and for all living creatures, it is not true love. And when love is not expressed in action or behavior, it is not real love but an image of love. An abstraction bears the same relation to reality that a mirror image does to the object before it. They may look alike, but they sure don't feel alike.

These considerations force us to look at the issues dialectically and in energetic terms. Every impulse can be viewed as a wave of excitation that begins at some center in the organism and flows along a designated path, which is its aim, toward an object in the external world, which is its goal. But it is also true that every impulse is an expression of the human spirit, for it is the spirit that moves us. However the spirit doesn't move us only in one direction. Impulses flow upward toward the head end and also downward toward the tail end. When the flow of feeling is toward the head, the feeling has a spiritual quality. We feel uplifted and excited. The downward flow has a sensuous or carnal quality, since this direction brings the charge into the belly and toward the earth, giving us the feeling of being relaxed, rooted and released.

Human life pulsates between its two poles, one located in the upper or head end of the body, the other in the lower or tail end. We can equate the upward movement with a reaching toward heaven, the downward movement with a burrowing into the earth. We can compare the head end with the branches and leaves of a tree, the lower end with its roots. Because the upward movement is toward light and the downward one toward darkness, we can relate the head end with consciousness and the lower end with the unconscious.

The pulsation and the relationship between the poles can be shown diagrammatically in terms of the body or dialectically. In the body these two directions of flow are found in the movement of the blood, which after it leaves the heart flows upward through the ascending aorta and downward through the descending aorta.* Normally the flow of

* In my first book, *The Physical Dynamics of Character Structure*, I postulated the thesis that the blood was the carrier of Eros, the feeling of love. The heart is the source of love. That book is available in paperback under the title *The Language of the Body*.

blood in the two directions is balanced, but one direction or the other may predominate in certain situations. We are familiar with the rush of blood to the head in anger and its strong downward flow in genital excitement. We know that too much blood leaving the head tends to cause a loss of consciousness. Figures 1 and 2 show some of these relationships.

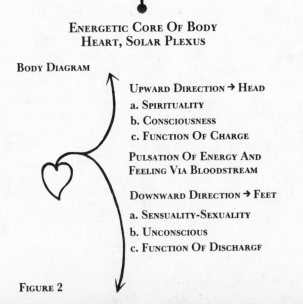

DIALECTICAL DIAGRAM

UPWARD FLOW	DOWNWARD FLOW
a. SPIRITUALITY	a. SENSUALITY
b. CONSCIOUS	b. UNCONSCIOUS
c. EGO	c. BODY
d. HEAVEN	d. EARTH

FIGURE 1

**ENERGETIC CORE OF BODY
HEART, SOLAR PLEXUS**

BODY DIAGRAM

UPWARD DIRECTION → HEAD

a. SPIRITUALITY
b. CONSCIOUSNESS
c. FUNCTION OF CHARGE

PULSATION OF ENERGY AND
FEELING VIA BLOODSTREAM

DOWNWARD DIRECTION → FEET

a. SENSUALITY-SEXUALITY
b. UNCONSCIOUS
c. FUNCTION OF DISCHARGE

FIGURE 2

If we can conceive of the body as being divided in its midsection by a ring of tension in the diaphragmatic area, the two poles would become two opposing camps rather than opposite ends of a single pulsation that moves in both directions simultaneously or as the end points of a pendular swing that moves between them. Now, it is a fact that some degree of diaphragmatic tension exists in most people. I pointed this out earlier in connection with the loss of belly feeling, *hara,* due to a restriction of deep abdominal respiration. It is also true that some degree of "splitting" is common to most people in Western society.* The effect of this splitting or dissociation of the two halves of the body is a loss of the perception of unity. The two opposite directions of flow become two antagonistic forces. Sexuality would be experienced as a danger to spirituality just as spirituality would be viewed as a denial of sexual pleasure. By the same token, all the other antithetical pairs of functions are seen as being in conflict rather than in harmony. The logic of this analysis becomes clear if we look at the two diagrams again with a block introduced to show where the disruption in the flow of excitation occurs. Figures 3 and 4 show these relationships.

BODY DIAGRAM

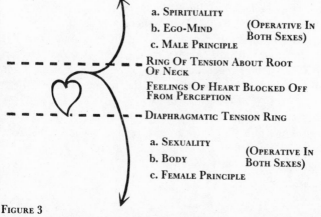

a. SPIRITUALITY
b. EGO-MIND   (OPERATIVE IN
c. MALE PRINCIPLE   BOTH SEXES)

RING OF TENSION ABOUT ROOT OF NECK

FEELINGS OF HEART BLOCKED OFF FROM PERCEPTION

DIAPHRAGMATIC TENSION RING

a. SEXUALITY
b. BODY   (OPERATIVE IN
c. FEMALE PRINCIPLE   BOTH SEXES)

FIGURE 3

* See *The Betrayal of the Body.*

Dialectic Diagram

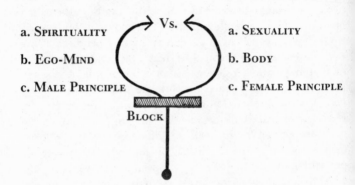

a. SPIRITUALITY   Vs.   a. SEXUALITY

b. EGO-MIND   b. BODY

c. MALE PRINCIPLE   c. FEMALE PRINCIPLE

BLOCK

ENERGETIC CORE OF BODY
HEART, SOLAR PLEXUS

FIGURE 4

I have had a poster in my office for some years depicting the flow of feeling in the body. One side shows the kinds of feelings one has in the different segments of one's body when the flow of excitation from the heart is full and free. The diagram is schematic, but it is as close as I can come to localizing these feelings. When there are no blocks to disrupt the flow, the feelings have a positive sign or quality. On the other side of the poster are the feelings which develop when the flow is blocked by chronic muscular tensions. Not only is the flow interrupted, but within each segment there is a stagnation of the excitation which produces bad feelings that have a negative sign. For convenience and clarity I have shown this difference by two separate charts. The lines curled in upon themselves indicate patterns of holding and stagnation. See charts 1 and 2.

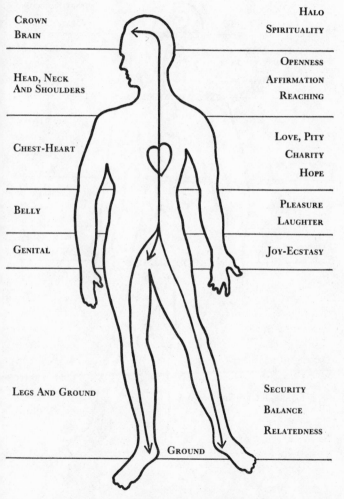

UNINTERRUPTED FLOW OF FEELING FROM THE HEART

SEGMENTS

CROWN
BRAIN

HALO
SPIRITUALITY

HEAD, NECK
AND SHOULDERS

OPENNESS
AFFIRMATION
REACHING

CHEST-HEART

LOVE, PITY
CHARITY
HOPE

BELLY

PLEASURE
LAUGHTER

GENITAL

JOY-ECSTASY

LEGS AND GROUND

SECURITY
BALANCE
RELATEDNESS

GROUND

THE FLOW AND THE FEELINGS OF FAITH

Disruption Of Flow Of Feeling By Chronic Muscular Tensions

BLOCKS   SEGMENTS

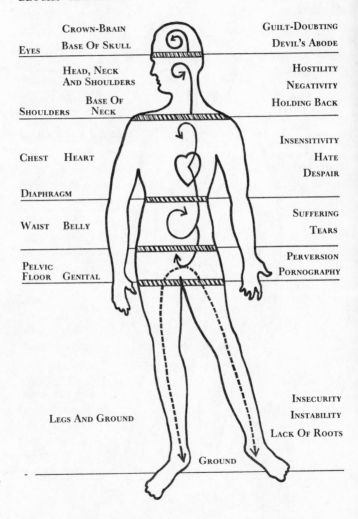

	CROWN-BRAIN	GUILT-DOUBTING
EYES	BASE OF SKULL	DEVIL'S ABODE
	HEAD, NECK AND SHOULDERS	HOSTILITY
		NEGATIVITY
SHOULDERS	BASE OF NECK	HOLDING BACK
		INSENSITIVITY
CHEST	HEART	HATE
		DESPAIR
DIAPHRAGM		
		SUFFERING
WAIST	BELLY	TEARS
		PERVERSION
PELVIC FLOOR	GENITAL	PORNOGRAPHY
		INSECURITY
LEGS AND GROUND		INSTABILITY
		LACK OF ROOTS
	GROUND	

The feeling of faith is the feeling of life flowing in the body from one end to the other, from the center to the periphery and back again. When there are no blocks or constrictions that disturb and distort the flow, the individual experiences himself as a unity and as a continuity. The different aspects of his personality are integrated, not dissociated. He is not a spiritual person as opposed to a sexual person, nor is he sexual on Saturday night and spiritual on Sunday morning. He doesn't talk from the two sides of his mouth. His sexuality is an expression of his spirituality because it is an act of love. His spirituality has an earthly flavor; it is the spirit of life that he respects as it is manifested in all earthly creatures. He is not a person whose mind dominates his body nor is he a body that has no mind. He is a person who minds his body.

But equally important is his sense of continuity. He derives from the past, he exists in the present, but he belongs to the future. This last thought may seem strange to those who follow the current fad of thinking that it is only the here and now that counts. But my thought came from the idea that life is an ongoing process, a continuous unfolding of possibilities and potentialities that are hidden in the present. Without some hope for and commitment to the future one's life would come to a standstill, as happens with depressed people. Biologically every organism is committed to the future through the germ cells he carries in his body.

The sense of continuity is also horizontal. We are connected energetically and metabolically with all living things on the earth, from the earthworms that aerate the soil to the animals which provide our daily food. To feel this sense of being connected and to act in accordance with it is the mark of a man of faith, a man who has "faith in life." One's faith is as strong as one's life because it is an expression of the life force within the person.

People with a true faith are distinguished by a quality we all recognize. That quality is grace. A person with faith is graceful in his movements because his life force flows easily and freely through his body. He is gracious in his manner because he is not hung up on his ego or his intellect, his position or his power. He is one with his body and, through his body, with all life and with the universe. His spirit is lighted up and glows with the flame of life within him. He has a place in his heart for every child, for each child is his future. And he has respect for "the elders" because they are the source of his being and the foundation for his wisdom.